NAME DROPPING:
MY LIFE IN
HOLLYWOOD
AMONG CELEBRITIES WHO WON'T REMEMBER ME!

Doug Smart

a publication of

Mustard Seed Workshops

Name-Dropping

Copyright © 2021 by Doug Smart

All rights reserved. No part of this book may be reproduced or used in any manner without written permission of the copyright owner except for the use of quotations in a book review.

First Edition October 2021

The events and conversations related in this book have been reported to the best of the author's ability, based upon personal experience and recollection. And while the description of these events and conversations reflect only the author's point of view, great care has been taken to relate them as accurately as possible.

Book cover design by teddiblack.com
Cover artwork created by Sandy Silverthorne
Interior formatting by Megan McCullough
Copy edited by Melissa Landon
Author Photograph by Sarah Hogencamp

ISBN (ebook): 978-1-7378298-0-5
ISBN (paperback): 978-1-7378298-1-2

CONTENTS

1. **Desi Arnaz and Lucille Ball**
   "You be careful, compadre. Remember, tha's my 'Babalu money' you got there!" 3

2. **Mae West**
   *"Why don't you come up and see me sometime?..."
   Thanks, I'd love to!* 27

3. **The Lawrence Welk Show**
   Can you even play "Shake Your Booty" on the accordion? ... 43

4. **Betty White**
   My embarrassing first encounter with Betty began over a croquet set… 87

5. **Henry Winkler**
   You meet the nicest people on a Harley. Or do you? 96

6. **Olivia Newton-John**
   Is that lovely young woman smiling at <u>me</u>…? 109

7   Cher
    Who invites the paparazzi to a hot tub party? 119

8   John Rich
    *Old joke: "Where does a 900-pound gorilla sit?
    Anywhere he wants."* 133

9   Jerry Seinfeld
    *One of us is remembering it all wrong.
    Or is it both of us?* 168

10 Newhart
    *The ballad of Larry, Darryl, and Darryl…
    and Randy* 177

11 The Golden Girls
    *It's funny how your life can take a turn just by
    answering your phone…* 194

12 George Clooney
    *Who forgets spending a week with George Clooney?
    Me, apparently…* 210

13 Suzanne Somers and *She's the Sheriff*
    *Doing a show with chimps in it? Call Doug.
    He's your guy!…* 215

14 James Earl Jones
    The night Darth Vader met the psychotic rabbit… 237

15 Danny Thomas
    "You should be ashamed of yourself, young man!" 246

16 Empty Nest
    "Life goes on, and so do we…" 266

FOREWORD

I began this project because one day it occurred to me that my five wonderful grandchildren–Megan, Madelynn, Seth, Grayson, and Colton–had all been born after I had left network television to begin my "second act" teaching television and film production classes at Southern Illinois University, the State University of New York at Oswego, and at Asbury University. They've only known "Paw Paw Doug" as a college professor, so I thought it might be fun to share with them some stories from my life and career in Hollywood.

I started thinking about which stories I wanted to tell. After compiling a fairly extensive list, I narrowed it down to sixteen stories which I felt would be interesting, funny, and offer real "behind the scenes" glimpses into the television industry. At the top of my list were stories involving those industry icons and pioneers who were inspirational to me during my formative years, and who later became my mentors. It became a humorous collection of milestones; small, sweet moments; embarrassing situations; lessons learned; and countless blessings.

Blessings. My life has been filled with them. I hope they are evident in my stories (either in the words or "between the lines"). People who read the first few said, "These are really good! And funny! This should be a book!" So now it is. But I want to pass my blessings on to others. Therefore, 100 percent of whatever profits this memoir generates will be given to a recognized charitable organization. Every penny. That is my pledge to you.

So if you are reading this page because you purchased the book, thank you. Thank you for your interest in my memoir and thank you for your contribution. Together we have made a difference in the life of someone in need.

Thank you for helping me to pass on the blessing!

Doug Smart (aka "Paw Paw Doug")

DESI ARNAZ AND LUCILLE BALL

*"You be careful, compadre.
Remember, tha's my 'Babalu money' you got there!"*

Truth be told, *I Love Lucy* was one of the reasons that as a kid, I dreamed of someday getting into the television industry. I was about two years old when my grandparents got a TV set. It was a massive chunk of mahogany and walnut veneer that seemed to dwarf the tiny picture tube contained within it. But as a young boy, I was fascinated by that box sitting next to the fireplace in the corner of their family room. A few years later, my dad bought us our own TV set *(although not nearly so impressive as my grandfather's)*. But that same magical world came into our box as well, flickering to life on that tiny screen. In the morning, I would join *Captain Kangaroo* and all of his friends in the "Treasure House." After school, I would be transported to the great city of Metropolis for *The Adventures of Superman*. And I would make sure my homework was done, so that after dinner, with my trusty Mattel Fanner 50 cap gun at my side *(still the world's greatest toy cap gun)* I could "Return with us now to those thrilling days of yesteryear! The Lone Ranger rides again!"

But as much as I loved shows like *The Adventures of Superman*, I knew that I could never **really** grow up to become a superhero who was "faster than a speeding bullet, able to leap tall buildings in a single bound!" And nobody was ever going to point up in the air and yell, "Look, up in the sky! It's a bird! It's a plane! It's **Doug**!"

But I started to think that maybe I *had* been blessed with a "power" of sorts, and that was the ability to make people laugh. It seemed that I was born with it, as a God-given gift. And while I would never be able to "change the course of mighty rivers," or "bend steel with my bare hands," I was starting to see that I could use my special gift to make friends *(crucial for a boy who was perennially the "new kid" in school)*, or to cheer up someone who was sad, or to sometimes even get myself out of trouble *(a bully is less likely to beat you up, or your parents are less likely to spank you if they're too busy laughing at something you said or did!)*.

And because I seemed to have a knack for making people laugh, I was fascinated by the genre of situation comedy. And even though I was just a goofy little kid, I began to notice that *I Love Lucy* was different somehow from the other popular sitcoms such as *Leave it to Beaver*, *Father Knows Best* or *The Adventures of Ozzie and Harriet*. To me, those sitcoms looked more like a movie, whereas *I Love Lucy* somehow looked more like a stage play. As I got a little older, I discovered that this was because *I Love Lucy* essentially **was** a stage play. The actors performed in front of a live studio audience while the crew filmed the TV show.

And although those other sitcoms also used a laugh track, I could hear that it wasn't quite the same. Even as a child, I could discern the difference between the predictable "canned" laughter on *Leave It to Beaver*, and the impromptu audience laughter I could hear on *I Love Lucy*. It seemed to me that *I Love Lucy* had an energetic quality about it that the others did not. It eventually began to dawn on me that this energy I was sensing was actually coming from the live studio audience present during the filming. Even though I couldn't possibly have been able to put this realization into words at the time, I had somehow made the connection that the actors appearing on *I Love Lucy* were actually feeding off the energy coming back to them from the audience, which was having an effect on their performances within the show itself. For example, sometimes the actors waited for the laughter to subside before delivering the next line of dialogue. This was a pretty huge discovery for a kid who hadn't yet mastered the grammatical intricacies of reading *Fun with Dick and Jane*!

And then I had the "great awakening." I couldn't have been more than about six years old when it began to dawn on me that everyone involved in the production of *I Love Lucy* wasn't doing it just for fun. *I Love Lucy* was their job! So, at the tender age of six, I had figured out my answer to the question that adults ask every single kid: "What do you want to be when you grow up?" The answer was simple. I was going to work on a TV comedy just like *I Love Lucy*! All I had to do now was figure out how to get to Hollywood. And I reasoned that once I was old enough to: 1) drive, and 2) read a map, getting out to Hollywood would be a piece of cake. Because I now had my entire future career path all figured out, the next step was to share this good news with my parents, who of course would be thrilled.

Oddly enough, they did not seem to share my enthusiasm..[*]

....

Now at this point, there's about a fifteen-year gap, most of which is not directly related to either Lucille Ball or Desi Arnaz. However, during that period certain events ***did*** take place that would eventually result in my coming face to face with Desi, and through him, I would also encounter Lucy. Here is the fast-forward version of these events:

In November of 1964, my family was living in Winter Park, Florida, which pre-Disney, was a pretty sleepy little town. I used to joke that in a state surrounded by water on three sides, Winter Park was about as far from the ocean as you could get and still be in Florida. But what it lacked in beaches, it made up for in humidity. And bugs. And snakes.

---

[*] *I refer you to the Chapter devoted to Cher...*

In February of that year, the Beatles had made their first appearance on American television on *The Ed Sullivan Show*. So, "Beatlemania" was at its peak, even in a place as remote as Winter Park. But apart from that, not a lot was going on. I played snare drum in the junior high school marching band, and with some buddies formed a small jazz combo, the "Rebel Rousers." My dad, who at this time was working for A & W Root Beer, came home from a business trip and told us he'd been offered a job promotion at the company's headquarters in Santa Monica, California. He said that we'd be moving to Los Angeles *(I know for a fact that he said "Los Angeles," but I swear I heard "Hollywood")*. And just like that, the "how I'll get to Hollywood" part of my future career plan had resolved itself.

So, in June of 1965 after the school year was over, we moved to southern California. Dad was already in LA working and looking for a house, so Mom drove us out in our old clunker of a Buick. Six days *(and one breakdown in Tucumcari, New Mexico)* later, we were negotiating Los Angeles freeway traffic. Imagine my excitement as we drove right through the heart of downtown LA when I got my first look at Los Angeles City Hall. I, of course, instantly recognized it as the "Daily Planet" building from *The Adventures of Superman*. How about that! We'd only been in LA for an hour, and we were already driving past an iconic piece of scenery from one of my favorite childhood TV shows! It was actually happening. The Hollywood dream I'd been holding onto since I was six years old was becoming a reality!*

Our new home was a chicken-wire and stucco condominium in the Zuma Beach area of Malibu, which compared to Winter Park, might as well have been another planet. It was a classic case of culture shock, and I was a madras button-up shirt and a pair of Bass "Weejun" penny loafers that had suddenly been dropped into a world of horizontally striped T-shirts, surfer "baggies," bell-bottoms and sandals. But, when in Rome…right? I got myself some striped T-shirts, a pair of baggies and a well-used Jacobs surfboard on the cheap and hit the beach. That summer of 1965, while transistor radios filled the air with the Beach

---

* *Some years later, while living in the San Fernando Valley, I would also find "Lone Ranger Rock," a distinctive rock formation immortalized in the main title sequence of "The Lone Ranger" TV series. "Hi-Yo Silver! Away!"*

Boys singing, "I wish they all could be California girls," I was literally surrounded by them on Zuma Beach. I couldn't help thinking it was all a bit surreal. I wasn't a particularly good surfer. Actually, I was terrible at it, but I had a lot of fun trying. Let's just say I drank my fair share of the Pacific Ocean.

For the next three years, I attended Santa Monica High School. Once again, I played snare drum in the school's marching band. Realizing there was more money (and more chances to meet some of those California girls) in rock music as opposed to jazz, a few of us started a rock and roll group, The Clique. It fizzled. A couple of us from The Clique started another band, The Mass Confusion Rock Band (the name came to us from the chaotic sounds of our first rehearsal). It took off. We got signed by a record label. We made a record. It sold well around the Santa Monica Bay area, but then fizzled. I like to refer to us not as the "one-hit wonders," but rather as the "no-hit wonders." Our record label went belly-up. The summer after graduation, so did The Mass Confusion Rock Band. It didn't look like music was going to open the door for me to get into the television business. As it turns out, I was wrong about that. It did. But more about that elsewhere…*

I was accepted into UCLA, and I spent two years there absolutely loving it, but UCLA was a film school. Film schools had been around since the days of silent movies, but in the late 1960's, not many schools offered a degree in Television Production, and TV was my passion. I tried my best to embrace the filmmaking process, but it just seemed so slow and tedious compared to the fast pace of episodic television, which demanded a new episode each week. And since my dream since I was six had been to work in television, specifically in situation comedy, I couldn't afford to get sidetracked. I felt I was too close. Something big was around the corner. I just *knew* it.

I consulted with my academic advisor, who informed me that San Diego State College offered a degree in Television Production, and on the spot, I made the difficult decision to begin the process of transferring from UCLA to San Diego State. For reasons that I discuss elsewhere, I did not consult my parents about any of this. Once I had been officially accepted at San Diego State, I simply informed them

---

* *More on this in the chapter devoted to The Lawrence Welk Show…*

that I was transferring schools.* Looking back on it, the decision to leave UCLA and attend San Diego State was perhaps my first major "adult decision," and it was a painful one, but it would turn out be a pivotal decision that affected my life from that point on.

As it turned out, San Diego State's Telecommunications and Film Department was everything I'd hoped it would be. They had a wonderful, dedicated and experienced faculty, and they also had Television Studio A, where students could work "hands on," putting into application what they were learning in the classroom.

Now, if I'm being completely honest, to describe Studio A as "ramshackle" would be appropriate, maybe even bordering on complimentary. If the 1950's "Golden Age of Television" had ever held a garage sale, the result would have been Studio A. The multi-camera studio and control room was held together with crazy glue and twine from a mismatched assortment of ancient black and white cameras, TV monitors, switching equipment, and videotape recorders that had been donated (more like cast off) by the networks during the transition to color TV in the mid-1960's. Two of the cameras were old RCAs with "turret" lenses, meaning you had to physically rotate the wheel of assorted lenses attached to the front of the camera if you wanted to change the shot from wide angle to telephoto or vice versa. And if I'm remembering correctly, Studio A's third camera was built by Marconi (the company founded by Guglielmo Marconi, the man credited with inventing the wireless telegraph, so that should tell you how old this camera was!) But it actually had a zoom lens that you could crank by hand–clockwise to zoom in, counterclockwise to zoom out.

The best that can be said about the microphones was that they worked. The microphone boom stand was old and rickety, and it required the operator to "ride" up on it in order to manipulate the microphone above the actors' heads. We all took turns doing it, but we usually held our breath, fearing that it might collapse beneath us at any moment, sending us tumbling down to the hard studio floor. The large studio lights that hung from the overhead grid were old and quite fragile, and the dimmer board that controlled them looked

---

* *Again, I refer you to the chapter devoted to Cher...*

as though it would have been right at home in the laboratory of Dr. Frankenstein in one of those old classic black and white horror films.

But none of that mattered to us. The first time I stepped into Studio A, it felt as comfortable as an old sweater. It felt like…home. And it basically *would* be my home for the next two years since I spent so much time there. Studio A was where I forged some lifelong friendships with my fellow students Packy, Bill, Judy, Sandy, Bruce and Tom. We would often work late into the night hanging lights, building and painting scenery, or trying to become proficient on the rickety equipment. Studio A was where I learned how to create a television show from the ground up. And it was in Studio A that I got the chance to direct my first TV sitcom. And the person who gave me that chance was Desi Arnaz.

In the fall of 1971, during my senior year, it happened. One day in class our professor, Dr. Wylie, announced that Desi Arnaz, the man who created *I Love Lucy*, would be coming to San Diego State for the spring semester of 1972 to teach a special course in sitcom production. But this wasn't going to be an ordinary class. It was going to be a workshop in which the class would be organized as a de facto production company, with Desi in charge, and the class members functioning more like a "production team" of employees rather than students. And we would be responsible for producing an actual multi-camera sitcom! The moment Dr. Wylie made the announcement, I couldn't sign up for the workshop fast enough! It was almost as if the six-year-old me had foreseen this moment coming all those years ago…

The TV show Desi had chosen for the workshop to produce was based on a script from an unsold TV pilot he had produced for Carol Channing, the very talented Broadway actress most famous for her leading role in "Hello Dolly." Each member of the class was assigned a position on the crew. To this day, I don't know why Desi chose me to be the show's director, but it was definitely a turning point in my life. It's one thing to work under the supervision of your college professor. It's another thing altogether to work under a legendary figure like Desi Arnaz.

And just like that, Desi became my first sitcom mentor, and I could not have asked for a better one. While the public mostly remembers Desi for his role as Lucy's TV husband, the conga-playing band leader

Ricky Ricardo, most TV historians credit Desi with actually inventing the multi-camera format which was used to film *I Love Lucy*. Desi's innovative ideas in multi-camera production proved to be so successful that they have been used in the production of some of the most iconic sitcoms in the history of television. *The Dick Van Dyke Show*, *Happy Days*, *The Mary Tyler Moore Show*, *Taxi*, *Friends*, *Cheers*, and *Seinfeld* were all filmed in the multi-camera format originally developed by Desi. Even today, when shooting on film is being replaced by digital video and audio recording, the basic techniques regarding how such popular sitcoms as *The Big Bang Theory*, *Last Man Standing*, or *Mom* are rehearsed and recorded are essentially unchanged from the methods pioneered by Desi during the development of *I Love Lucy*. And he taught those production techniques to me.

If I were to attempt to convey to you all of the knowledge regarding sitcom production that Desi shared with us, this chapter would read more like a textbook on TV production rather than a memoir. And since all of that information is available elsewhere (such as in actual textbooks on TV production!), I'll try to stay focused on lessons I learned from him that had more of a personal effect on me which, ironically, I was mostly unaware of at the time. But more on that later…

Desi told me that the TV sitcom format was modeled after the radio sitcoms that had preceded it. He said that the live audience for Lucy's popular radio sitcom *My Favorite Husband* had been instrumental in that show's success. And both he and Lucy felt that if their new TV venture *I Love Lucy* was going to be successful, it needed to be performed in front of an audience. Filming the show without an audience and using "canned laughter" like *Father Knows Best* was not an option. On this point the network executives at CBS agreed with him. However, they were simply thinking that *I Love Lucy* would be broadcast live over the airwaves while it was being performed, in the same way that Jackie Gleason and Milton Berle were broadcasting their popular shows (and the way that Saturday Night Live still does today).

But Desi had a different opinion. Namely, he believed there might be monetary value in retaining a permanent copy of each episode. And if *I Love Lucy* were broadcast live, in the same manner as Milton Berle's *Texaco Star Theater* or *The Jackie Gleason Show*, then once each episode was aired, it would essentially be lost forever. And whatever monetary value the episode contained would be lost with it.

In the early 1950's, videotape had not yet been perfected as a recording medium, and no other viable format was available for recording live television shows. Sometimes crude "kinescope" recordings of shows were made for archival purposes, but no serious thought was given to the idea of using kinescopes to actually pre-record a program for a later broadcast. The quality just wasn't there.

And besides, Desi said that both he and Lucy felt that the "live sketch" approach was too restrictive. The scripts being developed for *I Love Lucy* required costume changes, scenery changes and the setup of the numerous physical gags Lucy would encounter (things that could be easily imagined on radio with sound effects, but needed to be physically constructed to be seen on TV). As a result, Desi and Lucy had both decided that broadcasting their new sitcom live was not going to be an option.

So, if producing *I Love Lucy* as a live broadcast was out, their only other option was to pre-film each episode using 35-millimeter film cameras in front of a live audience, recording their laughter and applause along with the actors' dialogue, and then broadcast the pre-filmed show over the CBS network to the home viewing audience. But the problem was, how?

And this one of the first great lessons I learned from Desi, which he applied to TV, but is actually universal in nature: *a good producer can identify the problem, but a **great** producer can identify the problem and figure out a solution!*

And Desi, along with cinematographer Karl Freund, figured out that solution. They devised a system by which *I Love Lucy* could be recorded on film using four motion picture cameras on wheeled dollies simultaneously. The show's script would help the director determine where each camera needed to be at various points during each scene to get the correct shot. So, Desi and Karl devised a system of marking the floor with a unique set of marks for each of the four cameras for each scene. Using a script, a "camera coordinator" would guide each camera silently and efficiently to its next mark at the appropriate time to get the right shot without having to stop the scene. This allowed the cast to play out an entire scene uninterrupted in front of the audience, while the four cameras provided the necessary coverage required in order for the editors to be able to efficiently cut the show together for broadcast a few weeks later.* Karl Freund also developed a method of lighting each scene so that it could be shot from multiple angles (and from both close up and wide angle) simultaneously.

Rather than use a converted theater that already had audience seating, Desi's plan involved renting a motion picture soundstage and erecting elevated seating on scaffolding for the audience. Unlike in a theater, this arrangement would allow the audience to look *over* the camera crew on the stage floor below them and give them an unobstructed view of the actors on the set. He would have microphones installed above the audience and record their laughter and applause, while the four cameras simultaneously recorded the actors. This was the plan he and Lucy proposed to CBS for the production of *I Love Lucy*.

And this was another lesson I learned from Desi: *when people underestimate you, and tend to write you off, you can often use that to your advantage.*

Desi told me that a number of the network executives at CBS regarded him as simply a "conga playing Cuban" who was married to a movie star, and believed he was in over his head as a producer. They believed that Lucy had set him up as a partner in their production company Desilu† Productions just to give him something to do. And according to Desi, he was happy to go on letting them believe that. He would chuckle when he recalled that every time the execs proposed something he didn't like, he would simply start babbling in Spanish, pretending that he couldn't understand what they were saying. Desi was quite comfortable with letting the network execs believe that they were "putting one over" on the ignorant musician from Havana. After all, Desi had never produced a TV show before, and here he was, proposing that they waste the network's money by shooting *I Love Lucy* on film rather than simply broadcasting it live. As he put it, CBS believed Desi's

---

* *Desi also came up with the idea for a "multi-synced" Moviola (industry standard film viewer), allowing the show's editors to be able to screen the output from three film cameras simultaneously, dramatically speeding up the editing process.*

† *The name "Desilu" is simply a "mashup" of their two first names, "Desi" and "Lucy"*

ego far outweighed his experience, which he laughingly admitted to us was actually a very correct assessment on their part.

Not surprisingly, the network balked at Desilu's proposal to shoot the show on film, regarding it as an unnecessary expense. And according to Desi, this is where he turned the situation to his advantage. He proposed a deal in which Desilu, not CBS, would cover the cost of filming the show. But in return, after the show's contractual network run, CBS would turn the ownership of the original film masters of *I Love Lucy* back over to Desilu.

The CBS executives, believing that Desi had vastly overestimated the value of his product, agreed to the deal. After all, what value was there in re-broadcasting a program once it had already aired on the network? Everybody who had been interested in it had already seen it. So, after the initial network run, CBS signed over the ownership of all of the original *I Love Lucy* episodes back to Desi and Lucy.

Not only had Desi solved the problem of how to pre-record a live TV sitcom for broadcast (establishing a production method that has become an "industry standard" and innovating how TV shows would be edited from now on in the process), but also in this one negotiation, he had created the "re-run," a concept that would prove to be a financial boon to program producers to this day. In 2012, sixty-one years after it first aired, CBS reported that *I Love Lucy* was still making $20 million dollars a year being re-run on cable. Syndicated re-runs have become such a lucrative revenue stream that today potential syndication income is factored in at the very beginning of negotiations for the development of a new program. And this income can be staggering. Syndication revenue from hit sitcoms such as *Seinfeld*, *Friends*, and *The Big Bang Theory* is in the billions.

The ownership of the film masters also ensured that *I Love Lucy* would be seen by generation after generation around the globe *(and that Lucy and Desi would be millionaires many times over!)*. I've heard it said that *I Love Lucy* has been on continuously somewhere in the world ever since it ended its original network run. I don't know if that is true or not, but I wouldn't bet against it...

Some years later, I would be sitting in an editorial suite with my boss at the time, Tony Thomas (of Witt-Thomas-Harris, and the son of early TV sitcom pioneer Danny Thomas). I had just finished showing Tony the first edit of his latest sitcom pilot, which we'd shot a few days earlier. The filming had been fraught with problems, making the job of assembling the various takes into a cohesive show a real challenge. But after several very difficult and stressful days in the editorial suite, I believed that we had actually put together a really solid show. So, I called the Witt-Thomas-Harris production office to let Tony know that we were ready to screen a "first cut" for him.

Tony had come to the screening feeling somewhat pessimistic, but now he was smiling. He really liked what he'd just seen on the TV monitor in the edit suite. And he was impressed. As Danny Thomas's son, he'd basically grown up in the business and realized the skill level required for us to be able to "pull off" this kind of edit. He turned to me, and said, "Great job, Doug. How long have we worked together?"

I said, "About three years, give or take."

He pondered for a beat. "Hmmm. Well, I think I may have been underestimating you all this time," he said laughing.

I laughed back and replied, "Thank you, Tony. That's nice of you to say. And yes, you have been!" We laughed again, and got on with his notes, which were minimal. During our three years together, I had done my best to work efficiently and diligently for Witt-Thomas-Harris. It hadn't always been easy, but I loved the job I was doing. And I like to think I had somehow managed to put Desi's lesson all those years earlier about being underestimated into practice. As it turns out, I would wind up working for Witt-Thomas-Harris quite a few more times during my Hollywood career.

Another valuable lesson I learned from Desi was this: *always respect the audience.* You may think you're serving a production company or a network because they pay your salary or because they put up the money for your show's budget. But at the end of the day, you're really serving the audience. Because without the audience, you have no show. If no one watches your show, you'll quickly find yourself out of a job. So always treat the audience with respect. Desi was adamant about this, and it was a value that he shared with my subsequent mentors. And it has been one that I have done my best to uphold in my own career.

Filming *I Love Lucy* in front of an audience required that the audience members sit and wait during those breaks between the scenes, when the actors changed wardrobe, the camera operators reloaded their film stock, and the crew adjusted the sets and props. Desi impressed upon us the importance of not "wasting the good will of the audience" by making them sit too long while they changed the wardrobe or the sets. Speed and efficiency were of utmost importance. He believed that if these breaks between scenes took longer than five minutes, the audience would start to "cool off." Therefore, he trained me to run a stopwatch during the breaks, which is something I did throughout my career.

Desi also hired a "warm-up" person to tell jokes, answer questions, and generally keep the audience entertained while the crew worked in front of them *(a practice every multi-camera sitcom has adopted ever since)*. And while this warm-up person was very useful, Desi told us they quickly discovered that their studio audiences actually enjoyed watching all of the commotion on the set between the scenes. It was as if they had a special "back stage pass" to the production process. The audience also seemed to especially enjoy those moments during filming when a specially-rigged prop misfired, or when an actor (almost always a guest actor), would forget their lines, requiring a "re-take." The audience understood that these mistakes would be edited out of the broadcast version, so they had the opportunity to witness a part of the production that the audience watching at home on TV would never even be aware of.

Sometimes it was hard to separate Desi from the character of Ricky Ricardo. While Ricky Ricardo was a fictional bandleader, Desi Arnaz was a real bandleader prior to becoming an actor and producer. And they were both married to Lucy. So, for Desi Arnaz to play the part of Ricky Ricardo wasn't exactly a "stretch." You could certainly make the argument that the line between Desi and Ricky was blurred. And Desi Arnaz and Ricky Ricardo also shared that thick Cuban accent.

Because we were all in the "learning curve," there were a number of times during our class production in which one of us would do something that Desi considered to be less than professional, causing him to just scratch his head in frustration. At those times, I half-expected him to pull the offender aside and say, "Compadre, you got some 'splainin' to do!" The accent was definitely not an exaggerated affectation for his TV character. It was pure Desi.

So were his ever-present cigars. They were big, aromatic and if not actual Cuban cigars, they were mostly likely crafted by Cuban immigrants skilled in the production of quality hand-rolled cigars.* Today it would be quite strange (and quite politically incorrect) to step into a college classroom and see an instructor puffing away on a cigar as he stood in front of his students, but this was a very different time. And Desi was a very different kind of teacher.

But the accent and the cigars were not the only similarities between Desi Arnaz and Ricky Ricardo. Just like his alter ego on TV, Desi was also deeply tied to his roots as a musician and band leader, which were planted in the rich culture of his Cuban homeland.

Desi told us that when Batista came to power in Cuba in 1933, all of the Arnaz family property and fortune (which was considerable!) was confiscated by the new regime. He and his family were forced to flee to Miami with essentially nothing. As a young man, Desi embarked on a career in show business, and after years of hard work and perseverance, had established a name for himself as a musician and bandleader. And he kept a very tight grip on the money he earned as a musician, playing the congas, and singing songs such as "Cuban Pete," "Babalu" and "Holiday in Havana." But it was "Babalu" that most people associated with him.

And Desi did as well. Whenever he talked about his financial success as a musician prior to his television career, he always referred to those earnings as his "Babalu money." And it loomed large in his legacy. As it turns out, that "Babalu money" is what Desi used to cover the cost of filming *I Love Lucy* in the deal with CBS, giving Desi and Lucy eventual ownership of the show. His "Babalu money" funded the deal that would become a huge part of television history and would eventually provide the basis for all of Desi's future income.

He continued to keep close tabs on that money in the years that followed. I can remember one evening during our big production for Desi when the rehearsals were running late into the evening. We all

---

* *Cuban cigars were banned in the U.S. as a result of President Kennedy's 1962 trade embargo against the Castro regime, but it wouldn't have surprised me in the least if Desi had managed to create some sort of "pipeline" to smuggle him out a steady supply of real Cubans from Havana.*

had worked through dinner, trying to get everything done according to the schedule we'd created. We were very close to being finished, and everyone wanted to stay a bit longer in order to "make the day."* So, Desi asked me if I would mind making a "pizza run" for the cast and crew so that they could finish working. I told him I'd be glad to. And with that, he reached into his pocket and pulled out a money clip that was literally bursting with one-hundred dollar bills.

I'd never seen that much cash in my life! And with a loud **snap!** he artfully removed the wad of bills from the clip. I suspect that move was for effect. And if it was, it worked. With a similarly artful gesture, he peeled a couple of hundreds off the top, and handed them to me. I put them in my pocket, and as I turned to go, he put his hand on my arm, stopping me. And with that huge cigar planted firmly between his forefinger and middle finger, he pointed towards my pocket, grinned, and said in that thick Cuban accent, "And hey, compadre. You be careful with that, eh? Remember, tha's my Babalu money you got there!"

I grinned back, nodded and said, "You got it, boss!" and left. And I guarded that money with my life all the way to the pizza parlor and back.

Desi told us how they used to write the scripts for *I Love Lucy*. He said they would write each episode "backwards." Desi said that Lucy was so gifted at physical comedy, that he and the writing staff would sit in the writer's room and have brainstorming sessions. They'd play "what if," to come up with crazy bits of physical comedy that Lucy could do. Pretty soon the ideas would start flying around the writer's table. One writer might say, "What if Lucy and Ethel are on some kind of assembly line in a factory, and the conveyor belt keeps speeding up?" And another would take that idea adding, "Hey, what if it's a *candy* factory, and they're wrapping chocolates?" envisioning Lucy and Ethel shoving chocolates into their mouths as the conveyor belt ran faster and faster. Once everyone agreed on what the physical predicament would be, then the writers would work backwards, figuring out each of the sequential steps that Lucy and Ethel would need to take in order to wind up working in a chocolate factory. I found this process to be fascinating. The "write it backwards" method

---

* *A filmmaking term meaning the crew successfully completed shooting all scenes scheduled for that day.*

certainly wouldn't work for every sitcom, but it worked beautifully for a talented physical comedienne like Lucy.

....

As I mentioned earlier, Desi had selected me to direct the sitcom, an assignment I quickly discovered brought with it a fair amount of pressure from both the cast and crew. But to my surprise, one of the things I learned about myself during this process was that I kind of liked that pressure. To me, it was a feeling akin to riding on a roller coaster–scary but fun!

The student actors really threw themselves into their roles, and I learned another important lesson from Desi: *casting can make or break your production.* Under his guidance, we had assembled an excellent cast, and they really brought the dialogue and characters to life. Desi helped me understand not only the importance of casting, but also what to look for when auditioning actors. And I did my best to remember and apply that lesson throughout my career in Hollywood.

As the production progressed, I wanted to do something special for Desi, to show my appreciation for everything he had taught me. And I came up with an idea. The TV pilot was about the misadventures of a policeman, his wife and the wife's best friend—a very annoying houseguest who overstays her welcome. Halfway through the show, the houseguest accidentally knocks the policeman, who has just finished cleaning and reloading his gun, into the closet. From inside the closet, we hear a gunshot, followed by a cry of pain. When she opens the closet door, out hops the policeman on one foot. He's holding his other foot, presumably having just shot himself in the big toe. At the end of the show, the houseguest accidentally knocks the policeman into the closet a second time. Again, we hear a shot, a cry of pain, and once more out hops the groaning policeman, this time holding the other foot!

For the closing sequence of the show, I had designed a shot in which the camera starts on a close up of the policeman's face as he sits in his easy chair, reading as he recovers from the wounds to his toes. The camera then slowly tilts down, revealing a close-up shot of his two bare feet resting on a footstool, each big toe wrapped in a ridiculously large bandage. My leading man Sandy Silverthorne, who played the cop, really "sold the shot" by awkwardly wiggling each of his big toes just as the camera got down to them.

The end of the show is where the credits traditionally appear on screen. My credit would read "Directed by Doug Smart." Desi's would read "Executive Producer, Desi Arnaz." I couldn't believe I was actually sharing a credit on a show with Desi Arnaz, even if this was only a student production! That "six-year-old" me was living the dream. The idea I had come up with was to thank Desi by creating a "memorable" credit for him, something unique and hopefully humorous. So, I told the crew that we were to going wait until we got all the way down to the close-up of Sandy's two bandaged toes and then insert Desi's credit. One of the control room crew members asked, "Really? You want to put Desi Arnaz's name over the bottom of Sandy's feet?" I replied, "Yes! Exactly! It'll be cute. But no one tell Desi. I want to surprise him." They seemed only too happy to comply with my request. It was almost as if none of them wanted to be the one to tell Desi his name would appear over a shot of two bandaged feet. So as not to spoil the surprise, I rehearsed the closing credit sequence up to the point at which Desi's credit would appear, and then stopped. Unless you had been paying close attention (which Desi hadn't at that moment), no one would've noticed that we'd purposefully omitted his on-screen credit during rehearsal.

All the rehearsals were finished, and the time had finally arrived to record the show onto videotape. Amazingly enough, the taping went pretty well, especially considering it had been done by a cast and crew of student "first-timers." Looking back on it now (I have a copy on DVD), I cringe at some my choices in the camera coverage, but the cast and crew really pulled together, and as far as I was concerned, it was actually looking like something resembling a TV sitcom. I felt comfortable in the director's chair and was having no real problems keeping all of the various production elements coordinated.

During the taping, we had been joined in Studio A's antiquated control room by a number of faculty members who taught courses in TV production, TV direction, and Staging and Lighting. Desi's "Sitcom Seminar" had been the TV and Film Department's big experiment, and this production was the grand finale. No group of students at the university had ever attempted to produce and direct something as ambitious as a half-hour sitcom, and the faculty had come to see if we would be able to actually pull it off. They were all sitting against the wall behind us, watching over our shoulders—and silently rooting for us, as I later learned—during the show. And of course, Desi was there, standing right behind me, that giant cigar still between his fingers, watching the TV monitors and occasionally murmuring in Spanish, "thinking out loud." I guess I should've been nervous, but I wasn't. It was that "roller coaster" feeling again. I had no way of knowing it at the time, but I would experience that feeling numerous times in the coming years (such as when the ABC network Vice Presidents of Programming were all sitting right behind me during the Academy Awards, making comments to each other about the show while I was trying to work the live broadcast!).

With only a few minor fluffs, we'd finally made it successfully to the end of the program. Sandy had managed to "shoot himself in the foot" twice, and I had managed to get it all on camera. All that was left to do was to cue the closing theme music and roll the credits. Just like we'd practiced in rehearsal, when I gave the cue, the audio mixer faded in the theme music we had selected. Then one by one, I cued the technical director to insert the names of each member of the cast and crew onto the screen.

Finally, it was time for Desi's credit. The technical director punched up the tight shot of Sandy reading the book, and as rehearsed, the camera operator began the slow tilt down to reveal the close-up of his feet. When the shot settled, I cued the technical director to insert Desi's credit. And there, over an extreme close-up of Sandy's two bare feet, a ridiculous bandage on each big toe, appeared the words "Executive Producer, Desi Arnaz." Then right on cue, Sandy wiggled his two big toes awkwardly. The shot remained on the screen for a few seconds, and then we faded both the picture and the music out to black, ending the show. I thought it was perfect.

I was thrilled with the way it had all turned out. I took my headset off and turned to face the room behind me, waiting for their reaction. Everyone was still looking in the direction of the TV monitors now over my shoulder. The faculty was silent. For some reason, they all seemed to be holding their breath. Desi was also silent. He puffed on his cigar a couple of times. After a beat, he said, "Eh, that last shot. Whose idea was that?" Before I could even say a word, all of the students on the control room crew simultaneously pointed at me. "I wanted to do something special for you, and I wanted it to be a surprise," I said. "Do you like it?"

He replied, "Let me see it again."

We re-wound the videotape back a few seconds and hit "play." The theme music started playing. And there, on the TV screen once again was Sandy's face, then the tilt down, and then the close-up of his feet. And then the words, "Executive Producer, Desi Arnaz." Once again, the music and picture faded to black. I stopped the videotape playback, and turned again to Desi, waiting for his opinion.

A couple more puffs on that cigar. Finally, he said, "It's very funny. I love it. Nice job, compadre," and patted me on the shoulder. I think the faculty let out a collective sigh of relief. And with that, I had successfully directed my first TV sitcom, and for none other than Desi Arnaz!

....

It was through this apprenticeship with Desi that I encountered Lucille Ball. I use the word "encountered," because although Desi introduced us into Lucy's circle, we never actually got to spend any one-on-one time with her, as we had done with Desi.

At the time of Desi's production seminar at San Diego State University, Lucy was in production for her latest CBS sitcom. Lucy had been a fixture on TV ever since *I Love Lucy* premiered in 1951 until the end of its run in 1957. From 1957 to 1960, Lucy and Desi produced and starred in a series of popular *Lucy-Desi Comedy Hour* specials. But in 1960, after twenty years of marriage, Lucy and Desi divorced and went their separate ways. They both retained a shared interest in Desilu, and continued to be involved in television, producing or providing production facilities for a number of popular series such as *The Andy Griffith Show*, *The Untouchables*, and *The Dick Van Dyke Show*, to name a few.

According to Desi, he used this time to take a step back and assume more of a supervisory role with Desilu, leaving the daily "hands on" producing to others, such as Sheldon Leonard, Quinn Martin and Carl Reiner. But in 1963, Desi resigned as the head of Desilu, at which time Lucy took over as the president of the studio. Over the next few years Desi would occasionally be a guest star on series such as *The Kraft Mystery Theater*, *The Virginian*, and *Ironsides*. And he would resume "hands on" television production in 1967 with *The Mothers in Law*. Just like *I Love Lucy*, *The Mothers in Law* was a multi-camera sitcom shot in front of a live studio audience. It starred veteran comedic actresses Eve Arden and Kaye Ballard in the title roles, and was produced by his own company, Desi Arnaz Productions.

However, after their divorce, Lucy returned to TV almost immediately in 1962 with her very successful sitcom *The Lucy Show*, also starring her long-time *I Love Lucy* sidekick Vivian Vance (Vance would leave the show in 1965). By 1968 *The Lucy Show* was still performing well in the ratings. However, Desilu's deal with CBS did not give Lucy sole ownership of the program. So rather than continue, she chose to cease production on *The Lucy Show*, thereby ending Desilu's deal with CBS as well.

Lucy then immediately created a brand-new sitcom, *Here's Lucy*. This new show was not produced by Desilu, but instead was produced by Lucy's new company, Lucille Ball Productions. CBS negotiated a new deal with Lucy's production company for the broadcast rights to *Here's Lucy*, one which would grant Lucy sole ownership of the show.

And this time her co-stars would be her children, Lucie Arnaz (whom Desi often referred to as "Lucy Junior") and Desi Arnaz Junior. *Here's Lucy* also proved to be a hit, running from 1968 to 1974. Desi once joked about the titles of Lucy's succession of sitcoms. "It all started with *I Love Lucy*," he chuckled. "Next it was *The Lucy Show*. Now it's *Here's Lucy*. Her next show will probably be called *There Goes Lucy*, followed eventually by *Lucy Rises from the Grave!*" We all laughed. It was funny. But little did I realize that a few years later my next encounter with Lucy would involve the production of Lucy's next sitcom…*

---

* *I discuss this next encounter with Lucille Ball in the chapter on John Rich.*

During my time in the workshop with Desi, Lucy was filming her show *Here's Lucy* on a soundstage at Universal Studios in Los Angeles, and Desi had arranged for us to go up to LA and spend a day on the set, where we could observe the show in rehearsals. I couldn't believe my good fortune. Finally, after all these years, I was actually going to be on a sitcom set with *the* Lucille Ball! To say that I was excited would be an understatement. I was flying high!

Desi had made all of the arrangements but did not accompany us on the trip up to LA. He never said why he wasn't going, and none of us ever asked him. Several faculty members came with us to make sure we didn't get lost, and that we behaved ourselves. However, during our day at Universal Studios, my buddy Packy and I did manage to engage in some harmless mischief, but that's probably a story best told elsewhere.

When we got to the soundstage at Universal, we were ushered in and escorted to our seats in the audience bleachers, where we would have an unobstructed view of the entire set. The cast was in the middle of rehearsing a scene. Most movies and TV shows rehearse on what's known as a "closed set," meaning no visitors are allowed, and *Here's Lucy* was no exception. However, since we were there by special arrangement from Desi, we had received permission to "break the rule" and sit in on the rehearsal. Once we were seated, some brief introductions were made reminding Lucy, the director, and the rest of the cast just who all these scruffy-looking college kids were, and why we were observing their rehearsal.

The director, whose name I recognized as a seasoned veteran of many popular sitcoms (hoping to become a director myself, I had developed the habit of reading the credits of my favorite shows, to see who directed the episode). Lucy greeted us and said a few words of welcome. Then the director greeted us and politely cautioned us to be quiet, so we wouldn't interrupt the rehearsal process. If we had any questions regarding any aspects of the process, we were to make a note of them until an official break had been called, at which time he would come over and answer our questions. We were only too happy to comply with his request.

As I mentioned earlier, I was flying high as I entered that soundstage. However, it didn't take long for me to come crashing back down to earth. It seemed that almost everything I had imagined about what it would be like to direct a sitcom--and certainly every pre-conceived notion I'd had about Lucille Ball—was false! I was certainly inexperienced, and other than what Desi had shared with us, I possessed no real knowledge of the day to day workings of a network sitcom. But as the "perennial new kid" in school growing up, I *did* have some first-hand knowledge of what it's like to encounter a bully. And in my eyes, Lucille Ball was acting like a bully on the set that day.

Now, to be fair, Lucy *was* the expert on "Lucy." After all, by 1971 she'd been playing some version of herself on TV for two decades. Even as naïve as I was at the time, I could appreciate that there would be no need to try and tell Lucy how to play "Lucy." And since her co-stars were her real-life children, I can understand how she might address them more bluntly (as moms often do with their children) than she might address a co-star to whom she is not related. But what I found to be really disheartening was what I perceived as the disrespectful way in which she treated the show's director.

Several times this sitcom veteran attempted to actually do his job and direct the rehearsal, guiding the cast through their "blocking" (movements within the set) as they would rehearse each scene. And each time he tried Lucy would balk at his suggestions, letting him know that *she* would work out what the cast was going to do. At one point he said, "Okay, let's try this," only to have Lucy turn on him and say, "No! We're not doing that. I'll work out what we're doing, and then I'll let you know. You just worry about your cameras. Got it?" I was stunned. Lucy was bullying this man not only in front of the rest of the cast, but in front of us as well. I was heartbroken, both for him, and for myself. Was *this* what it was like to be a sitcom director? Was this kind of treatment at the hands of the actors what I had to look forward to?

As promised, at the next break, this very kind man came over to answer our questions. The question I most wanted to ask him was, "Why do you let her treat you like that? Do all actors treat their directors that way, or just Lucy?" But I knew better than to ask. If I did, it would not only embarrass him, it would also embarrass Desi and San Diego State and get us all kicked off the studio lot. In school, I had earned the reputation of being somewhat of a smart-alec. But even I wasn't *that* much of a smart-alec.

So, I sat quietly and politely and continued to watch the remainder of that day's rehearsal, trying to pick up whatever bits of knowledge I could about the production process that Desi might not have covered in our seminars. But I was no longer enthusiastic about being there on the set with Lucy. *Here's Lucy* had become just another show to me, one I would no longer bother to watch.

I made a couple of promises to myself that day. First, I would somehow find a way to politely ask Desi, doing my best not to offend him, if Lucy's treatment of this director was the way all TV directors are treated. When I finally *did* work up the courage to ask him, he sensed where my question was going, and was way ahead of me. After all, he'd been married to Lucy for twenty years! Before I could say anything about what I'd observed of his ex-wife's professional demeanor that might offend, he told me that the dynamic I'd observed all depended on the actor and director involved. He told me that some actors who've been at it a long time need little, if any direction, and often resent any attempt to be "directed," especially by a less-experienced director. Conversely, less experienced actors are usually more insecure, especially if they're new to television, and tend to welcome any and all direction from their director, no matter how inexperienced he or she may be. This proved to be quite true. Even as a young director, I sometimes had actors come up to me asking for guidance on all kinds of things, such as how they should manage their retirement investment portfolios!

He said he'd also worked with enough directors to understand that some were more "take charge" on the set while others were more "laid back." And that there were actors who worked best with a "take charge" director, while others preferred the more "laid back" style. He said it was a matter of "chemistry" and that it was not uncommon for a multi-camera sitcom to utilize a number of directors before finding one that has the right chemistry with the cast and the production company. Years later, I would observe first-hand the truth of Desi's words.*

---

* *I refer you to the chapter on The Golden Girls.*

I felt encouraged by what Desi had told me. Directing a sitcom didn't have to be the way it was that day at Universal. Desi helped to restore my belief that, when the chemistry was right, working on a sitcom set could be fun. The career train was back on the tracks!

But I made a second promise I made to myself that day at Universal. I resolved that, if I could at all help it, I was never going to allow myself to be in a position in which I would be treated the way Lucy treated her director. If that meant turning down a show that I knew was a bad fit, then so be it. A few years later, that resolve would be tested. And ironically, it would be tested by none other than Lucille Ball herself…*

---

* *Again, I discuss this next encounter with Lucille Ball in the chapter on John Rich.*

MAE WEST

"Why don't you come up and see me sometime?..."
Thanks, I'd love to!

As it turns out, I can remember the exact date that my path intersected with that of Mae West: it was February 29, 1968 – Leap Year Day. Looking back on it now, it's still hard for me to believe that I would cross paths with such a famous Hollywood icon, especially considering that in 1968, Mae West was in her mid-70's, and I was only in my late teens. And yet that's exactly what happened.

I realize that the more "mature" *(my polite way of saying "older")* readers among you may have some vague awareness of Mae West, but you're most likely unfamiliar with her stature in the history of Hollywood. And I'm guessing that the rest of you have probably never even heard of Mae West, which is certainly understandable. Not your fault, you're just too young. So allow me to briefly fill you in.

Mae West was more than just a famous actress, celebrity, and sex symbol. She was a global cultural icon whose career spanned seven decades on stage, in movies, nightclubs, and on radio and television. And although her fame never really diminished throughout her lifetime, it was during the 1930's and 40's that she became what we refer to as a "superstar."

Mae West was born in 1893. My grandfather wasn't even born until 1899. By 1926, she was starring in her first Broadway play, which was the year my grandmother gave birth to my mom.* In 1933, her movie *She Done Him Wrong* saved Paramount Pictures from bankruptcy. The film not only earned millions of dollars at the box office but also received an Academy Award nomination for Best Picture. The executives at Paramount were so grateful to Mae West that they named a building on the studio lot after her.†

She also claimed to have "discovered" Cary Grant. Prior to 1933, the young journeyman actor had only managed to obtain a few small parts in films. But Mae West insisted that Paramount give him a leading role in *She Done Him Wrong*. As she liked to tell it, she spotted Grant one day as he was walking along one of the studio streets and was so taken by his good looks that she told a Paramount director, "If he can talk, I'll take him!" Whether or not her version of the events is an accurate account doesn't really matter. The fact remains that at her insistence, Cary Grant was indeed given a starring role opposite her in *She Done Him Wrong*, and the rest, as they say, is classic Hollywood lore.

In 1933, Mae West was one of the largest box office draws in the country. By 1935, she was the highest-paid woman in the United States, and the second highest-paid person overall. Only newspaper tycoon William Randolph Hearst was making more money than Mae West.‡

But as I mentioned earlier, Mae West wasn't just an actress. She was an internationally recognized icon of popular culture and quite a

---

* The play was titled "Sex" and while it was popular with the public, Mae West was arrested for "corrupting the morals of youth." Rather than pay a fine, she chose to serve 10 days in jail, knowing that the publicity would boost ticket sales. During her brief incarceration, she had dinner each night with the warden and his wife.
† The "Mae West Building" remains a fixture on the Paramount studio lot to this day
‡ Many historians credit Hearst, along with Joseph Pulitzer, with creating the "yellow press" or tabloid journalism. Many also believe that Hearst played a major part in escalating the conflict in Cuba leading up to the Spanish-American War knowing that a war would sell papers. Hearst, with his California estate San Simeon, was the inspiration for the character of Charles Foster Kane in Orson Welles' Oscar-winning film "Citizen Kane"

sex symbol. In World War II, Allied pilots and flight crews nicknamed their inflatable life preservers "Mae Wests." The nickname jokingly referred to the notion that when the air bags on the life vest inflated, the wearer suddenly bore a striking resemblance to the actress whose busty, curvaceous "hourglass" figure was an integral part of her sensual on-screen persona.

The great American composer Cole Porter mentions Mae West by name in the lyrics of the title song of his Broadway musical *Anything Goes*. Spanish surrealist artist Salvador Dali not only painted a portrait of her but also famously created a sofa in the shape of her lips.[*] The Max Fleischer Studios paid homage to Mae West in *She Done Him Wrong* with their animated "Betty Boop" cartoon, *She Wronged Him Right*.[†] In 1967 The Beatles included a life-size image of Mae West on the cover of their ground-breaking album *Sgt. Pepper's Lonely Hearts Club Band*.[‡] It was a testament to the staying-power of her continuing global cultural impact.

So now that you have a better understanding of who Mae West was, let's get back to the story...

I mentioned at the beginning of this chapter that the day my path crossed that of Mae West was February 29, 1968 – Leap Year Day. And the reason I can be so sure after all these years is simple. February 29, 1968, was the day I made an appearance on a nationwide television broadcast, and a cute blonde cheerleader from Whittier High School asked me, "If you could be any famous woman throughout history, who would you be?"

I answered, "Mae West."

Even in the wildest stretch of my imagination, it never crossed my mind that Mae West might actually be watching the show!

---

[*] *The "Mae West Lips Sofa" has remained popular, and modern versions of it are for sale worldwide*

[†] *In addition to the "Betty Boop" cartoons, The Max Fleischer Studios also produced the "Popeye the Sailor" series of cartoons, the "Superman" cartoons, and the animated feature "Gulliver's Travels"*

[‡] *She initially refused the bands' request saying, "What would I be doing in a lonely hearts club?" So the Beatles wrote her a personal letter, stating that they were great admirers, and asked her to please reconsider. She did.*

I was making that appearance on TV as a contestant on the ABC game show, *The Dating Game*. The premise of the show, which was videotaped in front of a live studio audience, was simple: a young lady would pick one of three men to accompany her on a chaperoned "dream date" to be provided by the program. The gimmick, of course, was that the young lady could not actually <u>see</u> the three men who were vying to be her prospective date, nor could they see her. The three men were separated from the young lady by a wall. The studio audience, of course, could see all of the participants, as could the viewers at home. The "bachelorette" would ask the "bachelors" a series of questions, and based upon the answers they provided, would then select one of the three to accompany her on their "dream date." I happened to be "Bachelor Number Two."

So when the cute blonde cheerleader from Whittier High School asked, "Bachelor Number Two, if you could be any famous woman throughout history, who would you be?" I just said the first name that popped into my head: "Mae West." My answer must have caught the studio audience off guard because they all laughed, cheered and applauded. I imagine they had been expecting me to say something along the lines of "Joan of Arc," "Amelia Earhart," "Rosa Parks," or some other remarkable woman who had made an impact on history. But I hadn't. I'd said, "Mae West."

But why had I answered, "Mae West?" That's a fair question, and one that deserves an explanation.

Shortly after moving from Florida to southern California in 1965, some of my new friends from Santa Monica High School who shared my love of movies introduced me to the many "revival" theaters that were scattered throughout the Los Angeles area. These theaters featured classic films from the "Golden Age of Hollywood" and often screened double and triple features of a certain artist or genre. I couldn't believe my good fortune. I was the proverbial "kid in the candy store."

Movies I had previously only seen as tiny images on a TV screen, interrupted by countless commercials, were now available to me in a theater on the big screen as they were originally meant to be seen. As a result, it was as if I were seeing many of them for the very first time. Plus, I now had the opportunity to see movies that I had only heard about, but which had been unavailable to me as a kid growing up in the southeastern United States.

On a Friday or Saturday night, we would pile into someone's car and drive across town to see a "triple bill" of the classic Universal horror films, *Frankenstein*, *Dracula* and *The Wolfman*. Another time it might be an evening of Marx Brothers films, *A Night at the Opera*, *A Day at the Races*, and *Duck Soup* (it wasn't until I saw Groucho Marx on the big screen that I realized his moustache had simply been painted on with greasepaint!). It was thrilling to see *King Kong* larger than life (as opposed to the tiny TV image) or Humphrey Bogart playing the "hard-boiled" detectives Sam Spade in *The Maltese Falcon* and Phillip Marlowe in *The Big Sleep*.

But some of my all-time favorites were the comedies of W.C. Fields. To this day I still love watching the bulbous-nosed comedian playing the shady carnival owner Larson E. Whipsnade in *You Can't Cheat An Honest Man*, or Harold Bissonette, a grocery store owner who invests his life savings in a run-down orange grove in *It's A Gift*, or Egbert Souse (pronounced Sou-sé), a hen-pecked husband who accidentally thwarts a bank robbery and becomes an unwitting hero in *The Bank Dick*. My friends and I saw every W.C. Fields film we could and delighted in trying to imitate the comic actor's unique way of speaking, which always showcased his love affair with the more quirky applications of the English language: *"Don't be a luddy-duddy! Don't be a mooncalf! Don't be a jabbernow! You're not those, are you?"*

But in 1940, Universal Studios paired W.C. Fields with Mae West to both co-write and co-star in *My Little Chickadee,* a comedy set in the old west of the 1880's. And it was through this film that I was "officially" introduced to Mae West as both a writer and an actress.

In the movie, Mae West plays Flower Belle Lee, a sultry singer heading west under suspicious circumstances. Along the way she meets a con man, Cuthbert J. Twillie, played by Fields. He quips, "Flower Belle. What a euphonious appellation!" And although I had an awareness of who Mae West was, this was the first time I had actually seen her in a movie. And I was quite taken by her on-screen presence and her dialogue (not to mention her ability to hold her own with a notorious scene-stealer like Fields). Her "one-liners" were crisp and literally drenched in sexual double entendre.

In the film, Flower Belle is kidnapped by "the masked bandit," the film's villain, who quickly finds himself enamored of her beauty and sensuality. It doesn't take long for the captor to fall completely under the spell of his charming "victim." Sometime later Flower Belle walks into town completely unharmed, telling the worried townspeople, "I was in a tight spot, but I managed to wiggle out of it."

Later, in a courtroom scene the judge angrily asks her, "Young lady, are you trying to show contempt for this court?" to which she quickly replies, "No, I'm doing my best to hide it." Fields manages to get in some iconic lines as well. When he's mistaken for the masked bandit and about to be hanged, he's asked if he has any last wish. In response, Fields utters the classic line that is probably most often associated with him. "Yes. I'd like to see Paris before I die. Philadelphia will do."

But it was clearly Mae West who had the sharpest, wittiest one-liners. And her delivery was always spot on. I found myself wanting to see more of her films when they hit the revival theaters. They did not disappoint. In a scene from her first film *Night After Night*, a hatcheck girl comments on her jewelry, saying, "Goodness, what beautiful diamonds!' and Mae West responds, "Goodness had nothing to do with it, dearie." In *I'm No Angel*, she tells Cary Grant, "When I'm good, I'm very, very good. But when I'm bad, I'm better." And when a fortune teller says to her, "I see a man in your life." Her comeback is "What? Only one?" In *Belle of the Nineties*, she's standing at a bar, and suddenly notices that all of the men are staring at her, admiring her figure. She says coyly, "Well, it's better to be looked over than overlooked."

But the line of dialogue people usually attribute to Mae West is the one she purred provocatively to Cary Grant in *She Done Him Wrong*: "Why don't you come up and see me sometime?" But like Humphrey Bogart, who never actually said, "Play it again, Sam" to piano player Dooley Wilson in *Casablanca*, Mae West never said, "Why don't you come up and see me sometime?" And yet that misquoted line of dialogue has become synonymous with Mae West ever since the film was released in 1933. The line she *actually* said to Cary Grant was, "Why don't you come up sometime and see me? I'm home every evening."

What I found to be remarkable about Mae West was that she wasn't just an actress in her films, but she wrote all of her own dialogue as well. In an era in which the powerful studio bosses exerted total control over the actors they had under contract, Mae West refused to be controlled. She created her own image, rather than allowing the studio to create an image of who *they* thought she should be (or an image through which they intended to "market" her as a product for public consumption).

So while I didn't fully comprehend or understand certain aspects of her admittedly bohemian lifestyle, I admired the fact that Mae West knew exactly who she was, believed in herself, and had the confidence to tell the studio bosses in effect, "If you want me to star in your movie, then this is who you get. Take it or leave it."

And *that's* why on *The Dating Game* when the cute blonde cheerleader from Whittier High School asked, "Bachelor Number Two, if you could be any famous woman throughout history, who would you be?" I answered, "Mae West." And when she followed up with, "Why Mae West?" I replied, "Because she's someone who's always believed in herself and had the confidence to stand her ground, no matter what." And that was all I ever said about Mae West. Just a two-sentence exchange over the course of a half-hour TV game show.

Oh, and just in case you were wondering, the cute blonde cheerleader from Whittier High School ended up choosing me to accompany her on the "dream date." We were picked up by limousine and taken to Hollywood where we had dinner at the world-famous Brown Derby restaurant.[*] Later that evening we attended the opening night performance of the new Neil Simon comedy *The Star-Spangled Girl*. Afterwards we were escorted backstage to meet the star of the play, Tony Perkins.[†]

On the limousine ride back, I asked the cute blonde cheerleader from Whittier High School which of my clever answers had piqued her interest enough to select me over the other two "bachelors." Her answer surprised me. "Oh, none of them," she said. "To be honest, I was so nervous about

---

[*] *The Brown Derby was a famous Hollywood landmark associated with the "Golden Age of Hollywood." Shaped like a derby hat, it first opened in 1926, and is purported to be the birthplace of the Cobb salad.*

[†] *This is the same Tony Perkins who played the psychotic killer Norman Bates in Alfred Hitchcock's thriller, "Psycho." I admit it was a bit unsettling to see Norman Bates on stage in a light-hearted romantic comedy.*

being on TV that I couldn't keep track of who said what." Then before I could even ask, she spilled the beans. "I brought my two best friends along with me to sit in the audience where I could see them. Our plan was for them to signal me which one of you was the cutest by holding up one, two or three fingers. And they both held up two fingers."

I couldn't believe what I was hearing. The "fix" had been in. She hadn't picked me because I'd impressed her with my answers. She'd picked "Bachelor Number Two" simply because her friends had both held up two fingers. Three high school girls from Whittier had figured out a way to rig a network television game show.

I was kind of hurt and yet flattered at the same time. On the one hand, I thought I'd done an admirable job of coming up with witty, "off the cuff" responses, especially considering that I'd had the added pressure of doing so on network television. So it was kind of ego-deflating to hear that none of my clever answers had registered with her. But on the other hand, I'd received a unanimous verdict of "cutest bachelor" from her teeny-bopper jury of BFF's sitting in the audience. And in case I failed to mention this before, the blonde cheerleader from Whittier High school was quite cute herself. And we'd just spent a lovely evening together. So I really had no reason to complain, did I?

I never saw the cute blonde cheerleader from Whittier High School again after that night. And after the show aired on Leap Year Day of 1968, I just assumed that was the end of it. My appearance on *The Dating Game* had simply been something fun to do my senior year of high school. Besides, I had other things on my agenda that spring: my upcoming high school graduation, preparing to enter UCLA in the fall, and rehearsing and polishing the original songs that my rock and roll band, The Mass Confusion Rock Band were going to record for the Malibu Records label, which would be released that summer.*

But a few weeks after my appearance on *The Dating Game*, I received a large manila envelope in the mail. Inside was an autographed picture of Mae West. Interestingly, in the photo she appeared to be playing a Fender Telecaster electric guitar. The inscription read, "Doug Smart

---

* The two songs we recorded, "Mass Confusion" and "The War Rages On," were released in the summer of 1968. A short time later Malibu Records went out of business. It turned out to be the only record the band ever recorded.

– Mmmmm, The Dating Game." And she signed it, "Sin-cerely, Mae West," which certainly seemed to be in keeping with her reputation as a sex symbol.

I should probably note here that while my appearance on *The Dating Game* was *broadcast* on February 29th, the show had actually been videotaped about a month prior. And at some point during that interval, I must have discussed my appearance on the show with my next door neighbors (and my unofficial "aunt and uncle,") Max and Irenea Lamb.[*]

Unbeknownst to me, Max Lamb had a college buddy named Stan Musgrove, who as it turned out just happened to be Mae West's publicist. And also unbeknownst to me, Max had called his old buddy Stan and relayed to him what I had said about Mae West on *The Dating Game*, and that the show would be broadcast on February 29th, Leap Year Day. And further unbeknownst to me, Stan Musgrove had arranged for Mae West to be watching the broadcast. That's a heck of a lot of unbeknownsts! I later found out that Stan Musgrove had not told Mae West why he had wanted her to watch *The Dating Game*. But when she saw me speak admiringly of her on the show, she apparently was delightfully surprised and touched by my remarks.

And I, in return, was delightfully surprised and touched to receive the signed photograph, which I immediately framed and hung in my room. And once again, I assumed that was the end of it. Silly me.

Fast-forward about a year. It was a spring afternoon in 1969, my freshman year at UCLA. I had joined the Alpha Tau Omega fraternity and was living on campus at the house. That particular afternoon, I was in my room studying when one of my fraternity brothers stuck his head in. I could hear a hint of excitement in his voice. "Hey, Doug. You have a phone call."

"Thanks," I said, rising from my desk.

My fraternity brother went on. "He said his name is Stan something and that he's Mae West's publicist!"

I suddenly felt like a bolt of electricity had just shot through me. "Stan Musgrove?" I asked.

"Yeah," he said. "That's the guy."

---

[*] *I discuss my relationship with Max and Irenea Lamb in greater detail in the chapter devoted to Lawrence Welk.*

I literally sprinted the length of the hallway down to the pay phone at the far end.[*] Picking up the dangling receiver, I said, "Hello, this is Doug Smart."

"Hi, Doug. Stan Musgrove here." The voice at the other end of the phone had a certain polished quality to it. The voice sounded professional and somehow exactly like what I imagined "Old Hollywood" might sound like. Mr. Musgrove said that he had gotten my number at school from Max Lamb and was calling to say that Mae West was shooting a new movie at 20th Century Fox.[†] And then he hit me with the kicker: "Ms. West will be shooting some of her scenes tomorrow and would like to invite you down to the studio as her guest. She wants to meet you in person." I could hardly believe what I was hearing!

He asked if I was free the following afternoon, and I assured him that I was. As luck would have it, I only had morning classes the next day. But let's face it, that really wouldn't have mattered. I would have gladly skipped class for the chance to spend an afternoon at 20th Century Fox with Mae West! "There will be photographers there," Stan added. "Do you have a suit, Doug?"

Uh, oh. I didn't own a suit. I hoped this wasn't going to be a deal-breaker. "No sir, but I have a blazer, a tie, and slacks. Will that do?"

"That's fine," he said reassuringly. "Why don't you come down around 2:00 p.m.? I'll leave a drive-on pass for you at the Pico Blvd gate."

Fortunately, the 20th Century Fox Studios are only about a fifteen minute drive from the UCLA campus in Westwood. So at 1:45 p.m. the following day, I drove my little '57 MGA roadster through the Pico Blvd gate on the studio lot and found my assigned parking spot. I walked onto the soundstage at 2:00 p.m. sharp, where I was greeted by Stan Musgrove. His physical appearance was a perfect match to the voice I had heard on the phone a day earlier. He was polished and

---

[*] *In those days, it was unheard of for college students to have a private phone in their room. The common practice was to install pay phones in college dormitories, fraternity and sorority houses, usually with one phone per floor or wing. All students living on that floor or in that wing would share the pay phone to place or receive calls*

[†] *The movie Mae West was shooting was "Myra Breckenridge," a film adaptation of Gore Vidal's gender-bending novel. In addition to Mae West, the film also featured Raquel Welch, John Huston, John Carradine, and a very young Farrah Fawcett*

professional and appeared to be the personification of a Hollywood publicist (at least to me!).

As he had mentioned on the phone, there were photographers and members of the press milling around the soundstage, anxiously awaiting Mae West's arrival. He explained to me that the press was there because she was receiving the "Golden Apple" award from the Hollywood Women's Press Club, which would be presented to her that afternoon on the movie set.[*]

It was at that moment when "the light bulb flicked on" in my head. Stan Musgrove, the professional Hollywood publicist, had arranged for me to be there as part of a larger publicity event for his client. Not only would the press be there to witness Mae West receiving the "Golden Apple" award but also they would be witness to her "staying power" as the Hollywood icon played host to a new generation of youthful admirers (or at least this youthful admirer!). I had to admit that it was a clever move on his part. And to be honest, I didn't care that I was part of a publicity stunt. I was about to spend the afternoon with Mae West!

After a few moments, I noticed that there seemed to be a commotion among the photographers, who were now scurrying towards the large open "elephant door" at one end of the soundstage.[†] Stan Musgrove looked at his watch and said, "Oh, that must be her arriving now."

Mae West was indeed arriving at the studio. And did she know how to make an entrance! Outside the soundstage, a classic Rolls Royce limousine from the 1930's pulled up to a stop, and from the front seat a chauffeur hopped out. He looked like something right out of a movie himself. He was tall and handsome, and he was dressed in a double-breasted gray tunic, matching gray "jodhpurs," boots, gloves and cap. I had no doubt that he had been "cast" for the part.

---

[*] *The Hollywood Women's Press Club was founded by the famous (and feared) Hollywood gossip columnist Louella Parsons. The award was not based on performance, but rather behavior. The "Golden Apple" was awarded to actors who were considered by the press club to be easy to work with, while the "Sour Apple" was presented to those who were considered rude or difficult.*

[†] *The "Elephant Door" is the nickname for a large door at one end of a motion picture soundstage. While it is certainly big enough to allow an elephant to pass through, it is really used to allow large pieces of scenery, vehicles and equipment to be brought in and out of the soundstage.*

As the chauffeur opened the passenger door and extended his hand, a flurry of camera flashbulbs suddenly began erupting from the photographers, all clamoring for a "money shot" of the legendary actress. From the open limo door, a bejeweled hand reached out and took his, and out of the car and into the commotion stepped the one and only Mae West. She smiled and posed and flirted with the flashbulbs, giving the photographers exactly what they'd come for. And they were eating it up. And so was she.

Since she was scheduled to film her scenes that day, her trademark platinum blonde hair had been impeccably done by the studio's makeup department, as had her makeup. And she was already in her wardrobe, a cream white satin tunic and slacks ensemble that had been designed to her exact specifications for the film. But as I watched the strobing barrage of flashbulbs explode around her, something else caught my eye. It was a monkey, which was playfully perched on her shoulder. If I didn't know better, I would've sworn that the monkey was "playing to the cameras" as well.

It seemed to me that in that moment, Mae West was the personification of an opulent, almost decadent lifestyle that had once defined Hollywood but that now could only be found in movies, books, and in the memories of those who had lived it. But standing there, basking in the barrage of flashbulbs was no "Norma Desmond," the aging, forgotten silent movie actress living alone in a crumbling mansion in the film *Sunset Boulevard*.* Hollywood had definitely *not* forgotten Mae West.

At 76, she still had the "star power" to command top billing in the film. And she was receiving a salary of $350,000 dollars, twice that of Raquel Welch, Hollywood's current "sex symbol" whom the studio had cast to play the title role of Myra Breckenridge. She had also been given the creative freedom to re-write her dialogue. And Mae West

---

* *In the Academy-Award winning film, "Sunset Boulevard," Gloria Swanson plays silent-movie actress Norma Desmond, whose star has faded and who has been forgotten by Hollywood. In the film, we first meet Norma Desmond on the grounds of her crumbling mansion, where she is burying her beloved pet chimpanzee. Ironically, Billy Wilder first offered the role of Norma Desmond to Mae West, but she turned it down. She felt the storyline was "pure pathos," and out of keeping with her image as more a comedic actress. The role was subsequently offered to Mary Pickford, who also passed on it, and finally offered to Gloria Swanson.*

still wielded enough influence with the studio's casting department to convince them to give a small part in the film to yet another handsome young man who had "caught her eye." That handsome-but-unknown young actor made the most of that opportunity and has done quite well for himself ever since. His name is Tom Selleck.

The rest of the afternoon flew by. After all of the initial commotion at her arrival, the press retreated to an area of the soundstage that had been set up for the presentation of the "Golden Apple." Mae West had settled into her canvas studio chair with her script, going over her scenes and waiting for the film's assistant director to let her know that they were ready for her on the set. She would occasionally slip a small treat to the monkey, who was still happily perched on her shoulder.

Once she had settled in, Stan Musgrove escorted me over to meet her. He said, "Mae, I'd like you to meet Doug Smart." Now at that young stage of my life, I was totally naïve regarding "the ways of the world." I had no concept of what it might be like to have a woman "take me in" with her gaze. But if there actually is such a thing, then this had to be it.

She looked up from her script until her eyes were looking directly into mine. Then she slowly turned her gaze downward, as if she were visually scanning me from head to toe. And then she looked up once again, smiled and said, "Hiya, kid. How're you doing?" Her voice had that same silky, sultry "come hither" quality about it that I'd heard her use in the movies.

I'm amazed that I was even able to muster up an answer. "I'm fine, thank you. It's an honor to meet you, Ms. West."

She smiled. "My pleasure, kid," she replied. "And by the way, I enjoyed seein' you on The Dating Game. It was…sweet." She made the word "sweet" sound sexual somehow.

"Thank you," I said. "And thank you for the autographed picture. I knew you sang from your movies, but I had no idea that you could play the guitar."

"Yeah, I made a rock and roll album," she said, laughing.* "So I went out and bought a guitar and got me a few lessons." Then she laughed

---

* *In 1966 she recorded the rock and roll album "Way Out (Mae) West," backed by the band Somebody's Chyldren for Tower Records, a subsidiary of Capitol Records. The album featured the original song "Mae Day," and covers of hit songs such as "Twist and Shout," "When A Man Loves A Woman," and "Day Tripper."*

again and said, "It was the only time in my life that someone had to show me what to do with my hands." I had absolutely no idea how to respond to that. So, like an idiot, I just stood there smiling. "Listen kid," she said. "They're not gonna need me for a while. Why don't you pull up a chair so we can chat?"

She didn't have to ask me twice. Stan Musgrove found me an empty canvas chair and set it up next to hers, facing the opposite direction. This allowed us to sit "loveseat" style facing each other. She wanted to know a bit about me, but I was much more interested in learning more about her, and what it was like to make movies in the 1930's and 40's. And I just sat there, fascinated, as she related stories of working with Hollywood legends such as Cary Grant, Randolph Scott, and, of course, W.C. Fields.

When it came to Fields, she didn't pull any punches. He wasn't her favorite co-star by a longshot. Having enjoyed seeing the two of them together in *My Little Chickadee*, I was a bit disappointed, but understood. W.C. Fields was a notorious alcoholic and was well known for getting drunk on the set, a habit she considered both unprofessional and annoying. She suggested that I watch the film again and count the actual number of times that she and Fields appear on-screen together in the same shot (the number is surprisingly low).

Stan Musgrove came over to tell Ms. West that they were ready to present her with the "Golden Apple." As we stood, he mentioned that he'd like me to accompany her over to the presentation area and pose for some photos with her. Before I knew it, she was standing in front of a drape which had been hung for the occasion, accepting her award while dozens of flashbulbs lit up the scene. The next thing I knew, I was standing by her side while those same dozens of flashbulbs were suddenly going off in *my* face. Behind the commotion of all of the flashbulbs popping, I could vaguely hear someone say, "Hey, Stan, who's the kid with her?"

And then it was over. The press had gotten all of the coverage they needed, and the assistant director had arrived to escort Ms. West across the soundstage to shoot her first scene of the day. As they started off, she turned back and asked, "You're gonna stay and watch me work a bit, aren't you kid?"

I immediately answered, "Of course! I'd love to!" But I suspect that she already knew that before she'd even asked.

For the remainder of the afternoon, I watched as they filmed several of her scenes for the movie, taking mental notes regarding how things were accomplished. Since I hoped to be doing something very similar someday, I was trying to take full advantage of the opportunity that had been afforded me. I noticed that the lighting crew took great care with Ms. West's lighting and that the camera crew was paying very close attention to their choice of lenses during filming. I could see that they were determined to present the 76-year-old actress in the most flattering way possible on screen.

The day's filming wrapped much too soon. I found myself wishing I could've stayed longer, just to soak it all in. As the film crew began to stow their gear, I thanked Stan Musgrove for making such a "once in a lifetime" experience possible. He replied that he was happy to do it and asked if my home address was still the same. I said that it was. "Good," he said. "I'll see if I can get you a copy of one of the pictures they took today." I thanked him again.

I went over to Mae West to thank her for being so generous with her time. She said, "My pleasure, kid. It's nice to know I still have young fans." But instead of "good-bye," the next thing she said caught me by surprise. "Is there anything you didn't get to ask me before that you'd like to ask me now?" she said. "Here's your last chance."

I thought for a second. "Well, there is one thing, but you'll probably think it's silly, so I'm not sure—"

"Relax, kid," she purred, cutting me off. "I'm guessin' that there's nothing you can ask me that someone else ain't already asked."

She'd given me permission, so I decided to go for it. I held my breath and asked, "Would you say the famous line to me that you said to Cary Grant in *She Done Him Wrong*?"

She smiled a knowing smile and patted me gently on the cheek. "Sure, kid." And then in a voice even more sultry she looked into my eyes and said, "Why don't you come up sometime and see me? I'm home every evening."

If there's such a thing as a perfect ending to a perfect day, this would be right at the top of my list.

"Thank you for everything, Ms. West," I said. "You've given me an experience I'll never forget." She smiled, winked and said in that silky, sultry tone, "I know. Men have been tellin' me that my whole life."

And they would be right.

P.S. While writing this chapter I was prompted to dig through my boxes of old photographs. Inside one of the boxes I found a black-and-white photograph of Mae West, dressed in a white tunic and slacks, standing in front of a drape. Standing at her side is a 19-year-old kid, dressed in his best blazer, tie and slacks, gazing at her with admiration. A slightly faded reminder of a perfect day with a perfect ending.

THE LAWRENCE WELK SHOW

Can you even play "Shake Your Booty"
on the accordion?

I realize that many of you may not even recognize the name Lawrence Welk. Others of you may have some vague awareness of *The Lawrence Welk Show*, but you've never actually seen it on television. Perhaps you caught a glimpse of the show in re-runs on PBS (as I'm writing this, the show is still in syndication on PBS) while visiting an elderly relative. Or maybe you're old enough to remember seeing actor/musician Fred Armisen do his impression of Lawrence Welk in a series of comedy sketches on *Saturday Night Live* between 2008 and 2013. But I imagine that for most of you, *The Lawrence Welk Show* was probably just "that corny show I think my grandparents used to watch," or maybe even "that corny show I think my *great-grandparents* used to watch." However, the fact remains that *The Lawrence Welk Show* has rightfully earned its place in the history of television, and Lawrence himself was both then and now an iconic figure. The show could also be appropriately described as an example of "Americana."

But I would have no story to tell about *The Lawrence Welk Show* were it not for Jim Hobson, the show's producer and director. I owe my place as a member of Lawrence Welk's "Musical Family," and more importantly my career in television to Jim. He not only gave me my start in network television but also took me under his wing and became my greatest mentor and teacher—and one of my dearest friends. I can only hope that when I left network television to become a college professor, I was able to repay him by being the kind of teacher and mentor to *my* students that Jim was to me.

I first met Jim and his wife Elsie in the summer of 1968 in Malibu, California, at a dinner party hosted by our neighbors, Max and Irenea Lamb. Max worked in the film industry, and the Lambs and the Hobsons were longtime friends, going back to their days together at the Pasadena Playhouse in the early 1950's. Max and Irenea had no children, and in 1965 when my family moved from Florida and next door to them in Malibu, they sort of "claimed" my sister Donna and me as their surrogate niece and nephew. Donna and I responded in turn by addressing them fondly as "Uncle Max and Aunt Rene."

In that summer of 1968, I had just graduated from Santa Monica High School and was bound for UCLA in the fall. My rock and roll band, The Mass Confusion Rock Band, had just released its first (and as it turned out, only) record, which had done okay, selling out its first (and again, only) pressing in the Santa Monica Bay area.[*] I was proud of that record and, of course, had given Uncle Max a copy.

The Lambs had invited their old friends the Hobsons over for dinner, and, knowing that I was interested in both television and music, decided to invite me to join them as literally the "fifth wheel." And since I had grown up watching *The Lawrence Welk Show* with my family every Saturday night, I was both excited and nervous at the invitation to have dinner with the show's producer-director.

---

[*] *Our record label, Malibu Records, knew how to make records. But as it turned out, however, they didn't know how to actually sell records, and ran out of money before a second pressing of our record could be made.*

However, as the dinner progressed, my nervousness regarding the Hobsons began to subside somewhat. Both Jim and Elsie were very engaging, and I found myself growing more and more at ease around them as we talked about television, film, music, and Jim's love of aeronautics. It turned out that Jim was actually one of the early pioneers in the sport of hang gliding and ultralight aircraft. An article featuring his home-made "Rogallo Wing* Hang Glider," which he adapted from a NASA concept and had crafted from bamboo poles and an old swimming pool cover, had been published as early as 1962 in *Sport Aviation*, the official magazine of The Experimental Aircraft Association. Jim had the foresight to predict the tremendous recreational and sport potential of the flexible delta-shaped wing NASA had been developing for the Gemini spacecraft.

Dinner was followed by dessert, which was comprised of coffee and cookies. We were all still sitting at the dinner table, and Aunt Rene and Uncle Max had seated me next to Elsie Hobson, who was charming and quite vivacious. Elsie, who was originally from Yazoo City, Mississippi, had been an actress with a very successful career in radio, television, and feature films, including a supporting role in the motion picture comedy *Rhubarb,* starring Ray Milland[†] and Jan Sterling. She was also an avid golfer, playing regularly at the Brentwood Country Club where she and Jim were members.

We all sat around the dinner table, enjoying the coffee and conversation. Uncle Max was smoking his pipe, while Jim, Elsie and Aunt Rene preferred cigarettes (remember, this *was* 1968 after all!). Elsie was using her coffee saucer as an ash tray, and as her cigarettes burned down, she would gently flick the ashes onto the saucer. And after a while, that pile of cigarette ash had become fairly substantial.

During the coffee and conversation, Aunt Rene passed around a plate of cookies. I took one and passed the plate to Elsie, who also took one and passed the plate to Uncle Max, who passed it on to Jim. Elsie

---

[*] *A flexible Parawing, invented in 1948 by NASA engineer Francis Rogallo and his wife Gertrude. It was developed in hopes of replacing traditional parachutes for Gemini space capsule re-entry. If you look up the Rogallo Wing in Wikipedia, you will find Jim Hobson mentioned as a pioneer of its use as a hang-glider.*

[†] *Ray Milland won an Academy Award for his portrayal of an alcoholic writer in "The Lost Weekend."*

was animatedly engaged in the conversation and without even looking put her cookie down on her saucer, inadvertently inserting it quite deep into that substantial pile of cigarette ash that had accumulated there.

I couldn't help but notice this, and concerned that she might unwittingly bite into a cookie completely coated with cigarette ash, I just kind of instinctively leaned over to Elsie and said very softly, "Excuse me, Mrs. Hobson, but you've put your cookie in your ashes." She immediately turned to me with a twinkle in her eye, put her hand up to her face in mock indignation and said quite loudly, "I beg your pardon, young man! I've stuck my cookie in my *what*?"

And as quick as that, Elsie the actress had seized upon my awkward, unsolicited "rescue" attempt, and had flipped it back on me for maximum comic effect. The table exploded into laughter. "Jim," she said in an exaggerated Mississippi drawl, "I think this young man's trying to tell me just where I should stick my cookie!"

As you can imagine, I was absolutely horrified at my sudden dinner party faux pas. "What? No! Oh, no! Oh, I'm so sorry!" I sputtered, turning various shades of red. "That's not what I meant!" I pointed to her cookie, still sitting deep in the pile of ashes in her saucer. "It was just that…your cookie—"

Elsie laughed heartily, cutting me off. "Relax, darling boy," she said, gently patting me on my arm. "I heard exactly what you said. And it was very sweet of you to warn me. But if you think I was going to pass up a great set-up like that, you don't know me very well!" Everyone laughed again. She put her arm around my shoulder, gave me a hug and said, "Come to think of it, you *don't* know me very well, do you? But to use a golf analogy, if you keep teeing it up for me like that, I'm just going to have to keep you around as my personal caddy!"

Fortunately, the rest of the evening was much less embarrassing as the party moved from the dining room to the living room. One of the things I learned during the evening's conversation was that just like Uncle Max and Aunt Rene, the Hobsons also had no children. But Jim was like a big kid himself when it came to the subject of hang gliding, a sport which I was hearing about for the very first time. We also talked about music. Uncle Max played him my band's record. He seemed to genuinely like it. He asked which instrument I'd played on the record, and I told him it was a 12-string guitar, but that I also played the drums. Later on, Jim asked me what I intended to study at UCLA. I told him that I was hoping to major in Television and Film Production, which naturally led to the subject of his position as producer-director of *The Lawrence Welk Show*.

As the dinner party was breaking up, Jim asked me if I would like to be his guest at the ABC Television Studios and observe *The Lawrence Welk Show* being videotaped whenever I was on a break from school. Believe me when I tell you that I couldn't say "yes" fast enough! He gave me his phone number and told me to call him whenever I was out of school, and he would arrange for me to come down to the studio.

Although I couldn't fully grasp the significance of it at the time, that dinner party turned out to be a major turning point in my life…

Over the next four years, both at UCLA and later at San Diego State, I took Jim up on his generous offer. Whenever I had a break from college, I would call Jim and ask if it would be convenient for me to come and observe the show. And if the show was taping during that time, his answer was always, "Sure, come on down." Then he'd follow up with, "Just let me know when you're coming, and I'll leave a drive-on* for you with the security guard at the gate."

I can't tell you how exciting it was for a kid who was barely out of high school to drive up to the security gate at the ABC Television Center that very first time, lean out of my car window and say to the guard, "Hi. My name is Doug Smart, and I'm here to see Jim Hobson with the Lawrence Welk Show."

I was afraid the guard was going to take one look at me and say, "Who do you think you're fooling, kid? You're way too young to have any business with him!" But he didn't. He just picked up his clipboard, moved his finger down the list of names, and said, "Oh, yes, Mr. Smart. I have your name right here."

Then he pulled a parking pass from his clipboard, handed it to me and said, "Just put that on your dashboard." He pointed towards the "visitor" section of the parking lot. "You can park in any spot that doesn't have a name on it." Then he pointed the opposite direction,

---

* A *"drive on"* is a permission slip arranged through the studio's security detail, allowing a visitor to bring their vehicle through the security gate and onto the studio lot.

toward a small avenue between the cluster of soundstages, each one identified by a large number painted on the side of the building. "The Welk Show is taping on Stage 55. After you park, just go down that street to the courtyard and turn right. You can't miss it. Have a nice day." And just like that, I was "on the lot" at ABC!

There's no need to discuss my college years in detail. I highlight portions of them elsewhere in this book.* Let's just say I used that time to take full advantage of Jim's very generous offer. Over the next four years I became a human sponge, soaking up every bit of knowledge I could regarding how *The Lawrence Welk Show* was put together. I learned how it progressed from "script to screen," and the process of converting musical scores into a "shooting script" for the TV camera crew at ABC.

I observed how Jim, as the show's director, interacted with his associate director and technical director in the control room, along with his camera operators and stage managers down on the studio floor. And each time I came to observe the show, Jim introduced me to more and more people in both the cast and on the crew. Thanks to Jim, I was able to begin developing personal relationships with many of them. And they were very gracious, always willing to take a little time out of their day to answer my questions about their specific areas of responsibility to the show. And by the time I graduated from college, I knew how all of the pieces fit together.

....

Shortly after graduation I found employment with Warner and Associates,† a small independent film company in West Hollywood. We produced what was known back then as "Industrial Films," shot inexpensively on 16-millimeter film stock as opposed to the more expensive 35-millimeter film used to shoot feature films (for you younger readers, this was how it was done before the development of portable video recording equipment!).

---
* Refer to the chapter on Desi Arnaz and Lucille Ball.
† Warner & Associates had absolutely no affiliation with Warner Bros. Studios, although company owner Jerry Warner would never volunteer that information to his clients. He would only admit it if someone made a point of asking.

We made these films for companies and organizations that needed an employee training film, or maybe an OSHA-approved "safety in the workplace" film, or a "highlight" film touting a company's success, in order to assure investors or stockholders that their investment in that company was a sound one. It wasn't really the kind of production I wanted to be doing, but at least I was learning the craft of filmmaking. There were just three "associates" at "Warner & Associates," and the three of us did everything. And I was getting paid…barely. I was making the princely sum of $110 dollars per week…*before* taxes! To make ends meet, I was living in a $75 dollar-per-month studio apartment that had been converted from a 2-car garage, cooking on a hotplate, and washing what few dishes I had in the bathroom sink!

However, one major advantage of that job was that our offices were just a few blocks down Santa Monica Blvd from the Radio Recorders Annex, a famous recording studio originally built by the RCA Victor company.* And the Annex just happened to be where *The Lawrence Welk Show* rehearsed their TV show until late in the evening every Thursday. The band and singers also used the studio's state-of-the-art recording equipment to pre-record any big "production numbers" the TV microphones couldn't adequately capture when they taped the show live in front of an audience at ABC the following Tuesday. And just like at ABC, Jim Hobson had extended an open invitation for me to come by and observe at the Annex as often as I wanted and to stay as long as I liked.

And that's exactly what I did…

Every Thursday afternoon, just as soon as my responsibilities at Warner & Associates were complete, I would hop on my little Honda 350 motorcycle (which was all I could afford on $110 dollars per week) and scoot east up Santa Monica Blvd, turning south one block past La Brea Ave onto Sycamore Ave, and then down Sycamore a block to the Recording Annex. There I would spend the rest of my evening, with Jim and all of the other members of Lawrence Welk's "Musical Family" of musicians, arrangers, singers, and dancers.

---

* *In 1986, the Annex was bought by The Record Plant as its west coast studio and has been used by numerous recording artists over the years, including Beyoncé, who recorded parts of her "Lemonade" album there.*

The environment at the Annex was completely different than at ABC, because it was really a place where the cast members and musicians were all working things out, rehearsing, and refining their featured numbers for the upcoming show. So while I was able to develop relationships with the TV crew at ABC, it was at the Annex where I was able to really begin establishing relationships with many of the show's singers, dancers, and musicians.

As the director, Jim was the only member of television production crew at the Annex. He would spend much of his time in the studio's control booth, where recording engineer Thorne "Thorny" Nogar would make him low-fidelity reference recordings, or "ref tapes" of each musical number they were rehearsing or pre-recording for that week's show on audio cassettes.[*]

Jim would then take these recordings down the hall to his office space, where he would "transcribe" the recordings into a hand-written shooting script that could be used for TV.[†] Using the audio cassette player on his desk, Jim would playback each "ref tape" in short sections, one section at a time, counting the measures of music as he listened. He would then stop the tape and write down what he had heard on the recording. He would sit at his desk transcribing in pencil as he recited aloud what he'd just heard in phrases like, "four bars of trumpet, then two bars of trombone, into an eight-bar piano solo…"

This was a painstaking process, and Jim would often still be at that desk very late into the night, long after the musicians and singers had gone home, while Thorny and the studio crew put away all the gear. But I'd been coming down to the Annex and observing this time-consuming process for quite some time now. And I realized that there was an opportunity to stop being just an observer and start making myself more useful to Jim.

One Thursday night I made my pitch. "Jim," I said, "You know I can't get over here until five o'clock, when I'm done at work. But when I *do* get here, what if I stayed in the booth with Thorny and waited

---

[*] *Audio cassettes were the most popular medium for music recording and playback in the 1970's and 1980's, bridging the gap between the era of vinyl records and that of the digital compact disc, or CD.*

[†] *An office secretary to would take Jim's hand-written copy and then create a typed script for photocopying and distribution to the TV crew.*

for the ref tapes, and then brought them to you so you wouldn't have to keep running back and forth? That way you'd be able to work on your scripts without being interrupted, and maybe you'd be able to get out of here earlier."

Jim said, "Oh, man, that would be great!" So that's what we did. As soon as I got to the Annex each Thursday, I would check in with Jim, and then I'd head across the recording studio floor to the booth and sit at the mixing board with Thorny. As soon as the band and singers had finished rehearsing a number, Thorny would pop the ref tape out of the cassette recorder, and I would hustle back across the recording studio floor to Jim's office and hand him the tape for transcribing. Doing this accomplished two things: 1) hustling the tapes from the studio to Jim's office really did save him valuable time, and 2) continually walking back and forth across that busy recording studio in front of all the musicians and cast members dramatically raised my visibility among them!

We'd been at it a few weeks, and Jim seemed genuinely pleased with the results, joking that Elsie was delighted to see him home so early on Thursday nights. He said she was now teasing him about having been "sandbagging it" for all those years. I decided to see if I could press my luck a bit further. After one Thursday night session, I said, "Jim, I've been thinking. Would it be okay with you if next Thursday I brought in a second cassette player and tried my hand at transcribing some of these songs myself? Each one I could do would be one less that you'd have to do."

"Do you think you know how?" he asked.

"Yes," I replied. "Jim, you've let me come down and observe. And I've observed. I'm sure I can do it. But we could start with some of the simpler songs, if you'd like. When I'm done with a song, you could just check my breakdown against the ref tape and make any minor corrections or adjustments you think are needed. With two of us doing it, you could get home to Elsie even earlier!"

So that following Thursday, I brought in my own cassette player with me to the Annex and in addition to "schlepping" the tapes from Thorny to Jim, I started transcribing some of the musical numbers in the show. I began with short, simple songs at first, such as solo vocals by Norma Zimmer, the show's "Champagne Lady" and Irish tenor Joe

Feeney, or duets sung by the husband-and-wife team of Guy Hovis and Ralna English. After a couple of weeks, I was able to start adding small group numbers, such as up-tempo songs performed by the "Hotsy Totsy Boys," a combo of four or five band members named in honor of Lawrence's original band.

Once I had mastered those, I tried my hand at transcribing some "audience dance" numbers. These were bright, up-tempo instrumentals that allowed the TV studio audience to get up out of their seats and dance on the studio floor while the band played. Each episode of the show contained at least one, but more often two "audience dance" numbers. Most of these songs were only around two minutes in length, adhering to Lawrence's edict to keep the show moving along at a brisk pace. Transcribing these shorter instrumentals afforded me the opportunity to become more competent at the process.

After a while, I was proficient enough to handle what the staff of musical arrangers referred to as the "epics." These were much longer specialty numbers, often running four to five minutes, usually changing both time and key signatures at various points. On show night, George Cates, the show's musical director, would conduct the epics on-camera and they would always involve the entire orchestra, often including our cast of singers as well, adding a choral element to the production. These epics would often showcase a medley of songs written by one of Lawrence's favorite composers such as Irving Berlin or Cole Porter. Other times they might feature a salute to a popular stage or movie musical, or a well-known band leader. I began to enjoy taking on the challenge that they presented.

Jim seemed to be genuinely pleased with my efforts, and with each passing week, he was making fewer and fewer changes to my breakdowns. Then one Thursday night, it finally happened. Jim and I had just finished the evening's work and were packing up to leave. He closed his briefcase, turned to me, and said, "Doug, you're here every week, and to be honest, I'm starting to count on you being here. So I've been thinking that maybe we should make it official. What I'm saying is, would you like a job on the show as my production assistant?"

My response was immediate. "Jim, I thought you'd never ask!" He laughed. Hard. He told me he'd thought about asking me sooner, but had stopped himself, thinking the show might be too "corny" for my tastes.

"Well, I'll be honest with you, Jim," I said. "I'm not a fan of the accordion. To me it's the musical equivalent of fingernails on a chalkboard. But I love this show and would be thrilled to be a part of it!"

And so as far as Jim and I were concerned, it was settled. But there were a few details that needed to be ironed out. Jim said, "The show has never had a PA before. You'll be our first."

"Wait, you're making up a job for me?" I asked. "Will Lawrence be okay with that?"

"I'll just tell him I need you, which is the truth. Hiring you will make my job easier. That shouldn't be a problem. But before I talk to Lawrence, we need to decide what your double is going to be."

"My double?" I asked.

"Yeah, it's like this. Lawrence only hires people who can do more than one thing. That way he always gets "two for the price of one." All of our musicians can either "double" on a second instrument, sing, or dance. Likewise, our arrangers can also play an instrument or sing. The singers either play an instrument or they can dance a little. Even I'm both the producer *and* director. Everybody doubles at something. Now as I recall, you play guitar and drums, right?"

"Right," I said. "But drums are my main instrument."

"Fine. Are you in the union?"

"Yes, I'm in Local 47 here in Hollywood." I had joined the musician's union in Los Angeles during my days playing in a rock and roll band. When the band folded, I considered whether or not I should continue paying my membership dues to the AF of M.[*] When you're only making $110 dollars a week (and you're no longer playing in a band), it's tempting to think of something like union dues as a non-essential expense. At that moment I was very thankful that I had resisted that temptation.

"Perfect!" Jim said. "Then when Lawrence asks, and trust me, he *will* ask, I'll tell him I'm hiring you as my production assistant, but

---

[*] *The American Federation of Musicians, or AF of M. It is the labor union representing musicians who work professionally in theatrical productions, motion pictures, television, radio and concert performances.*

that you're also a card-carrying professional drummer. That will satisfy him that you're a good hire."

So that was it. On the basis of our handshake agreement, I gave my two week notice at Warner & Associates, and that following Thursday night at the Annex, Jim told me he'd met with Lawrence, who had approved of hiring me. It was official. As we shook hands, he said, "Oh by the way, last week you and I never discussed your salary. Lawrence offered you $150 per week."

But before I could even say, "Thank you!" Jim cut me off, adding, "But I told him I didn't think you could live on $150, so he agreed to pay you $175 per week, okay?"

"Okay? Jim, that's fantastic! That's $65 dollars a week more than I'm making now!"

"I know," he said, grinning. "But it wouldn't look good for my new production assistant to keep on living in a garage."

Later that evening, as I was "schlepping" the ref tapes back and forth across the studio, I apparently couldn't contain my excitement, because Barney Liddell and Kenny Trimble, two trombone players who had been with Lawrence for decades, pulled me aside. Both Barney and Kenny were accomplished musicians but were also well-known among the cast and crew for their humorous, and sometimes outrageous antics. Barney said, "Doug, what's up with you tonight? You look like the fox in the henhouse!"

"That's because I've just been officially hired on the show!" I blurted. "I'm the new production assistant!"

"What do you mean, you've just been hired?" Kenny said. "Man, you've been here for ages! Everybody knows you. We all just assumed you were already on the staff."

"Yeah," Barney added, laughing. "As a matter of fact, Kenny and I have been trying to figure out what kind of prank we were going to pull on you!" They both laughed and slapped me on the back in congratulations. Later that evening, Jim came out to the studio floor and "officially" welcomed me in front of everyone as the show's new production assistant.

So I became the newest member of Lawrence Welk's "Musical Family" with Jim Hobson as my new boss. But much more than that, Jim was also my mentor and my friend. He not only took me in and created a job for me where none had previously existed but also negotiated my first pay raise! Thanks to Jim, my television career was off to a "Wunnerful, wunnerful"* start! (Sorry. I know it's corny, but I just couldn't resist!)

....

And so, during my very first week as Jim's assistant, I suddenly found myself in a place so exclusive that even many of the show's veteran performers had never been there: *The Lawrence Welk Show*'s weekly production meeting.

The Lawrence Welk Show was taped in front of an audience at the ABC Television Center on Tuesday nights. Still adhering to the model that had been used since the 1950's, when all TV variety shows had been broadcast live, our tapings would begin precisely at 8:00 p.m., and end just as precisely fifty-eight minutes and thirty seconds later. Once the show started, no one except Jim Hobson was allowed to yell "cut" and stop the taping. If the musicians played a wrong note, they "owned it." If the singers forgot the lyrics, they hummed the melody until the words came back to them. The show was performed "live on tape" in just under an hour. Even the opening titles and closing credits were inserted "hot" during the taping, as well as all of the required commercial breaks. Therefore, no post-production editing was required. Once the show was "in the can," the performers and the audience all went home, and the TV crew disassembled the set. By 9:00 p.m. on Tuesday night, each episode was complete and ready for distribution to our syndicated network of 150 TV stations in the United States and Canada.

At 9:00 a.m. the following Wednesday morning, the process of planning and assembling future episodes would take place in Lawrence's

---

* *Comedian Stan Freberg famously mocked Lawrence Welk's dialect in his signature phrase "Wonderful, Wonderful" by mispronouncing it "Wunnerful, Wunnerful," in a classic comedy sketch. Afterwards, a number of other comedians and impressionists followed suit. But in reality when Lawrence used the phrase, it would actually come out more like "Wun-da-ful, Wun-da-ful."*

suite of offices in Santa Monica, at the corner of Ocean Ave and Wilshire Blvd, overlooking the iconic Santa Monica Pier and the even more iconic Pacific Ocean. But Lawrence didn't just rent this office space. He was an ownership partner of the entire high-rise tower complex. However, most people were unaware that Lawrence Welk owned the building, since the exterior bore the name of its major tenant, the General Telephone company. The office tower was simply known to the residents of Santa Monica as the GTE Building.

The production staff who attended these weekly meetings represented several areas of expertise and decades of experience. On the "television" side of things, was, of course, Jim Hobson, the show's producer and director. Assisting him was Jack Imel, a "triple threat" performer who was not only an excellent dancer, but who could also sing and play the marimbas (occasionally at the same time!). During Jack's tenure on the show, he had displayed an interest in production, so Jim had made him the show's associate producer. I was now only the third member of the staff to represent the broadcast aspect of the show.

Representing the "musical" side of things was, of course, Lawrence himself. He was joined by George Cates, the show's musical director (and Lawrence's "black hat"),* arrangers Bob Ballard, Joe Rizzo and Curt Ramsey, and former trumpet player Gus Thow, who was responsible for Lawrence's dialogue in between the musical numbers, and then creating the cue cards that Lawrence would read on the air.

I really enjoyed being accepted as a part of the production staff, but I have to confess at times I really felt like a "fish out of water" with the people I fondly (but privately) regarded as the "group of old men." When I joined the show, Lawrence Welk was already in his early 70's. George Cates and Gus Thow were both in their 60's. Jim Hobson, Bob Ballard, and Curt Ramsey were all in their 50's, and Jack Imel was the "youngster" of the group, as he was only in his mid-40's. By contrast, I was barely twenty-four. That "group of old men" each had a lifetime of experience in show business. I basically had none. I had a lot to learn.

---

* *A "black hat" is someone involved in production who is willing to be the bearer of bad news. This person is usually employed by someone who always wants to wear the "white hat," and only bring good news to his or her employees. I discuss this in greater detail in the chapter on Jerry Seinfeld.*

The shows were planned weeks in advance, and each show revolved around some kind of theme. Some themes were obvious and would recur annually, such as our "holiday shows" for Christmas, Easter, and Thanksgiving. Others usually featured songs chosen around a theme such as "A Salute to Broadway," "Far Away Places," or "A Tribute to Duke Ellington."

We needed those weeks of advance planning in order to pull the various elements of each show together. Sets had to be designed and constructed, wardrobe had to be pulled from the warehouse and fitted, and each piece of music selected for the show had to be "cleared." Now I mentioned in a previous paragraph that I had a lot to learn. And one of the things I learned very quickly was that the Lawrence Welk people saw on TV, the down-home bandleader playing the accordion and dancing the polka was just one part of who he actually was. The Lawrence Welk that I was now getting the chance to know was also a very astute businessman, especially for someone who had left school in the fourth grade to work on his family's farm.

I couldn't help but notice the parallel between my new boss Lawrence Welk and my old mentor, Desi Arnaz. Desi had spent years working in nightclubs with his band and had saved up his "Babalu" money to launch *I Love Lucy* and Desilu Productions.* Similarly, Lawrence had spent years playing in ballrooms throughout the mid-west with his Hotsy Totsy Boys, and later the Champagne Music Makers. And like Desi, Lawrence had leveraged that hard-earned income to form his own company, Teleklew Productions (the "Tele" in Teleklew was from the word "television" and the "klew" was just "Welk" spelled backwards). Teleklew Productions made very profitable investments in southern California real estate† and acquired a large number of music publishing companies. Through Teleklew Productions, Lawrence had purchased more than 100 publishing companies and controlled more than 100,000 copyrights, covering every single genre of popular music!

---

* *I discuss this in greater detail in the chapter on Desi Arnaz and Lucille Ball.*
† *Lawrence also built the "Champagne Towers" apartment complex adjacent to the office building at 100 Wilshire Blvd in Santa Monica. His corporation also developed a golf resort in Escondido, CA, outside of San Diego, and a resort in Palm Springs, CA.*

Lawrence knew from his years in the music business that there was big money to be made in music publishing. Each time a piece of copyrighted sheet music is sold, a royalty is paid to the company that published it. The same holds true when that piece of music is recorded by any artist and sold as a record, or played on the radio, on television, or in a motion picture. Publishing royalties are even paid for "elevator music," the now-generic term applied to music you might hear while riding in an elevator, or in stores, or in restaurants, or even when you've been put "on hold" on your phone, waiting for "the next available operator to assist you."

Lawrence always referred to the musicians and performers on his show, and even those of us on his production and office staff, as his "Musical Family." And to him, we really were like a family. Lawrence assumed the role of the family patriarch, placing us in the role of his "children." And I think that in similar way, Lawrence perhaps viewed his organization as resembling a large house in which the Musical Family resided, with each group of "family members" existing and functioning within its designated room in that house.

For example, Jim and I resided in the "television room," which contained all of the elements pertaining to the weekly TV show. But the next room over might be the "recording room," where George Cates would oversee the production of the record albums and singles for sale and for radio distribution. There was also a "room" designated for planning out the schedule for our live touring shows, as well as a "real estate investment room," and of course a "music publishing acquisition room."

I developed this particular point of view over a period of time as I observed the way in which Lawrence would work closely with all of us in those meetings. I noticed that he preferred to keep as many of the various elements necessary for business "in the house" whenever possible. Let me give you just one example using music publishing.

Each one-hour show would feature approximately twenty musical numbers. As I mentioned earlier, with the exception of the "epics," Lawrence preferred that all songs performed on the show be no longer than two minutes. His "two-minute rule" accomplished two things: 1) it allowed us to do more songs in a show, which kept the pace lively (very important to Lawrence), and 2) having more songs improved our chances of being able to feature each performer on the show that week.

The cast were all paid a weekly salary, whether they were assigned a featured number in the show or not. And when the songs were being chosen for the show, Lawrence would always ask who would perform what. He really chafed at the idea that he might have to pay a week's salary to someone who basically had nothing to do in the show that week. So the production staff worked diligently to make sure that everyone was included in some way in every show.

But the cost of paying the publishing royalties on twenty songs per week was no small amount. Therefore, Lawrence had another rule. He would not feature any piece of music that cost more than $250 dollars in publishing royalties. This rule allowed the show to set a budget line item for music clearance royalties at roughly $5000 per episode.

But there was one obvious exception to this rule. And that exception was as follows: if a piece of music was owned by one of Lawrence's publishing companies, then the cost of the royalty payment was irrelevant, because it meant that Lawrence could keep the money "in the house." To pay the royalty, he just mentally moved the money from his "television room" into his "music publishing room." As far as he was concerned, his money never left the building!

Now, everyone in the "group of old men" was keenly aware of the "$250 rule" and also aware of the exception. As a result, they were always very mindful when selecting songs for the show. Whenever possible, they would try to choose either songs from one of Lawrence's publishing companies, or songs from other publishers that cost $250 dollars or less. Whenever a song was pitched in a meeting, the first thing Lawrence would ask was, "Do we own it?" If the answer was "yes," then we simply moved on to the next song. If the answer was "no," then Lawrence's next question would always be, "Then how much does it cost?" Again, once he was assured that it was $250 or less, we would move on.

In addition to those annual holiday-themed shows I mentioned previously, it seemed as though every season we would do a show featuring the music of stage and film composer Jerome Kern. I once asked Jim Hobson why Lawrence made a point of doing a salute to Jerome Kern every year. He just laughed and said, "Two reasons. First,

Lawrence absolutely loves Kern's music. And second, Lawrence owns the publishing rights to the entire Jerome Kern catalog!" He laughed again and added, "Oh, and reason number two is the reason for reason number one!"

....

It was mid-morning on a Wednesday, and we were in the middle of our weekly production meeting. Everyone was hard at work, deciding on the final show order for next Tuesday's taping, talking through Thursday's musical arrangements for the Annex, following up on the final wardrobe and staging details, and brainstorming themes for future episodes.

Lawrence was at his desk, mid-way through his first bowl of Kellogg's All-Bran (by the end of the day on Wednesdays he would usually have consumed at least three large bowls of All-Bran!). Suddenly he pointed his spoon at us and said enthusiastically, "Oh, by da way boys, I heard dis wondaful new song on da radio dis morning, and I think we should do it on da show. It could be a really cute number."

We all stopped what we were doing. Lawrence rarely pitched songs for the shows, preferring to let the staff pitch to him instead. And it was even more unusual for him to get this enthusiastic about anything new or current.

George Cates, the show's musical director asked, "What's the name of the song, Lawrence?" Lawrence said, "I had Lois (his secretary) find da title for me. She wrote it down, so I wouldn't forget." Still holding the spoon, he reached into his pocket, and pulled out a folded slip of paper. "Here it is. Da song is called…" He unfolded the paper. "…Shake Your Booty."

Yes, you read that right. The new song that Lawrence wanted to do on his show was "Shake Your Booty" by KC and the Sunshine Band. My immediate thought was: *Well, this should be interesting!* And it was.

"Do we have a copy we can listen to?" George asked. Lawrence replied, "No, not yet. Lois sent someone out to get us a copy. But it's a cute song, and da lyric "shake your booty" repeats over and over in da chorus." By now he was sort of waving that spoon around as if it were his conductor's baton. "So, I was thinking, we could give da song to da three girls Sandi, Gail, and Mary Lou, and have Rose (the show's costume designer) dress them in "Doctor Dentons." You know, those old-timey pajamas for children that have da little booties on der feet? And da girls could maybe dance around in kind of a conga line while dey sang. You know, sticking out der feet, and shaking der little booties!"

It was obvious that Lawrence was totally unaware of the real meaning of the song's lyrics, thinking that "Shake Your Booty" was most likely some new kind of twist on the old song "The Hokey Pokey." For those of you reading this who are unfamiliar with that song, it goes as follows: "Put your right foot in, put your right foot out. Put your right foot in, and shake it all about. Do the hokey pokey and turn yourself around. That's what it's all about." It's one of those songs that I think a lot of us probably learned as children.

I waited for someone to speak up, but no one did. Apparently, no one at the meeting except Lawrence and I had ever heard "Shake Your Booty," and between the two of us, I was the only one who knew what the lyrics actually meant.

I was a bit apprehensive about just what I should do next. As the youngest and least experienced member of the production staff, I had decided from the outset that my main responsibility at these Wednesday meetings was to just sit quietly, observe, and learn. And while I was able to contribute from time to time, it had been my practice to never enter into the conversation unless invited, and even then to only offer my input or opinion when asked (usually by Jim, who would take it upon himself to make sure I had an opportunity to contribute something at each one of the meetings).

However, since no one else in the room was offering Lawrence any kind of feedback, I felt a sense of duty as a member of the production staff to speak up. "Excuse me, Lawrence," I said, swallowing hard, "But I think that would be a mistake. That song is not right for your show."

Lawrence just looked at me from over his bowl of All-Bran. And I could feel everyone else in the room looking at me as well. Lawrence just sat there, rocking lightly back and forth in his executive office chair, tapping his cereal spoon on the armrest, studying me. From the expression on his face, I could only guess as to what he might be thinking. On the one hand, this new kid, this inexperienced youth, had never just spoken up to him like that. And now when the kid finally does speak up, he has the nerve to question Lawrence's judgment about a song. But on the other hand, the kid also appeared to have the best interest of his show at heart.

So he sat there, rocking, tapping his spoon and mentally weighing it all. After a very long pause he said, "I see. So, do you know something about dis song, young man?"

"Yes, sir. I do." I replied. "It's by a group called KC and The Sunshine Band." Since we had no copy of the song to play, I just sang the familiar chorus to Lawrence. "Shake, shake, shake. Shake, shake, shake. Shake your booty. Shake your booty."

Lawrence nodded, recognizing that I was indeed referring to the same song he'd heard that morning. He continued to tap his cereal spoon on the arm of his chair. And after yet another very long pause, he said, "Yes, dat's da one. Okay. So tell me, Doug. Why do you think dis song is wrong for my show?"

"Because the lyrics don't mean what you think they mean," I replied. "And if you put it on the show, the public reaction is going to be like 'One Toke Over the Line' all over again." At the very mention of that song Lawrence stopped tapping his spoon and stiffened up. So did everyone else in the room. Except me. I didn't have to. I was already scared stiff and had been since the moment I'd decided to speak up.

Back in 1971, Lawrence had heard the hit song "One Toke Over the Line" by Mike Brewer and Tom Shipley. And one of the lines in the song contains the lyric, "One toke over the line, sweet Jesus." Lawrence thought the song had a very catchy melody, and because the lyrics mentioned Jesus, he believed it to be a modern, up-beat take on a gospel spiritual. So he decided to feature it on the show as a duet for Dick Dale and Gail Farrell.[*]

Unfortunately, neither Lawrence nor anyone on his production staff had known that to "toke" referred to smoking marijuana, and that when Mike Brewer wrote the lyric "one toke over the line," he was actually recalling a time when both he and Tom Shipley had been really stoned.

---

[*] *A video clip of Dick and Gail singing "One Toke Over the Line" on the show is accessible on YouTube*

And to make matters much worse, Lawrence didn't learn the truth about the song's true meaning until after the show had already been broadcast on TV. By then the media was abuzz with stories speculating as to how a song that the Vice President of The United States[*] had publicly denounced as "blatant drug-culture propaganda" wound up being featured on the squeaky-clean *Lawrence Welk Show* of all places! Needless to say, Lawrence had been publicly embarrassed by the incident and wasn't the least bit anxious to repeat it.

"Go on," he said flatly.

I glanced over at Jim, who nodded his encouragement. "Well, Lawrence," I said, "you're under the impression that the lyric 'shake your booty' means 'shake your boots, or shake your feet.' But it doesn't."

"It doesn't?" he repeated.

"No, sir," I continued. "Far from it. In the context of the song, when KC keeps repeating the line 'shake your booty,' he's not telling the girl he's dancing with to shake her feet. He's telling her to shake her, um…well, to shake her butt. You see Lawrence, 'booty' is a slang term for a woman's butt. So each time he says 'shake your booty,' what he *really* means is that he wants her to wiggle her butt for him in a provocative way."

Lawrence stopped tapping the cereal spoon. He looked like he'd just swallowed a live goldfish. Or two. Or maybe five. "Is dis true? 'Shake your booty' means to wiggle your butt?"

"Yes, sir. 'Shake your booty' really means wiggle your butt."

"And you're sure about dis?"

"Yes, Lawrence. I'm very sure."

"Well dis is just not right. If I were to do a song like dis on TV, I could lose my show!" Lawrence quickly scanned the room, looking for any signs of confirmation on the faces of his staff. "So what do you boys think about dis?" he asked.

As usual, Jim Hobson spoke up. "I'd trust Doug on this one, Lawrence." The rest of the "group of old men" seemed to concur.

Lawrence picked up his cereal spoon and began tapping again, only this time he was smiling. Then he pointed his spoon at me and said to

---

[*] *Spiro Agnew, the Vice President serving during the Nixon Administration, also pressured the FCC to ban the song from the radio due to its drug references. Rolling Stone Magazine voted it "#6 All-Time Best Stoner Song."*

the others in the room, "You see? Dis is why it's good to have a young person on da staff!" And with that, he laughed and poured himself another bowl of All-Bran as we all got back to work. And the subject of putting "Shake Your Booty" on the show was never mentioned again.

....

During my third season on the show, the ABC network was enjoying a particularly successful run of both prime-time and daytime programs. The network had so many shows in production that year that none of the sound stages at the ABC Television Center were available because they were being used for the production of their own programs.

And even though *The Lawrence Welk Show* had at one time been a staple of ABC's prime-time lineup of programs, it was now just a "tenant," renting the facilities from ABC. Even though ABC enjoyed having us around, when it came to the allocation of studio facilities, their network shows were the top priority. As a result, *The Lawrence Welk Show* got "bumped" from our long-time home on Stage 55 and relocated across town to the Hollywood Palace Theater.

In addition to their studios at The Television Center in the Los Feliz area of Los Angeles, ABC also owned the former Hollywood Playhouse Theater in "the heart of Hollywood," on Vine Street just a few steps up from the intersection with Hollywood Blvd., and directly across from the iconic Capitol Records tower.* ABC had renamed the facility "The Hollywood Palace," which was the name of their Saturday night variety show that had originated from the theater in the 1960's. The facility had had been sitting vacant ever since *The Hollywood Palace* TV show had been cancelled in 1970, only being used occasionally. And since there was no studio space available at the Television Center, *The Lawrence Welk Show* was relocated to the Hollywood Palace facility.

But studio space wasn't the only thing lacking at the Television Center. ABC's heavy production schedule meant that the number

---

* *The corner of Hollywood Blvd and Vine St is the central point of the "Hollywood Walk of Fame." It has long been a staple of popular lore in Los Angeles that "If you stand on the corner of Hollywood and Vine long enough, you will eventually see everyone you have ever known."*

of available crew members on the network's payroll had also been stretched very thin. And as with their sound stages, when it came to providing crew personnel, the network shows were the studio's top priority. While they had enough camera operators, audio and video engineers, electricians, and carpenters on staff to support all of the shows in production (including ours), it turned out that there was one key area in which ABC was understaffed. And this turned out to be a very lucky break for me.

Because *The Lawrence Welk Show* now suddenly needed a stage manager!

In my two years as the show's production assistant, I had learned a great deal and had been trained in a variety of jobs (including occasionally writing and holding Lawrence's cue cards on the show!). And during that period, I had made a point of spending as much time as I could with the show's "directing team," which included our two stage managers, "Woody" Woodworth and Ed Duzik, as well as our associate director, Ron Bacon. These three men possessed an amazing amount of knowledge and experience, and they were willing to share it with me. And I was extremely grateful for the opportunity to be able to learn from these talented professionals.

During the hiatus between our production seasons, Jim Hobson had once again taken me under his wing, sponsoring me into the Directors Guild of America. And that spring he made me his associate director for a TV variety special promoting the grand opening of Knott's Berry Farm's new "Roaring 20's" section of their theme park. When he asked me if I'd like to be the new stage manager at the Hollywood Palace, I enthusiastically said, "Yes!" almost before he could finish the question!

I discuss the duties of the stage manager in greater detail elsewhere in the book, so I'll skip the longer description here.* But in short, the stage manager is the director's "proxy" on the stage, making sure that everything runs smoothly, and is also the director's "voice" on the set, conveying the director's instructions from the control room to the cast and crew working on the stage.

---

* *You'll find a more detailed description of the duties of the stage manager in the chapter on Cher.*

I was really enjoying my new position. It was exciting to finally be down on the stage, working in front of the audience with Lawrence, the orchestra, and the cast! And in doing so, I discovered that working week after week as the stage manager was raising my profile among the show's veteran cast members and musicians. I had apparently "paid my dues" as the PA and now the show's veterans regarded me as more of a peer. It was the first time I truly felt as though I had become a full-fledged member of Lawrence Welk's "Musical Family!"

The first half of that season flew by, and we had just finished taping our last show before taking a two-week break for Christmas. After the show, everyone was invited to gather upstairs in the Mezzanine lounge of the Hollywood Palace Theater, where the company had set out a very pleasant Christmas buffet of hors d'oeuvres, pastries, Christmas cookies, and punch.

Everyone was having a good time laughing, discussing holiday plans, and wishing each other "happy holidays." And as we were all mingling, I could see Lawrence walking towards me. He had a big smile on his face and was nibbling on a Christmas cookie.

Once he reached me, he took me by the arm and, still nibbling on the cookie, said, "Doug, I just want you to know dat I'm so very impressed with da job you've been doing. Watching you out der tonight, you were just so professional!"

I was both surprised and touched. "Thank you, Lawrence," I replied.

"Which is amazing," he continued. "Because you were nothing when I found you!" With that he smiled, squeezed my arm in a kind of fatherly way, took another bite of his cookie, and turned away to go and mingle elsewhere.

And that, in a nutshell, was the key to understanding Lawrence Welk. To say he was a master of the "back-handed compliment" doesn't really do him justice. Lawrence had this unique ability to pay you the kind of sincere compliment that would really lift your spirits, making you feel as if you were floating in a warm bubble. And then in the very next breath he'd say something that would burst that bubble, sending you crashing back down to earth!

But if you took the time to get to know Lawrence, then you understood that he was truly an "innocent," completely unaware that anything he might say would be construed as hurtful. In Lawrence's head and heart, he was telling me, "I've been impressed with how far you've come in such a short time!" But when he tried to put that thought into words, it just came out as, "You were nothing when I found you!"

....

Everyone in Lawrence's "Musical Family" eagerly looked forward to the taping of our annual Christmas episode each November because it was indeed a "family" affair. The Christmas episode gave all of the performers the opportunity to introduce *their* families to the television audience watching at home. Each year the spouses and children of the band members, singers, and dancers would all come down to the studio dressed in their Sunday best to appear on the show. And since the Christmas show was a staple of every season, the loyal viewers at home would literally be able to watch these children grow up and mature from year to year.

And Lawrence always enjoyed featuring his own family on the show as well. In addition to his wife Fern, Lawrence's two daughters Shirley and Donna (who always seemed as though they were uncomfortable being on television) would be there with their families. And, of course, Lawrence's son, Lawrence Welk Jr., would make an appearance alongside his two sisters with his own family as well.

But for Lawrence Welk Jr., the term "Musical Family" wasn't just a metaphor. Larry Jr. had married Tanya Falan, a lovely young singer on the show with big brown eyes and an even bigger voice. The two started dating shortly after Tanya joined the show and got married about a year later. And within a few years, Tanya had given birth to their two sons, Lawrence Welk III and Kevin Welk. So in this case, Lawrence Welk's "Musical Family" and his actual family were one in the same.

At a designated time during the taping of the show, each of the performers would present their families, introducing each individual family member as Jim Hobson made sure that the TV cameras were framing that person in a close-up shot. And since family was everything to Lawrence, he always beamed with pride when introducing his own family. But Lawrence's unique way of speaking would affect his introduction of his "namesake" grandson, resulting in an unintentionally humorous and somewhat embarrassing bit of television each year.

As I mentioned in an earlier footnote, Lawrence spoke with an unusual German-American accent, which was often mimicked by comedians and impressionists. This accent resulted from his upbringing in a tightly-knit German farming community in Strasburg, North Dakota. He didn't learn how to speak English until after leaving the family farm at the age of twenty-one.

Sometimes people would ask me what language Lawrence spoke, and I would jokingly respond that he spoke "Welk-lish." I likened it to "Spanglish," which is a combination of Spanish and English. In my mind, Lawrence's mixture of his family's unique North Dakota-German dialect combined with English resulted in "Welk-lish."

For example, in Lawrence's Welk-lish, the "TH" combination might sometimes be pronounced as "D," but other times might come out sounding like a "T." The letter "B" would somehow become "P," and various other little odd quirks. As a result, words such as "this" or "that" would become "dis" or "dat," and words like "think" or "thought" would become "tink" or "taut." And phrases like "everyone needs to be on time" would come out as "everyone needs to pee on time," (much to the amusement of the musicians and cast!)

All of which brings me back to my point. Each year on the Christmas show, when Lawrence would introduce his grandson Lawrence Welk III, in his mind he was telling the viewers, "This is my handsome grandson, Lawrence Welk the Third!" But in Welk-lish, what the television audience *actually* heard was, "Dis is my handsome grandson, Lawrence Welk da Turd!" (again, much to the amusement of the musicians and cast!)

Although he bears his grandfather's namesake legacy, Lawrence Welk III decided not to go into the "family business" in the music industry. Instead, as a young man he worked his way up through the ranks of broadcast journalism in Los Angles. He has had a very successful career as both a photojournalist and a news helicopter pilot. I'm sure that Lawrence would be very proud of the man his grandson has become. And I will always remember him fondly as the exuberant, cheerful, and energetic little boy who gracefully endured having his grandfather introduce him on national television as "Lawrence Welk da Turd!"

Since we're on the subject of Welk-lish, it feels like a good time to segue into the topic of Lawrence's frequent, and usually humorous, mishandling of the English language. He became quite well-known for his unintentional malaprops. Lawrence once told me that during NASA's early tests of its space shuttle program, he'd been frightened by the "masonic boom" the shuttle had created upon its re-entry in the desert outside of Los Angeles.

Yogi Berra, the Hall of Fame catcher for the New York Yankees, was famous for saying things like "You can observe a lot just by watching," and "It ain't over 'til it's over." And like Yogi, Lawrence Welk could also somehow mangle a phrase in an unintentionally humorous way. Biographies about Lawrence in print and on the Internet often note that he once famously said, "There are good days, and there are bad days, and this is one of them." But those of us who worked with him were treated to many more examples of these "Welk-isms," referring to the way in which Lawrence could unintentionally turn a phrase on its ear.

One time on the show, the "epic" number the band was performing featured a medley of songs from the World War I era. So when Gus Thow was creating the cue cards for Lawrence to read on the air, he simply wrote: "Now, here's George and the band bringing you a medley of songs from World War I." But when Lawrence introduced the number on the show, it came out as: "Now, here's George and the band bringing you a medley of songs from World War Eye."

These "Welk-isms" were like delightfully unpredictable little geysers. You just never quite knew when one would bubble up. One time it might be, "When you all band together, and everyone stands together, dat creates a house divided!" And another time it would be, "If you don't know da tune, just play da melody."

At a production meeting one Wednesday morning, he became frustrated with his arrangers while debating a song choice for the show and blurted out, "I think you're just trying to pull da wool over my ears!" And in 1976 during our country's bicentennial year, Lawrence said to me, "Doug, I want to send you out to shoot da four guys on da hill." Translation: "Doug, I want to send you out to film Mount Rushmore." It was a classic "Welk-ism." And to those of us who worked closely with Lawrence, they were always unexpected little treats. Sometimes when he would mangle the English language it was not only humorous but also be unintentionally racy or off-color. I submit the following story as an example…

....

We were nearing the finale of our live arena show in Madison, Wisconsin, one stop on our two-week June tour. Each year the entire "Musical Family" cast of musicians, singers, and dancers would tour the country in March, June, and August, playing "one-nighters" in cities large enough to have concert venues that could accommodate an audience of 16,000 people per show.

As the show's director, I was at my usual position half-way back in the audience at the arena's audio mixing board. Since the touring show never did a sound check with the band prior to the performance, I would assist the audio mixer (who was used to working with rock and roll acts) as he tried to balance the sound of a 24-piece big band "on the fly." From my location I could also direct the spotlight operators through each of their lighting cues for the 2 ½ - hour long show via a headset system.

We had come to the place in the show when the entire band needed to leave the bandstand in order to go backstage and change into red, white, and blue costumes for the show's patriotic finale. To fill the time while the band changed costumes, Lawrence would be onstage accompanied only by accordionist Myron Floren, as well as dancers Bobby Burgess and Cissy King. Lawrence would then invite members of the audience to come up onstage and dance with Bobby and Cissy while Myron played a polka on his accordion. Our "audience polka" segment was an audience favorite every night on tour.

So just like every night, as the band left the stage Lawrence asked me to bring up the "house lights" in the arena. Once the lights came up, he walked to the edge of the stage and using his microphone, asked if anyone would like to come up and dance a polka with Bobby and

Cissy. And just like every night, people jumped up from their seats and eagerly came up the aisles to the stage to dance with Bobby and Cissy. Once they had reached the stage, I would bring the house lights back down, now just using the spotlights. And as each person took their turn to dance, Lawrence would ask their names and engage them in a bit of light-hearted banter on the microphone before the polka began.

But on this night, when Cissy's last dance partner told Lawrence his name, there was an unexpectedly robust and enthusiastic reaction from the audience. Lawrence sensed that something was going on here. And as an experienced showman, he knew he should just go with it. "Wow!" he said, gesturing out towards the crowd in the arena. "Everybody here seems to know your name. Are they all related to you?" The audience laughed enthusiastically.

"No," the man replied. "But I own a large hog and dairy farm business, and all of the grocery stores in the region carry our sausage and dairy products. They recognize my name because it's on all of our products."

Lawrence turned and addressed the audience. "We've got someone famous here to dance with Cissy. But first we need to find out. Does he make good sausages?" The crowd roared their approval. Lawrence laughed and turned to the man, "Well, da people out der seem to think your sausages are pretty good!" Then he turned back out to the crowd. "Let's see if he's as good with da polka!" And with that, Lawrence cued Myron to start playing. With a bit of help from Cissy, the fellow managed pull off a pretty decent polka. The audience ate it up.

After they'd finished dancing, Lawrence addressed Cissy over the microphone, "Now as you know Cissy, we're here in Wisconsin, which is da heartland of America. And here da people still have da good manners. So I think it would be good if you escorted this fine gentleman all da way back to his seat." Both Cissy and I immediately picked up on Lawrence's ad-lib cue. So while Cissy took the fellow by the arm and started back through the audience, I made sure that the spotlights stayed with them.

But Cissy had only walked the fellow about twenty feet down the aisle when Lawrence suddenly called out to her over the microphone. "Oh, and Cissy?" he said, "If you're nice to him, maybe he'll slip you a sausage!"

At this point sixteen thousand people exploded with laughter at Lawrence's unintentional double-entendre. It would never have occurred to Lawrence that his off-hand remark that Cissy might be able to get a free breakfast sausage could also be taken as sexually suggestive. His mind simply didn't work that way. But from the crowd reaction, he knew he'd said something really funny. He just had no idea what it was. It was just one more reason I was so fond of him.

....

Sometimes communication with Lawrence would resemble playing the childhood game of "telephone," in which the final message has become so garbled in translation that it bears almost no resemblance to what was originally said. And this is exactly what happened one night while we were in the middle of taping our TV show. The result was hilarious to those of us who were involved, although somewhat off-color. The story requires a somewhat lengthy set-up, so please bear with me here.

About halfway through our season at the Hollywood Palace, our associate director Ron Bacon broke his arm and was unable to work. As a result, Jim Hobson asked me to fill in for Ron as the show's associate director until he could return. I had mixed emotions about my sudden promotion because Ron had become a good friend. While I was excited about this opportunity to gain some valuable new experience, I would have preferred that it not come as a result of a friend's injury.

One of my main areas of responsibility as the show's associate director was to make sure everything timed out properly. As I mentioned earlier in this chapter, *The Lawrence Welk Show* was done "live on tape," and each show had to be exactly fifty-eight minutes and thirty seconds in length. In order to accomplish this, I needed to run three separate stopwatches.

My first stopwatch timed the overall show itself. Each Tuesday night at exactly 7:59 p.m., I would give everyone in the studio the "one minute to air" cue over the headset. At that time Jim Hobson would call for the videotape machines to begin recording. Thirty seconds later, at 7:59:30 p.m., I would call, "Thirty seconds…start the bubbles," at which point the bubble machines behind the bandstand would start blowing bubbles into the air above the band.* At 7:59:45 pm I would announce "fifteen seconds," and five seconds later I would begin my countdown. "Fading up on camera two in 10, 9, 8…" And at exactly 8:00 p.m. Wally Stannard, our technical director, would fade the camera up from black, and I would start that first stopwatch. And if I did my job correctly, I would stop it exactly fifty-eight minutes and thirty seconds later, at 8:58:30.

My second stopwatch kept track of the show's three commercial breaks, which were scheduled at roughly fifteen-minute intervals, occurring near the fifteen, thirty, and forty-five minute marks in the show. Each of these commercial breaks needed be exactly two minutes and two seconds in length. No more, no less. When the time came for us to go to a commercial, I would count us down going *out* to the break, start watch #2, and then count us back *in* from the commercial break exactly 2:02 later. I would then re-set that watch back to zero in order to time the next commercial break.

Therefore, the timings for stopwatch #1 and stopwatch #2 were fixed and unchangeable. The timing for #1 must always be exactly 58:30, and #2 must always be exactly 2:02. Stopwatch #3 was a different matter altogether. Stopwatch #3 kept track of the duration of each program segment *in between* the commercial breaks. These show segments were constantly changing, depending on the songs that had been selected, the pace at which they were performed, and the amount of applause from the audience. By paying close attention stopwatch #3, I could continually monitor these fluctuating segment times. Then I would update my time calculations accordingly in order to make sure that the program always timed out at 58:30.

When you're doing a live show that absolutely must end at a predetermined time, you need to have a contingency plan to make sure that it does. On *The Lawrence Welk Show*, our contingency plan was the "Good Night" song.

---

* Yes, I was actually the guy responsible for starting up the famous bubble machines. The band members all hated the "bubble juice" which was sticky and would gum up horn valves and violin strings. So I would wait until the last possible moment to start the bubbles, and then make sure I turned the machines off as soon as I could after the show started

At the end of every show, the cast would assemble downstage of the band to perform a specially crafted closing song. They would sing, "Good night, good night until we meet again. Adios, Au Revoir, Auf Wiedersehn 'til then. And though it's always sweet sorrow to part, you know you'll always remain in my heart…" After the vocals, the band would continue to play the melody while the closing credits rolled on the screen, until the credits would fade to black at exactly 58 minutes and 30 seconds on the clock (if the associate director was doing his job correctly!).

We had three versions of the song: the "long good-nights" version, which contained one minute of vocals before the credits would roll, the "short good-nights" version, with thirty seconds of vocals before credits, and the "no good-nights" version, which contained no vocals, just the music for the credits.

As the show's time keeper, the decision regarding which version of "Good Night" we used each week was my responsibility. If the show was running short, I would call for the "long good-nights," so that the minute of vocals would make up for the missing time. Conversely, if the show was running long, I would call for the "short good-nights" or "no good-nights," depending on just how long the show was running.

This was an important responsibility, because both the "long good-nights" and the "short good-nights" meant that the vocalists had to get into their wardrobe and take their places on stage for the closing number. They also had to know if they were singing for a minute or for only thirty seconds. But if I called for "no good-nights," then the vocalists could remain in their dressing rooms, since only the band would be seen playing on stage. And every week it was different, since no two shows were alike.

During the rehearsals on show day, I would time each number with stopwatch #3 and then add all of those individual timings together to get an estimated length for the show. I would then factor in our estimated "audience spread," which accounted for the applause we expected each performance to receive from the studio audience during the show. While the "audience spread" timing was always a guess, it was an educated one based upon twenty years' worth of experience, and it rarely fluctuated more than five or ten seconds either way from show to show.

Okay, now that you know how we would bring the show in on time each week, I can finally get to the actual story I want to relate about Lawrence's unique ability to mishandle the English language (hey, I warned you it would be a long set-up, right?).

On this particular taping day, we had finished rehearsing each number in the show, and the cast and crew were getting prepared for our 5:00 p.m. dress rehearsal. But unlike our "stop and go" camera rehearsal during the day, the dress rehearsal consisted of running the entire show from top to bottom without stopping, but minus the studio audience.

We used this late afternoon break in between the camera rehearsal and the dress rehearsal to hold a brief production meeting. At the meeting I would report to Lawrence, Jim Hobson, and Jack Imel, our associate producer, updating them regarding the overall timing of the show. But on this day, when I added up all of the rehearsal timings I'd logged during the day and factored in the "audience spread," it was very clear to me that the show was about two minutes short.

So at the meeting I told Lawrence, Jim, and Jack that if all of the performances on the 8:00 p.m. show ran the same length as we'd just rehearsed them, we would be about a full minute short, even with the "long good-nights." Now one minute may not seem like much, but when you're the one staring into the lens of a TV camera with nothing to say, sixty seconds of "dead air" can feel like an eternity!

Lawrence asked me if I was positive about my timings, and I assured him that I was. The answer was obvious: we needed another song, something around a minute in length to fill the extra time. It was then that Jack Imel spoke up. "Lawrence," he said, "I have my marimbas here at the studio. I'm sure I can come up with a minute of something on the marimbas as a 'stand by' number at the end of the show if it turns out that we need it."

Now I should probably point out here that whenever Lawrence called Jack by name, it would come out sounding like "Shag." With his "Welk-lish," accent, "Jack" was "Shag" ("Shag" was also Jack's unofficial nickname among the rest of us as well). Lawrence liked Jack's solution to our problem. "Oh, fine Shag," he said. "Do you have a song in mind?"

Jack replied, "Oh, I'll just work up a chorus or two of 'Yellow Bird' or 'Tico Tico.' And towards the end of the show, I'll just stand next to Woody (our stage manager) off camera. Then we can roll the marimbas out quickly if we need to."

So it was settled. Our associate producer "Shag" Imel was our second contingency plan. As we went through our 5:00 p.m. dress rehearsal, my segment timings remained consistent with those I'd taken earlier in the day. We were still two minutes short. As we went into our last commercial break, I called for the "long good-nights" to give the cast time to get into wardrobe.

Just before we closed the show, Woody helped Jack roll his marimbas out on stage. Jack played a couple of choruses of "Tico Tico" so that Jim Hobson could see it on camera, and I could time it for the show. Jack finished the song with a flourish, and the cast sang the one-minute version of "Good Night. " As soon as the vocals were done, we rolled the credits and faded the camera to black, and I stopped watch #1 within a couple of seconds of being right on time. The plan was working.

At 6:30 p.m., we would always have another production meeting to discuss any problems that may have come up during the dress rehearsal and to make any final adjustments necessary for the 8:00 p.m. live taping. Lawrence was very interested in knowing if adding Jack's number to the dress rehearsal meant that we were back on time. I assured him that it did but added a caveat.

I told him, "Lawrence, if we do the same show at eight that we just did at five, then we'll be right on time. But you know that sometimes the eight o'clock show will spread. When we get a 'hot' audience, our singers have a habit of 'holding' their last few notes a bit longer than they did in rehearsal. Even George Cates will 'milk' it a bit when he's conducting the epic. Not to mention that the applause may last longer. So as it stands now, we're right on time. But it could change when the audience comes in. I'll have a better idea of where we stand when we're about halfway through the show." So that was where we left it. And at 8:00 p.m. on the dot, we started the show, and I started stopwatch #1.

As luck would have it, we did have a "hot" audience that night, and as I clocked each of the segments, I noticed that my show timing was indeed starting to spread a bit. As expected, the singers were "milking" their songs a bit more, and the audience was giving them enthusiastic applause. Fifteen minutes into the show, at the first commercial break, our timing was about eight or nine seconds longer than it had been in the dress rehearsal.

If the show continued to spread at that pace, we would only be about thirty seconds short, instead of one minute. So at that point in the show, I was calculating that with Jack's one-minute version of "Tico Tico," if I switched to the thirty-second "short good-nights" the show would come out right on time. But there was still a lot of show left.

We had reached the second commercial break and were halfway through the show. My segment timings were indicating that we were beginning to spread even more. I was now projecting that at the current pace, the show would come in around fifty seconds longer than it had in dress rehearsal. If this were the case, I had two options: 1) Jack could still play "Tico Tico" and I could call for "no good-nights" and go straight to closing credits, or 2) I could call "long good-nights" and not use Jack at all. Of course, there were still two more segments left in the show, and what if the pace were to suddenly pick up and go faster? Then I would definitely still need Jack and his marimbas.

Just then I heard Woody's voice in my headset. "Doug," he said, "I'm here with Lawrence. He wants to know where we stand with the show timing. He can feel that we've got a good audience, and he's asking if we still need Jack. He wants to talk to you, so I'm putting him on my headset."

After a second or two I heard Lawrence's voice in my headset. "Hello? Doug? Can you hear me?"

"Yes, Lawrence," I replied. "I can hear you."

"Oh, very good. It feels to me like we have a very good audience. Do you think we still need Shag?"

"It is a good audience, and the show is spreading a bit, but it's too early to say for sure. At this point it could go either way. So I would tell Jack that he still needs to stand by. But if we continue to spread at this pace, we most likely won't need him."

Lawrence responded, "Okay, I'll tell dat to Shag."

As it turned out, the rest of the show continued to spread, and we didn't need Jack to play "Tico Tico." Going into the last commercial, I called for the "long good-nights," and we finished the show right on time.

Afterwards, down on the studio floor, Jack was enjoying a cigarette break with Woody. As I approached, Jack grinned broadly, his cigarette clenched firmly in that grin, and said to me, "Doug, Woody and I would both like to know just what you said to the old man during the show." Jack gestured towards Woody and then turned back to me. At that moment he kind of resembled the Cheshire Cat, if the cat had smoked Lucky Strikes.

I looked at Woody, who was grinning as well. Clearly something was going on, but I had no idea what. "I told him that the show was spreading, but it was still too early to know for sure. So I told Lawrence to make sure you were standing by. But if the show continued to spread at the same pace, then we probably wouldn't need for you to go on."

Jack just continued to grin, the cigarette still firmly clenched in his teeth. He nodded to Woody, who smiled and nodded back.

"Why?" I asked. "What did Lawrence tell you?"

Jack's grin grew even wider. He took the cigarette out of his mouth with his right hand and put his left arm around my shoulder. "Well, I'll tell you, kid," he said, gesturing with the cigarette. "The old man gets off the headset with you and says to me…he says (imitating Lawrence's voice and accent), 'Shag, Doug wants you to pee on your toes. We may have to jerk you off later!'" And with that, both he and Woody burst into laughter. "Yessir. That's what the old man said to me! Doug wants you to pee on your toes. We may have to jerk you off later!"

Like I said earlier, communicating with Lawrence could often resemble a game of "telephone." Jack and I worked closely together both on the television show and the live tours, and "Pee on your toes" quickly became a staple of our "production vocabulary" for the remainder of my time with Lawrence's Musical Family.

....

Every summer we played the main showroom at Harrah's casino in Lake Tahoe for three weeks. We would do two shows per night, at 8:00 p.m. and midnight, forty-two shows over twenty-one nights. The showroom never took a night off or went "dark." The schedule at Harrah's was set up so that the incoming act would rehearse their show during the final day of the outgoing act. And then that night, the cast of the incoming show would be invited to attend the 8:00 p.m. show of the outgoing headliner. And this particular year, the headliner that preceded us at Harrah's was Sammy Davis, Jr. A couple of interesting things happened during our first two days at Harrah's, with the first occurring on the night of Sammy's last show, and the second on the following night during Lawrence's first show.

During the day of Sammy Davis Jr.'s last performances at Harrah's, we rehearsed our show on the main stage just as we had in previous years. But this year the showroom had installed a new hi-tech upgrade: pop-up microphones. The production crew at Harrah's had felt that it was awkward to have stagehands always running out on stage in full view of the audience just to set up microphones for the performers, and then running out again to remove them. So they had installed a number of motorized microphones specially designed to quickly "pop-up" through small trap doors located at key positions on the stage.

When not in use, these microphones would remain hidden beneath the stage. Whenever a microphone was needed, the sound technician simply had to flip a switch, and one would quickly pop up through its trap door anywhere on stage. It was a very efficient system.

Since Lawrence was now in his seventies, trying to "find his microphone" in the glare of the spotlights while on stage had become an issue. Jack Imel solved that problem for Lawrence by always marking the position of his microphone with a large "W" made from strips of bright red gaffer's tape.[*] Each night on tour Lawrence knew that all he had to do was find the "W" Jack had taped to the stage floor, and that's where his microphone would be.

And the show at Harrah's was essentially just like our touring show, except for this new hi-tech addition. There was a pop-up microphone located at the center stage position, directly in front of Myron Floren and the band. Myron was a skilled accordionist, and also served as the bandleader whenever Lawrence wasn't out onstage conducting the band himself. So Jack taped the familiar red "W" onto the stage

---

[*] *Gaffer's tape is a strong, cloth-backed tape similar to duct tape, but it leaves no sticky residue when removed. It is easily cut or torn into strips as needed and is used extensively by stage hands in the theater, and in film and television production.*

just about a foot "upstage" of that microphone's trap door. Jack had carefully positioned the "W" so that whenever Lawrence was standing on it, the microphone would pop up directly in front of him.

The rehearsal went smoothly, and after a few run-throughs, Lawrence got comfortable with having his microphone pop up in front of him then disappear each time he walked away from it. We finished our rehearsal around 3:00 p.m., giving everyone some free time before meeting back at the showroom as Sammy Davis Jr.'s guests for his 8:00 p.m. show. Some of our group went out to the casino to do a little gambling. Others grabbed a bite to eat. Still others went back to their rooms to grab a quick nap. And after we'd finished our rehearsal at 3:00 p.m., the Harrah's stage crew re-set the stage for Sammy Davis Jr.'s final two shows.

Sammy's show that night was terrific. Knowing that Lawrence and the rest of the cast were in the audience, he devoted part of his act to poking fun at our show, doing his hilarious impression of Lawrence in the process. It was all quite good-natured, and even while Sammy was having some fun at Lawrence's expense, it was clear that he had tremendous respect for Lawrence and everything he'd accomplished. It was classy, and vintage Sammy Davis Jr.

As was customary after the show, we were all invited backstage to Sammy's dressing room to celebrate with him on his final night. And there was definitely a party atmosphere in that room. The alcohol was flowing freely, and everyone around Sammy were celebrating their successful run at Harrah's, with only the midnight show still left to do. Sammy was a gracious host and seemed genuinely delighted that Lawrence had come backstage to congratulate him. A staff photographer from Harrah's was capturing the festivities and suggested a photo-op with Sammy and Lawrence together. And that's when the first funny occurrence took place.

As the two stood together for the picture, it was apparent that Sammy was in his element. Dressed in his tux and sunglasses, sporting several large rings on both hands and a Star of David hanging from a large chain around his neck, he was the personification of the famous "rat pack," exuberantly holding court in his dressing room. By way of contrast, Lawrence appeared to be out of *his* element. He didn't drink, he didn't "party," and his "Champagne Music Makers" were the polar opposite of Frank Sinatra, Dean Martin, Joey Bishop, and Sammy Davis, Jr., who together performed as "The Rat Pack." As they spoke, Sammy had his arm around Lawrence's shoulder. The photographer framed up the two of them, and said something to the effect of, "Okay now, give me big smiles on three. One…two…"

And in that split-second just before the photographer said "three," Sammy turned and kissed Lawrence forcefully on the cheek. Lawrence's eyes went wide as saucers with shock and surprise. And just as they did…POP! The camera's flash lit up the room, and that expression was now captured on film. The photographer loved the spontaneity of it all and handed me his business card in case Lawrence wanted a copy of the photo. Sammy shook Lawrence's hand and told him quite sincerely what an honor it had been to meet him in person. And Lawrence, to his credit, managed to regain his composure during that handshake, thanking Sammy for his kind words. But from the expression on Lawrence's face, I could tell that something was off.

As I was escorting Lawrence out of the dressing room and through the backstage area towards his table out in the showroom, he put his hand on my arm and said, "Doug, dis is not right. Da boys should not kiss da other boys. Especially without warning da other boy first!"

I took the staff photographer's card out of my pocket, smiled and said, "The photographer gave me his card in case you wanted a copy of the photo. Am I safe in assuming that you don't?"

"I do not," Lawrence replied.

"Very well," I said, and tore up the card, tossing the pieces in a waste basket on our way out.

The second amusing thing happened at our first show the following night. As it was opening night, the showroom at Harrah's which could accommodate fifteen hundred people for dinner, drinks, and a show, was completely sold out. The audience had been seated for dinner and drinks an hour earlier and were now eagerly waiting for the show to start. You could feel the anticipation in the room. It was showtime!

At 8:00 p.m. sharp, Myron cued the band to play the show's opening fanfare, followed by a pre-recorded announcement from the cast, "Ladies and gentlemen, Harrah's Lake Tahoe is proud to present Lawrence Welk and the Champagne Music Makers. And now here's the maestro himself, Lawrence Welk!" The audience broke into enthusiastic applause as the band played the rest of the fanfare for Lawrence's entrance.

The curtain rose, and the spotlights hit Lawrence as he entered from the wings and strode down to his "W" at center stage to greet the audience and welcome them to the show. There was just one problem. His pop-up microphone wasn't there. He looked over his right shoulder, to where Jack Imel and I were standing in the wings. We could see the panic in his eyes as he said, "Shag, where's da microphone?"

It was only natural that Lawrence would turn to Jack, since Jack was the one who made sure his microphone was always there. From the wings, Jack frantically made a big "W" sign in the air with his finger and stage-whispered, "Find your W, Lawrence. Find your W!" But Lawrence just shot back a frustrated look from the stage and pointed down at his feet. He was quite clearly standing on his "W." And then we saw the problem. The microphone couldn't pop up because Lawrence was standing on top of the trap door!

Remember when I told you that at the end of our rehearsal the day before, the Harrah's production crew had set the stage back for Sammy Davis Jr.'s shows that night? Well, it turns out that when they did, the stage hands had pulled up the "W" that Jack had stuck on the floor marking the spot for Lawrence's microphone. And then when the crew re-set the stage for our show, they accidentally put the "W" back in the wrong spot. Instead of a foot "upstage" from the trap door, they'd placed the "W" directly *on* the trap door. And since Lawrence had been trained to stand on his "W," he was in fact standing on top of the trap door, making it impossible for his microphone to pop up.

So again he asked Jack, "Where's da microphone?" all the while Jack was waving his arms around like a lunatic, trying to signal Lawrence to just take a step back. Not understanding what Jack was trying to tell him, Lawrence did the next logical thing. He turned towards the band and away from the audience to Myron Floren, his trusted "co-captain" on the stage and asked, "Where's da microphone?" But Myron could only shrug his shoulders as if to say, "Beats me, Lawrence. It should be there."

But as it just so happened, as he turned around to face Myron, Lawrence inadvertently stepped off of the trap door. And as soon as he did, his microphone immediately popped up into position. Unfortunately, since Lawrence was now facing the band and not the audience, he never saw it come up behind him.

Getting no answer from Myron (who couldn't see the now-present microphone because Lawrence was standing in between), Lawrence turned in frustration back towards the audience. And that's when all fifteen hundred people in the room suddenly heard Lawrence Welk yell, "WHERE'S DA MICROPHONE?" directly into his microphone.

....

One day during my fifth season on the show, I got a call from super-producer Marty Pasetta. He was in pre-production on several network variety specials, including the Academy Awards. He'd lost his associate director and wanted to know if I would like to come and work for him. I told Jim Hobson about Marty's offer, and he said that I should take it. But I wasn't so sure.

"Jim," I said, "You literally took me in and created a job for me. Then you got me into the Director's Guild and trained me as a stage manager and an associate director. You even bought me my first stopwatch! I owe you so much!"

And then Jim said something I'll never forget. "Doug, if you pass up this offer out of some misguided sense of loyalty to me or the show, I'll never speak to you again! You and I both know this show's only got a few years left. Don't stay with it until it's over. Working for Marty will take your career to the next level. A chance like this may never come along again. If you don't quit and take Marty up on his offer, then I'll fire you so you'll have to."

"But how will I ever pay you back?" I asked.

He replied, "Easy. Someday when you get the chance, just do the same for someone who's trying to get started in the business." And then he smiled at me. It was a warm, fatherly smile. Jim had taught me to fly, and now he was kicking me out of the nest for my own good.

So I left The Lawrence Welk Show and began working for Marty Pasetta. And Jim was right. My career (and my visibility within the industry) rose dramatically. We were doing huge network specials such as *A Country Christmas*, *The Concert for UNICEF*, and of course *The Academy Awards*. And I can't tell you how many times I relied on that stopwatch that Jim had given me to ensure that my show timings were accurate.

The next season I had a short break from my work schedule with Marty, and Jim called to ask if I was free for a couple of days. Apparently, there'd been a scheduling mix-up at ABC, and *The Lawrence Welk Show* suddenly found itself without an associate director for Monday's rehearsal and Tuesday's show taping. Jim wanted to know if I'd like to come back and do the show "for old times' sake." I told him I'd love to, and that I was bringing my stopwatch!

I was walking across the stage at ABC when Lawrence spotted me. He smiled and met me with a warm greeting. "Doug," he said as he shook my hand, "So good to see you. Are you back with us?"

"I'm just filling in for this one show, Lawrence," I replied.

"Oh, dat's fine!" And then he took a long look at me and in classic "Welk-lish" said, "Didn't you used to be taller?" Now, of course what he *meant* was, "I remember you as being taller." But it had come out as, "Didn't you used to be taller?"

I just smiled at him and replied, "Yes, Lawrence. I did."

He grinned and said, "Yes, I thought so."

He asked me what I'd been doing, and I listed a couple of the shows I'd done, including the Oscars. "Oh," he said, "Dat is so wondaful! I want you to know how proud I am of you! Because you know…"

I just laughed and finished his sentence for him, "I know. Because I was nothing when you found me!"

He let out a hearty laugh and said, "Dis is true!" We laughed again together and shook hands once more. It was good to be back, even for just one more show.

That was the last time I saw Lawrence. Not too long after that his memory began to fail, and those closest to him decided that it would be in his best interest to end production of the television show. So in 1982, after an amazing run of twenty-seven years on TV, *The Lawrence Welk* Show ceased production.

When the show ended, Jim Hobson retired, but we still made it a point to meet regularly for lunch. And there was one special day when we took that hang glider he'd made years earlier from bamboo and a swimming pool cover out to the beach, and I launched myself from a hill overlooking the Pacific Ocean. As I landed, as Jim came running up whooping and hollering, "I knew it! I knew it! I knew it would fly!" Despite the fact that Jim had designed and built his hang glider years earlier, apparently I was the first one foolish enough jump off a hill hanging by my armpits from a flying pool cover with a bamboo frame! Even after I went into teaching and moved away from Los Angeles, every time I was back in town with my students, I would make it a point to get together with Jim as many times as I could.

Lawrence Welk passed away in 1992 at the age of eighty-nine. In July of 2001, Jim lost his beloved wife Elsie. And then in April of 2013, I was awakened in the middle of the night by a phone call informing me that Jim had died, and asking if I would speak at his funeral. I caught a flight to Los Angeles the following day. In the chapel at Forest Lawn I shared my memories of Jim, holding tight to that stopwatch as I spoke.

They're all gone now: Lawrence, Jim, George Cates, and even Jack Imel. Aside from myself, no one remains from the "group of old men" that would meet every Wednesday at Lawrence's office in Santa Monica.

....

I realize that this has been a very long chapter. But *The Lawrence Welk Show* was both a milestone and a turning point in my life. The lessons I learned and the skills I acquired while working on the show laid the foundation for the rest of my career in television. Without Welk, I would never have been able to do the Oscars. The training I received working "live on tape" in front of a studio audience each week on *The Lawrence Welk Show* prepared me for everything else that followed throughout my career, including directing situation comedies.

And I also realized that the few anecdotes that I've shared with you are just the "tip of the iceberg." While writing this chapter, I came to the conclusion that I could probably fill an entire book just with funny stories from the TV show and the tours. But I also came to the conclusion that there isn't much of a market left for that book. Too much time has passed since Lawrence Welk was a staple of weekly television.

But I will always be honored to be a member of his "Musical Family." I say that in the present tense because a number of us have managed to stay in touch, either in person, on the phone, "video chatting" via Skype or FaceTime, or through social media. We've all shared a common experience and are life members of what many people regard as a pretty corny club. And while it may not be the hippest club around, it's a pretty exclusive one. There aren't too many people around who can say that they are one of Lawrence Welk's "Champagne Music Makers."

BETTY WHITE

*My embarrassing first encounter with
Betty began over a croquet set...*

It was in the mid-1970's, and I was working on *The Lawrence Welk Show*. We were taping at CBS Television City in Hollywood next to the Farmers Market. Back then, along with soap operas and game shows such as *The Young and the Restless* and *The Price is Right*, a number of the sound stages at Television City were dedicated to musical-variety shows, which were popular at the time. These included *The Carol Burnett Show, Sonny and Cher, Tony Orlando and Dawn,* and *The Smothers Brothers Comedy Hour*.

Now, musical-variety shows really only need a soundstage for two days per week: one day to set up and rehearse and another to camera block and shoot the show in front of a live audience. Since sound stages are expensive and rehearsal halls are cheap, it was more economical for a production company to only rent the expensive sound stage for the two days it was actually necessary and rehearse the show in a much less expensive rehearsal hall (often with just a rehearsal pianist) for the other three days.

But CBS needed to keep those expensive stages booked full all week, since an empty sound stage doesn't generate any revenue. Therefore, it was not uncommon for a facility like Television City to schedule two musical-variety shows on the same stage during the week, one on Monday and Tuesday, and the other on Thursday and Friday, leaving Wednesday for the stage and engineering crews to "turn around" the sets, lighting, and audio. The crews worked both shows, keeping them employed all week. This practice continues today, although now it's mostly just for game shows, since musical-variety has fallen out of favor.

At that time, *Sonny and Cher* and *The Lawrence Welk Show* were sharing Stage 31 at Television City. *The Lawrence Welk Show* used it on Mondays and Tuesdays, while *Sonny and Cher* were in a rehearsal hall, as was *The Carol Burnett Show,* which also taped on Fridays, but on Stage 33, next door to us.

I'm telling you all of this because my story begins on a Tuesday, meaning that *The Lawrence Welk Show* was using Stage 31. We were preparing to videotape our show at 8:00 p.m. that Tuesday night in front of a live audience and had taken our lunch break in the middle of the camera rehearsal. Since Christmas was about six weeks away, I decided to skip lunch and try to get a leg up on my shopping. My niece Mindy, who was around seven at the time, had asked for a croquet set for Christmas. I was using the phone in Stage 31's control room, calling all over Los Angeles trying to find her one.

I wasn't having much luck. I had called every toy and hobby store in the phone book (remember, this was the 1970's, when people still used phone books), and nobody had a croquet set. However, someone I talked to said they thought that Hollywood Sporting Goods carried croquet sets and suggested I give them a call.

So, I called Hollywood Sporting Goods and asked the man on the other end of the phone if they had croquet sets. Much to my delight he replied, "Yes, we do." It seemed my quest was over, as he assured me they had them in stock.

Almost as a formality I said, "Oh, by the way, how much are they?"

His answer stunned me. "One hundred and twenty-five dollars."

In the mid-70's, $125 would be the equivalent of approximately $585 today. There was no way I could afford that kind of money for a croquet set for a seven-year old! "A hundred and twenty-five dollars for a croquet set?" I gasped. "What do they come with? Teak mallets and rosewood balls?" He laughed, guessing that from my response, the price was a bit steep for me. I thanked him for his time and told him I would keep looking. He wished me luck. We hung up, and I assumed that was the end of it. But I was wrong. Very wrong.

Around 5:30 that afternoon, we were in the middle of the dress rehearsal, which was our last camera run-through before the live taping at 8:00 p.m. In the TV control room was our producer-director (and my second mentor) Jim Hobson*, the show's technical director, the lighting director, audio mixer, a couple of production assistants, and myself.

During a break in the rehearsal, the control room door opened, and in walked Betty White, big as life, just taking over the room with her effusive personality. She was in the building rehearsing for a guest appearance on *The Carol Burnett Show*, and it so happened that she and Jim Hobson were old friends from when they both worked at KLAC-TV, an early local television station in Los Angeles. And, as I mentioned above, all of the musical-variety shows at Television City shared crews, so Betty also knew everyone else in the control room as well. Everyone, that is, except me.

The entire control room crew was delighted to see her, as was Jim Hobson. She hugged Jim, with the kind of warm greeting you would expect of two old friends, telling him, "I'm here rehearsing, and when I heard that the Welk Show was taping today, I just had to drop by and say hello to my old friend." Jim was delighted, and they swapped a few stories from the old days. And then she tossed the grenade.

"But you know, Jim," she said with playful coyness, "I have a confession to make. If I'm being completely honest, I didn't come down just to see you. I *really* want to meet that hunky stud who was in here during lunch."

"Hunky stud?" Jim asked. "What hunky stud?"

---

* *I refer you to the chapter on The Lawrence Welk Show.*

"His name is Teak Mallets," she cooed lustfully. Her eyes widened in mock excitement. "And I hear he's quite the ladies' man. He has rosewood balls, you know!" Betty was well-known (and much beloved among the stage crews) for her racy sense of humor. And her grenade hit the mark, because the control exploded with loud, raucous laughter.

My face felt hot and flushed. I just wanted to find a hole and crawl into it. While I was on the phone at lunch, I had failed to notice that someone from the *Sonny and Cher* crew had left the control room intercom switch to the dressing rooms in the "ON" position. As a result, everything I had said on the phone in the control room could be heard in the dressing rooms. And Betty, who had taken lunch in her dressing room, overheard me speaking with the man from Hollywood Sporting Goods, asking if the expensive croquet set came with "teak mallets and rosewood balls." And so, she decided to have a little bawdy fun at my expense.

Jim asked, "Does anyone know what she's talking about?"

I raised my hand sheepishly, stood and said, "I do, Jim." I stammered, "See, it's like this. I was on the phone, trying to find a croq-"

But before I could get another syllable out, Betty jumped in and cut me off. She was having too much fun, and I was completely at her mercy. She took my hands in hers. "Teak? Teak Mallets? Is it really you?" she asked. "Funny," she quipped, "I thought you'd be taller. Oh, but that's okay. I'm guessing that the whole 'rosewood balls' thing probably compensates for a lot. Am I right?" She elbowed me and winked. The crew was laughing so hard they were crying. And now Jim was laughing right along with them.

Betty White. Sweet, adorable Betty White, had just skewered me good. There was no way out of this. I could see that any attempt on my part to explain was only going to make it worse, so I just took a deep breath and played along. "Actually Betty, it doesn't compensate as much as you might think," I grinned back. "Believe it or not, some people find the clacking sound really annoying." Betty was delighted that I was playing along with her! She laughed, a big robust laugh, her eyes twinkling. Again, the control room crew roared with laughter. Betty squeezed my hands to show her approval of my comeback line, and then crossed to the door, where she stopped and turned back to me, striking a melodramatic "come hither" pose in the doorway.

"I'll be in my dressing room, if you know what I mean," she said, in a mockingly seductive tone. Before I could respond, she said, "Oh, and Teak? No need to knock. With all of that clacking I'll hear you coming!" With that, she exited while the control room again exploded with laughter.

Everyone started slapping me on the back, or giving me a "thumbs up," saying things like "All right, Teak!" or "Way to go, Teak!" As far as they were concerned, I now had a new nick-name (which the crew made sure I would keep for the remainder of that season). Jim just smiled and put his hand on my shoulder in a fatherly kind of way. My first encounter with Betty White had certainly been a memorable (and embarrassing) one!

Our second encounter would come a decade later...

This time it was on the set of *The Golden Girls*. How I ended up working on the iconic sitcom just a few episodes into its very first season is a story of its own, which I've relayed elsewhere in this book.[*] So, on my first day at work on *The Golden Girls* my path crossed Betty's for the second time.

On a weekly sitcom, each new week starts with a "table read," where the cast gathers around a table on the stage and reads the script aloud for the first time for the writers and producers. Even though I was new to the show, I already knew most of the crew from working with them on *Benson* and some of the other shows I had done for Witt-Thomas-Harris in the past. Therefore, I basically just needed to meet the cast.

Tony Thomas,[†] the executive producer who hired me, introduced me to the group at the table. It was just a simple, "Folks, this is Doug Smart, and he'll be our Associate Director for the next few episodes." Everyone nodded or waved, and said some version of "hello," and we got right to work, with the cast reading through the script. But even though almost

---
[*] *I refer you to the chapter on The Golden Girls.*
[†] *Tony also appears in the chapters on John Rich, Danny Thomas, and The Golden Girls.*

ten years had passed, I thought I saw a glimmer of recognition from Betty, as if she were trying to remember where she'd seen me before.

Once the read-through was done, and we started setting up to rehearse on the stage, I approached the ladies and informally introduced myself to them again, letting them know how happy I was to be working with them, even though I was only there short-term. When I got to Betty, there *was* that expression of recognition on her face. "Doug, you look familiar," she said. "Have we worked together before?"

"No," I replied. "But we *have* met. About ten years ago at CBS Television City, with Jim Hobson in the control room of *The Lawrence Welk Show*. Except that day, you didn't call me Doug. You called me something else."

Her curiosity kicked in. "Really? Well, what a rude old broad I am!" she laughed, "What did I call you?"

I smiled and said, "You called me Teak Mallets."

Her eyes widened, and she broke into a huge grin. She remembered! She grabbed my hands and squeezed them, laughing, "Oh, my goodness! Teak Mallets! I remember!" And with that sweet, twinkling smile, and with that innocent-but-coy "girl next door" way about her, she pulled me close and whispered, "Tell me, Teak, do you still have those lovely rosewood balls?"

Have I mentioned that I just love Betty? Our next encounter was just a few years later...

This time I was directing an episode of *Empty Nest*, a spinoff of *The Golden Girls*. In that show, a widower pediatrician, Harry Weston (played by Richard Mulligan*) and his two adult daughters Carol and Barbara (Dinah Manoff* and Kristy McNichol*) all live in a house described as "around the corner" from the home occupied by Dorothy, Blanche, Rose, and Sophia.

As is often the case with spinoff shows, there were a fair amount of "crossover" appearances during a season, in which cast members from *Empty Nest* would be written into episodes of *The Golden Girls*, and vice versa. In addition, the episode I was directing was to be part

---

* *I refer you to the chapter on Empty Nest.*

of what NBC called a "seamless" night, meaning it contained a theme or an issue that would begin on *The Golden Girls* at 8:00 p.m., and would run through *Empty Nest* at 8:30 p.m., finally resolving itself on *Nurses*, another *Golden Girls* spinoff that followed *Empty Nest* at 9:00 p.m. The theme for this seamless night was the unusual things that seem to occur during a full moon.

The Golden Girls full moon episode involved Blanche throwing an all-male party at the house, thinking she'll have her pick of any number of eligible men. But to her bewilderment, all of the men who show up find themselves attracted to Dorothy instead. Meanwhile, Rose wins a honeymoon trip to Paris, and Sophia deals with a witch's hex. Harry Weston's two daughters from *Empty Nest,* Carol and Barbara, cross over to make appearances in the episode.

And in our episode, Harry accidentally takes a dose of the wrong medicine, causing him to act strangely, while daughter Barbara is convinced that the full moon has turned their dog, Dreyfuss, into a human (played marvelously by the late Chuck McCann). And Betty White was the crossover in our episode, showing up at the Weston's kitchen door. She only had a few lines, so it didn't require too much rehearsal.

Two old pros like Richard and Betty didn't require a lot of rehearsal for the short scene, so my directions to them were basically, "Okay, Betty knocks, and Richard crosses to the door and opens it. And then applause, applause, applause…and more applause, and then Richard says his line…" I was anticipating the ovation Betty would undoubtedly receive from the studio audience when they suddenly see Rose standing at the Weston's back door.

Betty, as usual, was comically self-deprecating, mockingly expressing her doubts that the audience would greet her so warmly. But I knew. And Richard knew. And, truth be told, I'm sure Betty knew as well. The audience loved Rose. And they love Betty.

The scene, from the terrific script written by Peter Gallay, went as follows:

> THERE IS A KNOCK AT THE KITCHEN DOOR. HARRY OPENS IT, REVEALING ROSE, STANDING IN THE DOORWAY.
>
>> HARRY
>> Rose. What are you doing here at this hour?
>
>> ROSE
>> I'm sorry to disturb you Harry, but I'd like to ask your opinion about something, as a man of science. I mean, **I'm** not a man of science. I'm the one who's asking. **You're** the man of science.
>
>> HARRY
>> Yes, Rose. I know who we both are. What can I do for you?
>
>> ROSE
>> Do you believe in full moons?
>
>> HARRY
>> Absolutely not.
>
> ROSE POINTS UPWARDS OUT THE DOOR.
>
>> ROSE
>> Well, then what's that big round shiny thing out there?

As you might imagine, when Betty delivered that line, the audience just roared with a long, hearty laugh that went on for quite a few seconds. And to no one's surprise, she did indeed receive a huge ovation from the audience when Richard opened the door, revealing her standing there. After that first reveal, and the audience knew Betty was there, we stopped and re-set for her entrance. Then we did a second take of Richard crossing to the door and opening it, this time going on with the scene without the ovation, which is the version the television viewing audience saw at home.

Although our rehearsals during the week were brief, we still had a great time together. Betty just always brings a bright cheerfulness with her that is infectious to those around her. It's hard to be depressed, angry, or upset when Betty's in the room. And as a kind of private joke, she would occasionally refer to me as "Teak" in conversation or during note sessions, which provoked some quizzical looks from some of the other cast members, writers, and producers. I just shrugged it off, telling anyone who might ask that it was just her nickname for me from a previous time.

However, Richard Mulligan, who was as perceptive as he was talented, could sense that there was more to the story than I was letting on. And I knew that it was just a matter of time before he wore me down. Sure enough, I eventually confided to him the whole story of "Teak Mallets with the rosewood balls," which he found quite amusing. But he also thought the story was, in his words, "sweet."

And thinking about it, if someone were to ask me to describe Betty White in just one word, a number of adjectives would come to mind, including "brilliant," "talented," and "hilarious." But "sweet" would definitely be right up there among the top. Thanks, Betty for the "sweet" memory…

5

HENRY WINKLER

> *You meet the nicest people on a Harley.*
> *Or do you?*

Let me just start this chapter by telling you that Henry Winkler, aside from all of his many talents (which are considerable), is one of the nicest, most decent, most honorable, kind-hearted people I've ever had the pleasure to work for. He's the kind of person whose team you just want to be on. He truly cares about the people in the cast and crew around him, and they in turn love working for him. As far as I'm concerned, if Henry's doing the show and I'm fortunate enough that he would ask for me, I'm in.

I'm guessing that most people my age probably still associate Henry Winkler with "Fonzie," the wildly-popular character he portrayed on the ABC sitcom *Happy Days*. However, Gen-Xers may associate him with somewhat more quirky characters, such as bumbling lawyer Barry Zuckerkorn in Mitch Hurwitz's loopy sitcom, *Arrested Development*, or as Coach Klein in Adam Sandler's movie *The Waterboy*. Millennials will probably know him best from his current Emmy award-winning portrayal of acting coach Gene Cousineau in the hit HBO series *Barry*, starring *SNL* alum Bill Hader.

As it turns out, I have absolutely no association with Henry through any of those projects. Nope, my history with him follows a somewhat different, less high-profile path.

I first met Henry in New York City in January of 1979. More specifically, we met at the United Nations. So, you might be wondering, "What the heck were Henry Winkler and I both doing at the UN, of all places?

And that would be a very good question.

I was there as the Associate Director for an NBC TV network special, *A Gift of Song, the Concert for UNICEF*, and Henry was there as one of the program's celebrity presenters. UNICEF was celebrating 1979 as "The International Year of the Child," and the TV special, which boasted an impressive line-up of international musical superstars, was to be the kickoff for that celebration.

The concert was videotaped from the floor of the UN General Assembly on Tuesday night, January 9th, and was broadcast on NBC at 8:00 p.m. EST the very next night. It was organized and hosted by famed British TV presenter David Frost, whose resume included the satirical news program *That Was the Week That Was*, interviews with celebrities such as Muhammed Ali, and the famous (or infamous) interview with former President Richard Nixon in the wake of the Watergate scandal.

The concert featured the Bee Gees (brothers Barry, Maurice and Robin Gibb); their younger brother, singer Andy Gibb; Rod Stewart; Kris Kristofferson; Rita Coolidge; John Denver; Donna Summer; Olivia Newton-John;* and vocal groups Earth, Wind and Fire, as well as ABBA. Elton John had also been scheduled to perform, but just days after we arrived in New York for the show, I heard from one of the producers that Elton John's management team had contacted them saying, "The gig's off," (which would explain why I didn't write a chapter in this book about Elton John!). The graphic artist who had already finished the publicity poster and album cover featuring caricatures of all of the musicians had to quickly remove the hand-drawn image of

---

* *I refer you to the chapter devoted to Olivia Newton-John*

Elton from the picture (no easy task back in the days when graphics were done with pens, brushes, paints, and ink!).

Each artist performed a specially-selected song for the televised concert. And when they finished their song, they would sign a special parchment donating all future royalties from that song to UNICEF, thereby generating a perpetual future revenue stream for the international children's charity. The program was a huge success, broadcast nationally on NBC on January 10th, 1979, and subsequently seen by more than 300 million people in over 70 countries. And according to some sources, it's been estimated that the royalties from the donated songs have generated over fifty million dollars for UNICEF in the years since the program was first broadcast.

But, as I've been known to do from time to time, this story is beginning to "wander out in the weeds," so let me get back on track.

As I said earlier, Henry Winkler was there as one of the program's presenters, along with screen legend Henry Fonda and comedienne Gilda Radner, a break-out star on *Saturday Night Live*. And by this time, Henry had become internationally famous (and much beloved) for his portrayal of Fonzie, the leather-clad biker on *Happy Days* who was the epitome of "cool."

As the associate director of the program, I had three main responsibilities. First was the rehearsal schedule and show sequence rundown. Throughout both the rehearsals and later the actual show, I worked with our stage managers to make sure that all of the talent were at the right places at the right times, coordinating when and where they would make their entrances, hit their marks, and then exit smoothly when their segment was finished. My second responsibility was coordinating the camera coverage for our director Marty Pasetta[*] during the rehearsals and the show, so that the correct camera angles and shot sizes Marty wanted were ready when he called for them. My third responsibility was to help edit the show down from three hours to 90 minutes so that it would comply with NBC's program format for broadcast on the network less than 24 hours later (which is a very scary story that could be a whole other chapter by itself!).

---

[*] *I discuss producer Marty Pasetta in greater detail in the chapters devoted to Cher and John Rich.*

So, in keeping with these areas of responsibility, the sum total of my interactions with Henry (as well as co-presenters Gilda Radner and Henry Fonda) during their time on the program basically consisted of a very brief "get acquainted" meeting, an equally brief talk-through-walk-through, and a couple of quick rehearsals.

It would all go something like this: we'd be standing on the stage together with our scripts in binders. Looking at my copy of the script in which I'd transposed Marty's blocking instructions, I'd say, "Okay Henry, at this point in the program, Don (Stage Manager Don raises his hand to ID himself) will bring you to the Stage Left entrance. When he gives you the cue to go, you'll enter, cross to the Down Left mark, and introduce Rod Stewart. When you hit the Down Left mark, Marty will have you on Camera 5, which is right there (I point out to him which of the nine cameras in the room is Camera 5) in the audience. That'll be your camera for Rod's intro. When Rod comes out and the music starts, you'll exit back up Stage Left where Don will be waiting to take you up to the interpreters' booths for your next segment."

And then we'd run that sequence once or twice with the cameras and cue cards if requested (I don't recall any of them asking for cue cards). And that was it. Once the actual show started, I was no longer physically in the building, but rather I was outside with Marty in the NBC network remote truck, and all communication with the talent at this point was relayed through the stage managers back in the General Assembly room via our headsets.

As celebrity host/presenters, Henry, Gilda, and Henry Fonda made their appearances in the show between songs, promoting UNICEF's mission to the global television audience. In retrospect, the mix of singers and presenters came off as kind of...oh, how shall I put it... weirdly eclectic? For example, the producers decided that Henry's presentation should take place in one of the UN interpreters' booths, located high above the floor of the General Assembly, which I felt made him appear somewhat isolated from the action on the stage below, since he was in a small room behind glass (however, he also introduced Rod Stewart from down on the main stage).

Henry Fonda and Gilda Radner both worked from center stage. Gilda's spot, which chronicled uplifting stories of how UNICEF helps children around the world overcome hardships such as malnutrition and disease, was preceded by Andy Gibb, lustfully gyrating and singing *I Go for You*, and followed with a love song duet between Andy and Olivia Newton-John (Gilda later introduced ABBA for their number). Henry Fonda read excerpts from *The Diary of Anne Frank*, followed shortly thereafter by Rod Stewart in a faux-leopard shirt and skin-tight spandex pants prancing around the stage singing, *Do Ya Think I'm Sexy?* Like I said…weirdly eclectic.

All three presenters joined the musical artists onstage for the closing number, in which the entire cast sang *Put a Little Love in Your Heart*, the hit song both written and made famous by Jackie DeShannon a decade earlier. On the broadcast, Henry could be seen behind Barry Gibb and Olivia Newton-John, clapping and singing along enthusiastically. Next to him was Gilda Radner, also clapping enthusiastically, and next to her was Hendry Fonda, always the professional, but appearing somewhat uncomfortable and out of place. Looking back on it now, it all seems a bit wonky. But back in 1979, when Disco ruled the earth, it somehow all seemed, I don't know….normal?

And then suddenly it was over. Around 10:00 p.m. Tuesday night, the concert ended, and David Frost wished everyone a "Good Night." The audience of invited dignitaries left, and the crew started tearing down the stage and packing up all of the television equipment. Marty, David Frost, and I took off in a taxi across Manhattan to EUE Screen Gems to begin the overnight edit in order to have the show ready for broadcast at 8:00 p.m. the following night, and all of the performers went to wherever they were scheduled to go next. Some stayed in New York for a few days, while others departed the very next morning.

I did not see Henry again until a year later, the following January. Henry was assisting his good friend John Ritter, co-hosting *Weekend with the Stars*, John's 24-hour weekend telethon for cerebral palsy, and I was directing the overnight portion of the program. *Weekend with the Stars* was the very first nationally-broadcast television program I ever directed.

As such, I would never expect Henry to recall that first time we worked together (or even later on *Weekend With the Stars*), but I'd like to think that he remembers me as his associate director on the sitcom he produced for ABC…

At the beginning of this chapter, I listed several of Henry's more well-known acting credits. But acting is only one of Henry's many talents. Henry and his partner Lin Oliver are also co-authors of the award-winning *Hank Zipzer* children's book series, chronicling the everyday adventures of a bright middle-schooler who struggles with learning challenges (taken from Henry's real-life struggles with dyslexia). In 2014, the *Hank Zipzer* books were made into a TV series in Great Britain.

In addition, Henry is also a very successful TV producer and executive producer, whose credits include *Better Late Than Never, Mr. Sunshine, Who Are the Debolts? And Where Did They Get Nineteen Kids?, So Weird, Sightings, The Hollywood Squares,* and *MacGyver* (both the 1980's series on ABC and the current series on CBS).

This brings us to the year 1986. Henry, along with Co-Executive Producer John Rich,* was about to start production on two new TV pilots for ABC: *MacGyver* and *Mr. Sunshine*. One of these two shows would turn out to be a tremendous hit, would be the darling of the network and the critics, and would become an iconic part of the cultural landscape, both then and now.

I worked on the other show.

Mr. Sunshine was a half-hour multi-camera comedy about Paul Stark, an irascible college professor who just happened to be blind. Now, up to this time, leading characters with disabilities or challenges in TV series were rare, and those who did appear were usually defined by their disability, such as a blind private investigator, or a paralyzed former police chief consulting with police to solve crimes from his wheelchair. So, the idea behind *Mr. Sunshine* was to create a comedy about a person who was not defined by his inability to see, but rather by his utter inability to interact with those closest to him. Paul Stark was blind, yes. But he was also acerbic, annoying, and quite often simply "out of sync" with everyone around him, thus earning him the ironic nickname, "Mr. Sunshine."

It seemed like an outstanding premise, offering opportunities for great storytelling and tremendous comic potential, as well as offering insight into those who live with physical challenges. But from what I

---

* *Refer to the chapter devoted to John Rich.*

could tell, the ABC network "suits" couldn't see that potential. "Suits" is a less-than-flattering term for network executives whose responsibilities include areas such as scheduling, programming, marketing, budgeting, etc. While the people wearing the suits quite often may be very intelligent, talented people, most of them have degrees in professional fields such as public relations, marketing, sales, finance, law, etc. Few, if any, have even the slightest experience in television production, nor do they possess even the basic skills required to successfully create or run a show. And from my experience, most of them wouldn't recognize "comedy" if it came up and bit them in the butt!

Just the idea of a sitcom featuring a blind leading character made the suits queasy. However, ABC was contractually bound to support the production. As part of Henry's contract re-negotiation with ABC to play Fonzie on *Happy Days* for several more years, the network had guaranteed to produce two pilots from his production company, which was housed on the Paramount lot where *Happy Days* was filmed.

Veteran director-producer John Rich, who had won both the Emmy and Golden Globe awards while helming such iconic TV sitcoms as *The Dick Van Dyke Show*, *All in the Family*, *Barney Miller*, and *Newhart*, also had a two-pilot guarantee with ABC for *his* company, John Rich Productions. Their mutual friend and agent suggested to Henry and John that they form a new company together, which he could then package to Paramount. So, Henry Winkler/John Rich Productions was created, capitalizing on their existing pilot guarantees from ABC. Love it or hate it, the suits at ABC were contractually obligated to the production of *Mr. Sunshine*.

The pilot was written by David Lloyd, the Emmy-winning writer whose credits include *The Mary Tyler Moore Show, The Bob Newhart Show, Taxi, Cheers,* and *Frasier*. He won the Emmy award for writing "Chuckles Bites the Dust," the episode of *The Mary Tyler Moore Show* that the readers of TV Guide voted the #1 sitcom episode of all time. Needless to say, the writing was first-rate: intelligent, with fully-formed, well-rounded characters, engaging stories, and crisp, witty dialogue (which, in my opinion, made it far superior to many of the sitcoms ABC currently had on the air at the time).

But none of that seemed to matter to the suits at ABC. It's kind of ironic, really. The very same network that had no problem airing an episode of *Happy Days* in which Fonzie jumps over a shark on water skis while still wearing his leather motorcycle jacket,* was having problems with a comedy featuring a blind leading character. But Henry and John managed to press forward, even though ABC was dragging its feet.

Henry, the optimistic diplomat, and John Rich, the cigar-chomping, opinionated "bull in a china shop," together resembled a producer's version of "The Odd Couple." To me, their dynamic often resembled something akin to "good cop, bad cop," with John very much at home in the role of "bad cop," raging and bellowing. Henry was required to play the "good cop," constantly acting as the peacemaker. But together they pushed hard for the elements they felt ideally represented excellence and quality in all areas of the production, and ABC pushed back.

Casting seemed to be a particularly acrimonious affair. Henry and John, quite naturally, wanted to assemble a cast made up of the finest talent available, who would create the kind of chemistry required for successful ensemble comedy. But John Rich confided to me that ABC seemed to be more interested in casting people who scored high in the "TV-Q."

The TV-Q is a popularity rating, calculated by a formula based upon how many people will identify a celebrity as a "favorite," divided by the total number of people who can simply recognize that same celebrity. The problem with the Q score is that it has absolutely no relation to someone's talents and abilities. It's simply an indicator of their name recognition and popularity. Therefore, an extremely talented, classically trained actor who plays a variety of popular characters, but who might not be recognized *out* of character, might have a very low Q score. Conversely, someone without a shred of discernable talent, but who merely seems to be "famous for being famous" could have a very high Q (a certain "selfie"- obsessed family who insists that viewers "Keep Up" with them comes to mind).

---

* *The episode of Happy Days in which Fonzie "Jumps the Shark" became synonymous with the point at which the writing in a TV series loses credibility with the viewers, marking the beginning of the show's decline in the ratings. The metaphor became so popular that afterwards it became customary for both the critics and viewers to try and identify a particular episode in which a television series "Jumped the Shark."*

Despite the ABC suits' efforts to cast high TV-Q'ers, Henry and John refused to knuckle under. They were looking for talent, not popularity. Both Henry, a classically-trained actor, and John, who had directed many successful sitcom pilots, knew that casting could make or break a show. They both knew they had to get it right, or it wouldn't work. The push-and-shove over casting seemed to be escalating in its intensity, which eventually lead to a heated shouting match in a conference room at Paramount.

During a particularly rancorous casting meeting, with Henry and John on one side of the conference table, and the network suits on the other, the two sides seemed to be at an impasse. Someone at the table (most likely Henry, ever the peacemaker) suggested that perhaps the best course of action would be to table the discussion to allow both sides to cool down. Now, John Rich was highly regarded in the industry for his considerable skills and talents. However, the ability to "cool down" was not one of them.

By the time the break was suggested, John was really fuming. He was chomping hard on his ever-present cigar, frustrated by the network's pushback against their casting choices. As the meeting adjourned, one of the network VP's foolishly decided he'd poke the bear, and said to John, "Geez, John. Why are you being so damn stubborn about this? I mean, it's not like it even really matters. Everybody knows that the TV sitcom is dead, anyway."

John whirled around, his eyes flashing with anger. He leaned in really close, poked the man in the chest, his cigar wedged tightly between his two poking fingers, and roared, "Yeah! And morons like you are the sons-of-bitches that KILLED it!" With that, he put his cigar back in his mouth and stomped out of the room, leaving the exec shaken and sputtering.

Eventually the cast was set, and it appeared that Henry and John had finally worn the network down, because they were able to assemble an outstanding cast, including Jeff Tambor as Professor Paul Stark and Emmy-winning actress Barbara Babcock as June Swinford, his landlady. The rest of the cast was equally accomplished, including Oscar and Tony nominee Leonard Frey, film and TV veterans Nan

Martin and Cecilia Hart,* and a couple of talented young newcomers, Molly Hagen and David Knell.

Once production began on *MacGyver* and *Mr. Sunshine*, Henry decided to host a party for the casts and crews of both shows at his home in a lovely area of Los Angeles not far from the Warner Brothers Studios. This suburb has been home to a number of famous residents throughout the years, including Bette Davis, Bob Hope, Bing Crosby, Ozzie and Harriet, Donnie and Marie Osmond, and Ron Howard.

It was a big, beautiful home in a neighborhood full of big, beautiful homes. But you certainly didn't need a "map of the stars' homes" to find Henry's house. His house was the only one on the street that had a life-sized, realistic fiberglass replica of a black and white Holstein cow "grazing" on the front lawn!

The party was in the back yard, and as we walked up the driveway, Henry was there to greet us, his arms open wide, a big smile on his face. "Welcome to the house that Fonzie built!" he said joyfully, offering all of us a tour of his home.

Later that afternoon, as the party went on, Henry introduced me to his parents, Harry and Ilse Winkler, who had come out for a visit from their home in New York City. During the course of the conversation, I thanked Henry for the tour of the house, remarking how lovely it was. I had barely gotten the words out when his mother, who spoke with a distinct Yiddish accent, said, "Ach, such a big, fancy house!"

Henry started to look just a bit uncomfortable. "Henry's father and I could never live in such a house," she went on. "Too big, too fancy. Do you know that Harry and I still live in the exact same apartment we had ever since Henry was born?"

But even before I could respond, she tossed in, "Of course now, our Henry owns the whole building!" Henry just grinned at me and shrugged, as if to say, "Parents. What are you going to do?"

Once *Mr. Sunshine* started production, we quickly fell into the weekly routine for a multi-camera sitcom shot in front of an audience. Monday would start with a production meeting, followed by a cast read through. Throughout the week, we would rehearse the show and fine-tune it. Our week would culminate on Friday night by taping

---

* *I discuss Cecilia Hart in greater detail in the chapter devoted to James Earl Jones.*

two separate shows, each in front of a live studio audience. The first show taped at 5:00 p.m. and the second show at 7:30 p.m. Allowing for wardrobe and set changes, it would usually take us about an hour to an hour and a half to tape each show.*

Around 9:00 p.m. on Fridays, after the audience had been dismissed, we would shoot any "pick-ups" that might be required. These might include any flubbed dialogue or bits of physical business a cast member have gotten wrong, or any props or wardrobe that had malfunctioned during the taping. Pick-ups might also include any shots the camera crew had missed, or any last-minute piece of new dialogue a writer thought up too late to replace a line that just hadn't worked in front of the audience.

Pick-ups usually lasted until around 11:00 p.m., making for a full day's work. After pick-ups were done, there was usually a brief period of socializing (the length of which depended on how well things had gone and everyone's general mood), after which everybody would go home, either to rest or to start working ahead on the next episode, which would begin on Monday morning.

It was during one of these "after show socials" that I finally got around to asking Henry a *Happy Days* question that had always bothered me. I said, "Henry, I know you're probably sick and tired of talking about *Happy Days*, but could I ask you about something about Fonzie that has always puzzled me?"

I half-expected him to politely refuse, and I would have completely understood if he had. By this time, he'd lived with the character of Fonzie for well over a decade and had been required to deal with all of the media interviews, questions, and requests for quotes and "sound bites" that came with it.

But instead, Henry graciously replied, "Sure Doug. What is it?"

"Well, you know I love motorcycles. I ride my bike to the studio every day."

He nodded and said, "Yeah, I know."

"So, the thing that's always puzzled me is this: since *Happy Days* was set in Milwaukee, which is the home of Harley-Davidson, and

---

* *I discuss this process in greater detail in the chapters devoted to* The Golden Girls *and John Rich.*

since Fonzie was supposed to be the quintessential American biker, why didn't he ride a Harley?"

Henry's response was an unexpected delight. With a quizzical expression he simply said, "Wait. Are you saying that wasn't a Harley?"

I laughed. I couldn't help it. "No," I replied. "It was a Triumph, made in England. And I've never understood why, in Harley-Davidson's hometown, Fonzie would ride a British motorcycle. And I'm even more surprised that Harley's marketing department didn't reach out to you or Garry Marshall for some kind of endorsement deal during the show's heyday."

At this point, *he* was the one who laughed. He said, "Maybe it's because someone from Harley-Davidson actually saw me ride!" He went on to tell me that he only rode the motorcycle one time very early on during *Happy Days'* eleven-year run. Because of his dyslexia, he mixed up the various hand and foot levers that controlled the accelerator, clutch, and brakes.

While filming a scene, he accidentally went past the camera, lost control of the bike, and wound up laying it down, almost taking out a couple of crew members in the process. After that, all of Fonzie's motorcycle riding was confined to Henry just sitting on a "tow bike," hitched behind the camera car that was filming him. He told the story with relish, and I enjoyed hearing it. Towards the end he just looked at me and said, "So, it really wasn't a Harley?"

"Nope," I said. "It was a Triumph Trophy." Then I smiled at him and said, "You know, like the one Steve McQueen rode in the movie *The Great Escape*."

He just laughed, and in character as Fonzie said, "Well, that's cool. McQueen's cool." Then he switched characters, affecting a bit of his mother's Yiddish accent, and said, "What can I tell you, Doug? I'm just a Jewish kid from New York who went to Yale Drama. What do I know from motorcycles?" He laughed again, slapped me gently on the back, and we both went off to mingle elsewhere.

Despite the outstanding cast and the high-quality writing, *Mr. Sunshine* failed to catch on. ABC honored its obligation to Henry and John but gave the show a time slot opposite two very popular, well-established hit shows: *Dallas* on CBS and *Knight Rider* on NBC. This was basically a death sentence for a new show in search of an audience. *Mr. Sunshine* was cancelled by the network after its initial run.

But soon afterwards, I got the chance to work for Henry again on another sitcom pilot titled *Starting Now*, starring Ricki Lake. Working on this pilot is how I met legendary actor (and voice of Darth Vader) James Earl Jones,[*] which I'll tell you about in another chapter.

---

[*] *I discuss this in greater detail in the chapter devoted to James Earl Jones.*

OLIVIA NEWTON-JOHN

Is that lovely young woman smiling at <u>me</u>...?

Olivia Part One: Beverly Hills, California

It was a lovely evening in the early spring of 1975, and I was attending a banquet in the spectacular grand ballroom of the Beverly Hilton hotel in the heart of Beverly Hills, surrounded by dozens of A-list celebrities. The occasion was the network broadcast of the very first *People's Choice Awards* on CBS. "Officially" I was there as a representative of *The Lawrence Welk Show*, which had been nominated for an award. But in reality I was simply invited by my boss and mentor Jim Hobson, the show's producer and director, to "tag along" to the event with him and Lawrence. Some of the other nominees and presenters in attendance that night included John Wayne, Barbara Streisand, Bob Hope, Mary Tyler Moore, Alan Alda, Carol Burnett and Sammy Davis, Jr. So it's no exaggeration for me to say I was *way* out of my element!

At that time I was just a lowly production assistant, and Jim thought I'd enjoy a chance to get dressed up and participate in the kind of experience usually reserved for Hollywood's more elite. *The Lawrence Welk Show* had been nominated for a People's Choice Award in the "Favorite Television Variety Show" category. The other two programs nominated in that category were *The Carol Burnett Show* and *Tony Orlando and Dawn*. With those two shows as our competition, it felt as though I were breathing that rarified air. Heady stuff, for sure.

As I mentioned, this was the very first presentation of the *People's Choice Awards*. And unlike long-running awards shows such as the Oscars or Emmys, this award show had no prior history or credibility. And it had no "academy" of acclaimed industry peers casting votes for these awards. As per the show's premise, the winners for each category were decided by public opinion, as tabulated by the Gallup polls. In reality, *The People's Choice Awards* was simply a brand new, made-up-for-television awards show for CBS Television to be broadcast a few weeks prior to *The Academy Awards* on competing network ABC, perhaps in an attempt to steal a bit of thunder from the Oscars.

I should point out that many celebrities are often reluctant to attend a new and unproven awards program with no history or "street cred" for fear of embarrassment. I mean, it's hard enough on a performer's ego to appear on an existing awards show and have the public see them possibly lose out on an Oscar, Emmy or Grammy. So why would they want to go on network TV and risk getting passed over for some new, made-up award that no one's even heard of before? So the producers of first-time awards shows often need to find ways to entice celebrities to show up.

One such enticement is to create a "party atmosphere" around the awards. Hosting a cocktail hour and dinner prior to the actual awards presentation itself allows people from the motion picture, television and music industry to co-mingle and "schmooze." And this is exactly what *The People's Choice Awards* did. Even in Hollywood you might be surprised at who will show up for a free meal, an open bar, and the chance to "schmooze" and establish contacts with industry professionals outside of their normal sphere of experience!

And as I mentioned earlier, I had no business even being there. I was just a production assistant and as such, I made no creative contribution to *The Lawrence Welk Show*. As a PA, my entire job consisted of simply doing whatever errand Lawrence, Jim Hobson or the production staff needed me to do. It's the very definition of an "entry level" job in television.

But Jim thought it would be a good experience for me, and since his wife Elsie had no desire to attend, Jim invited me to the awards banquet as his "plus one." Sitting there in my rented tuxedo, actually having dinner with Jim and Lawrence Welk, and literally surrounded by famous people I'd only ever seen in the movies or on TV, I couldn't help but feel a bit like Cinderella at the ball. But as exciting as it all was, I knew that by midnight it would all be over, and I'd go back to the reality of being the $175-dollar-per-week production assistant. But there was plenty of time later to turn back into a "pumpkin." For now, I was being seen as an equal among a room full of Hollywood's movers and shakers!

The cocktail hour was winding down. A number of the celebrities were still mingling among the tables, while others were beginning to take their seats for dinner. It was at this time that I noticed a very lovely young woman sitting a few tables over. Actually, the word "lovely" didn't do her justice, but somehow it just felt like the most appropriate description. I didn't recognize her, but she was absolutely beautiful, with blonde hair, big blue eyes, and a smile that I could only describe as "dazzling." And to my amazement she appeared to be looking my way, smiling and waving as if to say "hello there!"

I quickly looked around to see if she were waving at someone behind me, but I didn't see anyone waving back at her, or even looking in her direction. And Lawrence and Jim were engaged in conversation, not paying any attention to what was going on, so she couldn't have been waving at them. Was it possible that she actually *was* waving at me? I smiled and waved back at her. She appeared to acknowledge my return greeting, smiling once again in my direction.

I just sat there for a moment, trying to figure out what to do next. On the one hand, I was just a lowly PA in a rented tux who had been invited to dog-paddle around in the deep end of the celebrity pool for an evening. But on the other hand, here was this lovely young lady sitting across the room who apparently had just smiled and waved at me. What if she was trying to make contact with me, hoping I might come over and introduce myself?

At that point I realized two things: 1) yes, I was just a $175-dollar-per-week production assistant who had no business being here, and 2) in my rented tuxedo, and in this room, only Jim and Lawrence knew the truth about number 1. So I made up my mind. I was going to go over and say hello. I mean, the whole point of the cocktail hour was to mingle and "schmooze," right? And after all, Jim had waved his magic wand over me, which had gotten me into the ball in the first place. Maybe the magic was still working.

I summoned my courage, got up and made my way across the ballroom. I'll admit it took some self-control to try and casually "meander" and not to just flat-out sprint. As I reached her table, I extended my hand to her and said, "Hello. My name is Doug Smart. I'm with The Lawrence Welk Show, and I just wanted to—" Suddenly two hulking men seemed to appear out of nowhere. Either of these guys could have played linebacker in the NFL. Linebacker #2 grabbed my arm, actually lifting me off the floor and said, "Is this guy bothering you, Olivia?"

Olivia? **OLIVIA?** It hit me like a bucket of ice water in the face. This lovely woman who I thought had been waving at me, who I had just crossed the ballroom to meet, and who I was now being dangled in front of, was Olivia Newton-John! I instantly realized two *new* things: 1) whoever Olivia had been smiling and waving at, it certainly hadn't been me, and 2) I was a complete idiot for even considering that number 1 might have been possible in the first place!

I was in way over my head (which is exactly what can happen when you're in the deep end of the pool!). But to my surprise (and my undying gratitude to this very day), Olivia Newton-John was every bit as gracious as she was lovely. She called off the linebackers saying, "No, this gentleman's not bothering me at all." Linebacker #2 released his grip on my arm, and my feet could once again touch the floor. The feeling began to come back into my fingers.

Olivia said, "I'm sorry. You were saying?" It was my move. I knew from the evening's program that Olivia was a nominee, so I did my best to regain my composure. I smoothed out my now-rumpled tux and somehow managed to squeak out, "Um, I was saying…I'm here with the Lawrence Welk Show." I pointed back across the room at

Lawrence, hoping that if she recognized him it might offer me a hint of legitimacy. "Anyhow, before the show started I just wanted to come over and, um, you know, wish you good luck. So…um…good luck!" *Smooth, Doug. Real Smooth. You're the "Prince of the Schmooze!"*

"Thank you very much," she replied, shaking my hand. "That's very kind of you. And good luck to you as well." She smiled at me. I thanked her, turned and started making my way back to my table. My face felt hot and flushed with embarrassment. I was hoping it wasn't noticeable. But with each step I took back across that ballroom I felt a whole lot less like Cinderella an a whole lot more like a pumpkin (And yes, I do realize that in Cinderella it's actually the coach that turns back into a pumpkin. But that's Charles Perrault's version of the story. This is **my** version, and I'm sticking with it!). As I sat back down at our table, I was relieved when neither Jim nor Lawrence seemed to notice my chagrin.

Jim just said, "Where've you been?" I replied, "Oh, you know, just trying to mingle and schmooze a bit. Wish people luck. You know." I was praying that he wouldn't press it any further. Mercifully he didn't. I went quietly back to my dinner.

Olivia Newton-John didn't need any luck that night. She and Barbara Streisand were both awarded the People's Choice Award for "Favorite Female Performer" in a tie vote. In 1977, Olivia would win a second People's Choice award in that same category, and she would win a third in 1979 along with the People's Choice award for "Favorite Movie Actress" for her portrayal of Sandy in *Grease*, opposite John Travolta.

Now before I continue with Part Two of my Olivia Newton-John story, I have a little "side-bar" story about Lawrence Welk and *his* experience that night. Even at the height of its popularity, *The Lawrence Welk Show* was always considered fairly "lowbrow" entertainment within the industry. After all, in addition to hosting the show, Lawrence would also play polkas on his accordion (considered by many to be a "lowbrow" instrument). And Lawrence spoke with a quirky midwestern-German-American accent that was tailor-made for comic impressionists who would do satirical send-ups of him on TV variety shows (even decades later by Fred Armisen on Saturday Night Live).

And the show's squeaky clean image, which featured a nostalgic look back at the music of the big band era (complete with a bubble machine), appealed mostly to an older, less sophisticated viewing audience. So when awards season would come around, neither Lawrence nor the show were ever given much serious consideration. On those rare occasions when the show *was* nominated, it always lost out to a show aimed at a more contemporary, youthful audience.

Therefore, as a rule, Lawrence declined invitations to awards shows. It always made him feel like they only wanted him there as "window dressing," playing on his visibility as a recognizable TV icon, but with zero chance of winning. So then why was Lawrence even attending the first annual *People's Choice Awards* broadcast? I'm glad you asked. Remember when I told you that quite often a new and unproven award show needs to find ways to entice celebrities to show up? On this particular occasion, one of those enticements ended up playing out in a somewhat bizarre fashion.

As I stated above, *The People's Choice Awards* were based on the results of public opinion as tabulated by the Gallup polls. No "academy," no industry insiders. Just the public. And in this instance, someone from either CBS or from Bob Stivers Productions, the company producing the show for the network, not only told Lawrence that his show had been nominated for "Favorite TV Variety Show" but also they told him he'd actually won!

Jim Hobson said the show's producers had made it clear that unlike the Oscars or the Emmys, *The People's Choice Awards* were not bound by any rule that required them to keep the poll results a secret. Therefore, they were notifying all of the winners in advance. Jim said they wanted to make sure that the winners in each category would actually show up to accept their awards. I asked Jim about the other nominees; had they been told in advance that they *weren't* winners? "No," Jim said. "They told us that because this is their first presentation. They were only informing the winners. They are trying to make sure that whoever wins is present to accept their award on camera."

"Does Lawrence know he's won?" I asked.

"Of course," Jim replied. "That's why he's here. He wouldn't have come otherwise." I had to admit it was a novel approach. What better way to get celebrities to show up for a new and unproven award show than to let them know ahead of time that they've won. I mean, who wouldn't show up for that?

We were part-way through the evening, and a number of awards had been presented in various categories. And we had finally come to the segment of the broadcast in which they would present the People's Choice for "Favorite Television Variety Show." The famous actress Jaqueline Bisset stepped out from the wings with a sealed envelope and crossed down to the podium to announce the nominees.

I looked over at Lawrence. He was beaming. At the age of 72 and with a television career that was still going strong after more than twenty years the viewers—*his* viewers—had finally recognized him for his contribution to the industry. And he was ready for his big moment. He had his acceptance remarks written down on a 3 x 5 index card clutched in his hand, so that he wouldn't forget what to say at the podium. But Lawrence was in his seventies, and our table was some distance from the stage. So he decided to give himself just a *little* head start in order to reach the podium in a timely fashion to accept his award.

"And the nominees for the People's Choice for Favorite Television Variety Show are…" Bisset announced, reading from the teleprompter, "…The Carol Burnett Show…" Applause. Lawrence stood up. "Tony Orlando and Dawn…" A second round of applause. He buttoned his tuxedo jacket. "…And the Lawrence Welk Show." A third round of applause. As the applause subsided and Jaqueline Bisset began opening the sealed envelope, Lawrence had already begun making his way towards the podium.

He was halfway there when Jaqueline removed the card and read, "And the People's Choice goes to The Carol Burnett Show!" The room exploded into enthusiastic applause and cheers. The orchestra played *The Carol Burnett Show* theme, and from the other side of the ballroom Carol Burnett crossed to the podium to accept the award. Meanwhile, practically unnoticed in the commotion was Lawrence Welk. Not knowing what else to do, Lawrence just kept walking, never breaking stride, all the way across the ballroom and out the exit at the other side, as if he were going to the men's room.

Lawrence never returned to the table that evening. He was hurt and humiliated. Jim Hobson was furious, realizing they'd been "played." Someone involved in the production had lied to them, just to lure Lawrence into showing up. No one at CBS or Bob Stivers Productions ever admitted any responsibility. The following year, Lawrence was nominated once again, this time for "Favorite Musical Performer." Needless to say, he did not attend.

Olivia Part Two: New York City, New York

It was January 1979, almost four years after my first embarrassing encounter with Olivia Newton-John. I was no longer a lowly production assistant, and I was no longer working on *The Lawrence Welk Show*. I was now an associate director and was in New York with producer-director Marty Pasetta for *A Gift of Song: The Concert for UNICEF*, a huge TV concert special to be staged from the floor of the United Nations General Assembly for the NBC network. The concert featured some of the most popular acts in contemporary music. The concept for the show was that each act would perform one of their hit songs then donate all future royalties from that song to UNICEF, the United Nations International Children's Emergency Fund. In addition to the musicians, there was an all-star lineup of celebrity hosts including Henry Fonda, Gilda Radner, and Henry Winkler.[*]

As I said, the show featured some of the most popular musical acts in the world, including The Bee Gees, Earth Wind and Fire, Rod Stewart, Donna Summer, Kris Kristofferson, ABBA, John Denver, and of course, Olivia Newton-John.

As the associate director, my job entailed working closely with the performers throughout the staging and rehearsal process to ensure that the show ran smoothly from the stage, and then assisting Marty to make sure we had the proper camera coverage for each performance. I was excited to meet these world-famous performers, but I have to admit I was apprehensive about coming face-to-face once again with Olivia Newton-John.

---

[*] *I discuss this production in greater detail in the chapter dedicated to Henry Winkler.*

I was afraid that when I was introduced to Olivia, she would look at me, squint her eyes a bit, and then say, "Wait a second. You look familiar. Have we met? Oh, yes. Now I remember. Aren't you that awkward fellow who came over to my table at The People's Choice Awards a few years ago and tried to wish me good luck?"

At which point I would be forced to admit, "Yes, Olivia. That was me." And then I'd go crawl off into a corner somewhere and suck my thumb.

So when Michael Seligman, our associate producer came up to me on the stage and said, "Olivia Newton-John just got here. She's in the production office. We should go down so I can introduce you. Then you can go over the schedule with her," I'll admit I was pretty nervous. Okay, okay, fine! I was *really* nervous!

We stepped into our makeshift production office, and there she was, every bit as lovely as that night back at the Beverly Hilton, just more casually dressed. But those eyes were just as big and blue, and that smile was just as dazzling. We walked over and Michael said, "Olivia, I'd like you to meet Doug Smart, our associate director. He'll walk you through the rehearsal and shooting schedule and will work out all of your cues with our stage managers."

This was it: the moment I'd been dreading. I took a step towards Olivia, wondering what would happen next. But to my utter relief, nothing happened, other than Olivia extending her hand to me in greeting. I took hers in return, and as we shook hands, she looked me straight in the eye, smiled, and said, "It's lovely to meet you, Doug. I look forward to working with you."

"Very nice meeting you as well, Ms. Newton-John," I replied.

She shot me a very sweet "Oh, please" smile and said, "Just call me Olivia, okay?" I promised I would. There was that smile again. She was every bit as gracious and lovely as I had remembered from that night four years earlier.

She hadn't remembered me at all! A huge wave of relief washed over me. I was never so happy to have been completely forgotten by someone in my life! And I realized that while our meeting at the People's Choice Awards may have been an unforgettably embarrassing incident for *me*, for Olivia it had been nothing more than a blink of an eye, a casual greeting, no more memorable than the thousands of other casual greetings she'd likely experienced during the course of her career.

We got right to work, and Olivia was an absolute pleasure to work with; she was charming, easy-going, and prepared for whatever was asked of her. We were simply two professionals working towards a common goal. And at no point during our time together in rehearsal did she give the slightest indication that we might have met before. And I wasn't dumb enough to remind her. Nope, that was a "sleeping dog" that I was only too happy to just let lay.

The night of the concert Olivia delivered two outstanding performances. The first was her duet "Rest Your Love on Me" with Andy Gibb, younger brother of Barry, Maurice and Robin Gibb, the Bee Gees. Later in the program she took center stage on the floor of the General Assembly and, standing alone in the spotlight, charmed everyone with a tender, heart-felt performance of her hit song "The Key." At the end of the show, Olivia joined the rest of the cast on stage for the closing number, standing next to Barry Gibb of the Bee Gees, as they all sang "Put A Little Love In Your Heart."

That was the last time I saw Olivia Newton-John in person. In the years since that night, her numerous career accomplishments, her awards, her courageous battles with cancer, and her generous philanthropy have been well chronicled in the media. It's all a matter of public record.

When I first saw Olivia Newton-John across the ballroom that night back at the Beverly Hilton I couldn't help but think, "What a lovely woman!" I still can't help but think that same thing.

7

CHER

Who invites the paparazzi to a hot tub party?

Cher. That's it. Just her first name. Anything more is redundant. I mean, let's face it. Who on this planet doesn't know who I'm talking about?

I met Cher in the spring of 1980, in Monaco, in the south of France. We were on location shooting *The Monte Carlo Show* for FOX Television. *The Monte Carlo Show* was a musical-variety show in the classic sense, featuring an array of singers, dancers, comedians, magicians, and animal acts. Like the name suggests, *The Monte Carlo Show* was being produced in Le Salle des Etoiles *(Room Under the Stars)*, an open-air concert venue in the Sporting Club of Monte Carlo, overlooking the Mediterranean Sea.

Most of the acts appearing on the show came from Europe, but FOX made sure that each of the twenty-four episodes we were shooting featured a "headline act" that would appeal to its American viewers. These "headliners" included such well-known entertainers as Liberace, Glen Campbell, Ben Vereen, Mac Davis, and of course, Cher. In addition to her appearance on our show, HBO had contracted with Cher to shoot a 90-minute concert special using our venue and crew, which we did after the taping for FOX had been completed. But my "Cher story" doesn't begin in Monte Carlo in 1980. For that, we need to go back a decade earlier...

This story actually begins in the Crown Room at the famous Hotel Del Coronado on Coronado Island, just across the bridge from San Diego. The Crown Room is the luxurious dining room of the world-class "Hotel Del" and is famous for its high arched ceiling paneled in Oregon sugar pine and its crown-shaped chandeliers, which were designed by none other than L. Frank Baum, the author of *The Wizard of Oz*. Since the hotel first opened in 1888, the Crown Room has hosted banquets for the rich, the famous, and the royal, but on this particular evening in the spring of 1971, there were no such luminaries in attendance, and no such festivities on the agenda. No, this particular evening had been set aside for my parents to show me the error of my ways.

I was in the second semester of my junior year at San Diego State University, and I had been invited (or summoned, depending upon your point of view) by my parents to join them for dinner at the hotel. My father was an executive with A & W Root Beer and was in San Diego on business. Since the trip was on the company dime, Dad elected to stay at the Hotel Del and had brought my mother along with him, as she often joined him on his business trips.

My parents were very upset to discover that I was majoring in Television and Film Production. Actually, "very upset" is putting it mildly. They were furious with me, especially my father. But Mom was not far behind. They regarded my decision to study Television and Film Production as a foolish waste of a college education and had been insisting that I choose another "more sensible" major, such as Business (which did not hold even the slightest interest or appeal for me).

Now to be perfectly honest, I'd been dodging the issue for a while now. Since incoming freshmen were not required to declare a major for the first two years, I had simply opted to remain an undeclared major as a freshman and sophomore. And since the bulk of my courses during that period consisted of liberal arts "gen eds," I had been able slip the occasional screenwriting or film history courses into the mix without raising any red flags with Mom and Dad. But as I began my junior year, I finally had to officially declare to the world that I was in fact majoring in Television and Film Production (and had been all along, compounding my sin).

And as soon as it became official, my parents launched their campaign to convince me that I was making the biggest mistake of my life. And part of their strategy was to invite me to dinner at the Hotel Del Coronado and, over a delicious and very expensive meal, tell me what a huge disappointment I was to them. I knew all this when I accepted their invitation and was not particularly looking forward to what was in store for me, despite my love for a good prime rib.

So there we were, the three of us, sitting beneath those lovely chandeliers in the magnificent Crown Room at the Hotel Del Coronado. If part of Dad's strategy was to use the opulence of our surroundings to intimidate me, then I have to confess that it was working a bit. As a scruffy college student, I definitely felt out of my element. As soon as we had ordered and the waiter left with the menus, my parents began their campaign to convince me that I was being foolish. At first, they claimed that I had blindsided them by choosing Television and Film as my major. I responded, "How can you say that? Ever since I was a little kid all I've ever talked about is going to Hollywood and working in television. It's all I've ever wanted to do!"

Dad countered with, "But we thought that was just a phase. We thought you'd grow out of it. You know, like the kid who says he wants to be an astronaut or pitch for the Dodgers when he grows up."

"But Dad, some of those kids *don't* grow out of it. And they're the ones actually *become* the astronauts or major league ball players!" I shot back. "How do you know I'm not one of those kids?"

"Because you're not!" he said, slamming the table. And he meant it. My father didn't believe I would ever make it. "You need to grow up and stop throwing your life away chasing this silly, childish dream!"

It was getting tense. Real tense. My ear lobes felt hot. I took a sip from my water glass to keep from popping off with some remark I'd probably regret. But then my mom said something so bizarre, so off-the-wall, that all of the anger that had been welling up inside me just instantly and completely dissipated.

She said, "I'm just terrified that someday I'll pick up one of those gossip magazines from the supermarket checkout line, and there'll be a picture of you, in a hot tub with Cher!"

Her remark caught me so off guard that I almost did a spit-take with my water. My mom wasn't afraid that her son might become an alcoholic or a drug addict? She didn't lie awake nights, worrying that I might die destitute and alone? Nope. As far as Mom was concerned, the worst fate she could conjure up for her baby boy was that he might wind up in a hot tub with Cher.

I decided to counter her fear with logic. "Mom," I said, simultaneously laughing and choking on my water. "Two things. First, what on earth makes you think that Cher even has a hot tub? And second, and even more to the point, assuming there's a universe in which Cher actually *does* have a hot tub, of all the people she could invite over for a soak, why would she ask me? I mean, look at me, Mom. I'm not exactly leading man material."

Without skipping a beat she came back with something even funnier. "Have you ever taken a good look at Sonny Bono?" she quipped.

"Be that as it may," I replied, "I think you can take 'me and Cher in a hot tub' off your worry list, Mom." Me and Cher? That night at the Hotel Del Coronado I couldn't imagine a more unlikely scenario.

....

But then almost a decade later there I was, alone with Cher herself. It was just the two of us, sitting on the set of *The Monte Carlo Show*, talking through the show's rehearsal schedule. How had she and I arrived at this particular intersection in life?

Throughout the remainder of the 1970's Cher's star had continued its orbit in the celebrity universe. In addition to her continued success in music, she had also been an award-winning TV star, receiving a Golden Globe in 1974 for her performance on *The Sonny & Cher Comedy Hour*. In 1975, she married Gregg Allman, the co-founder of The Allman Brothers Band, and in 1976 gave birth to a son, Elijah Blue Allman. Cher and Gregg divorced in 1979, and afterwards she continued to produce a string of hit records. She also starred in two more television specials: Cher…Special *(1978)* and Cher…and Other Fantasies *(1979)*.

And I hadn't been exactly standing still, either. Within a year of graduation from San Diego State, I had gotten my foot in the door as a production assistant on *The Lawrence Welk Show*.* Through a combination of hard work and opportunities, I had advanced to become the associate director of the television show and the director of the live touring show.

In 1978, I was hired by the talented but volatile producer-director Marty Pasetta.† I immediately began working as his associate director on a number of musical-variety specials, including *A Gift of Song: the Concert for UNICEF*,‡ *A Country Christmas*, *The All Star Salute to Pearl Bailey*, and the *American Film Institute Life Achievement Awards* to Alfred Hitchcock and Jimmy Stewart. We had also done *The 51st* and *52nd Academy Awards* broadcasts together, with our second *Oscars* telecast taking place just the night before we made the transatlantic flight to France to begin production on *The Monte Carlo Show*. For me it had definitely been a long and winding road from that dinner at the Hotel Del Coronado to The Sporting Club of Monte Carlo.

But now here I was, sitting alone on stage in the Salle des Etoiles with Cher herself, just two professionals going about our business. And I was a bit surprised at how easily the conversation flowed. And she was so funny! As we sat together on stage going over the schedule, Cher was constantly serving up hysterical "one liners" regarding the general state of the chaos going on around us during the rehearsal. We laughed and joked our way through that meeting. I can't speak for Cher, but I was having a great time!

And even though it had been almost ten years, I could still hear my mom's voice just as clear as a bell: *"I'm just terrified that someday I'll pick up one of those gossip magazines from the supermarket checkout line, and there'll be a picture of you, in a hot tub with Cher!"* Life had presented me with a golden opportunity to prove to my mom that her worst fear was totally unfounded. And I was starting to feel comfortable

---

* *I discuss this in more detail in the chapter devoted to The Lawrence Welk Show.*
† *I discuss this in greater detail in the chapter devoted to John Rich.*
‡ *I discuss this special in greater detail in the chapter devoted to Henry Winkler.*

enough in the short time I'd spent with Cher to broach the subject. But how? That was the tricky part. We really had nothing in common… except we both had moms.

We'd hit a natural pause in our conversation. Cher took a sip from her water bottle, and I used the pause to try and bring up the subject of my mom. "Cher," I said, "Since we have a few minutes here, can I ask you a random question that has absolutely nothing to do with anything whatsoever?"

"Well, that's an intriguing proposition Doug," she said, giving me a side-eyed glance, followed by a grin. "Yeah, I guess so. As long as it's not too personal."

"No, I don't think so. It's not even really my question. It's my mom's. Honestly, I don't know how she comes up with this stuff."

She gave me that side-eyed grin again. "She doesn't need a reason. She's a mom." I wasn't quite sure if this was in reference to her relationship with her own mother, or because she was a mom herself. Either way, I pressed on.

"Good point," I replied. Since Mom's real concern was less than flattering, I confess that I put a "spin" on the actual question at hand. It came out more like this: "Anyhow, my mom has somehow got it in her head that you…well, you…like to throw hot tub parties."

"Hot tub parties?" She said, nonplussed. "I thought I'd heard it all. But I gotta tell you, that's a new one!"

"You have to know my mom." I said, wanting to keep it light. "Apparently she believes everything she reads in the supermarket checkout line." I just smiled at her, shrugged, and went palms up. "Anyhow," I went on, "when she heard that I was going to be working with you, she wanted me to find out if you really do have those wild hot tub parties she reads about in the tabloids!"

She laughed hard, shaking her head.

I shrugged. "I know. Bizarre, right?"

She laughed again. "Well, for the record, you can tell your mom 'no.' I don't throw wild hot tub parties. Or any other kind of hot tub parties. I've never really been a hot tub kind of gal." We both laughed, and I assured her that the next time I spoke to my mom, I would set her straight once and for all. We laughed again and got back to work.

I almost wished my mom had been there. If she had, she would've been able to see the *real* Cher, not the one plastered on the front pages of the supermarket tabloids. But here I was, actually getting to spend some time with the genuine article. Lucky me.

....

On this particular day there were two American pre-school children at The Sporting Club of Monte Carlo, and they were having a grand time running all around the Salle des Etoiles, playing on the set of *The Monte Carlo Show*. The cast and crew were hard at work getting that night's show ready, but these two children were much too busy having fun to pay much attention to the TV show being staged all around them.

One of those kids was Elijah Blue Allman, Cher's son with ex-husband Duane Allman of The Allman Brothers Band. Since he wasn't old enough yet to be in school, he had traveled with his mom to Monte Carlo. And instead of staying at the hotel or going to the beach, Elijah Blue had wanted to come with Cher to the venue while she rehearsed the show. Elijah Blue was just a shade under four years old, and was having a great time, exploring all the nooks and crannies of the huge set pieces, asking questions of the crew, and "marching" around the room while the show's orchestra rehearsed that evening's musical numbers.

The other child was Stacey Seligman, the daughter of our associate producer, Michael Seligman. Stacey was only about three years old at the time, and she was just as cute as she could be. Three months shooting on location is a long time to be separated from your family, so Michael had decided to bring his wife and young daughter with him. And on this day Stacey had accompanied her dad to The Sporting Club of Monte Carlo as well. Usually when she came to the set, she was the only child there, and she had completely charmed the crew, who doted on her. However, on this day Stacey actually had a playmate her own age, as Elijah Blue was marching around the set. And it wasn't long before the two kids were joyfully marching around the Salle des Etoiles together.

Cher and I were sitting in a corner of the set, going over her cues. The orchestra was just finishing running through the arrangement of one of her numbers when Elijah Blue marched up with Stacey, his arm around her shoulder.

"Mom," he announced, "This is Stacey. She's my new friend!"

Cher leaned in towards the little girl and extended her hand. "Well, hello there, Stacey." She took Stacey's hand and shook it very gently, and with a warm smile said, "It's so very nice to meet you." Stacey just giggled in response.

"Isn't she neat?" Elijah Blue asked.

"Yes," his mom replied. "She certainly is neat."

Elijah Blue looked at Stacey for a second then turned back to Cher and blurted, "Mom, can Stacey come to our hotel room tonight and sleep with me in my bed?" Again, Stacey just giggled.

Without even batting an eyelash Cher said, "We'll talk about it later, honey. Why don't you two go and play for a while until lunch?"

"Okay," he said. And the two of them turned and marched off, still arm-in-arm, to another adventure.

As soon as they were out of earshot, Cher shot me a huge side-eyed grin. "That kid is just like his old man," she said slyly. "He's known her for what, five minutes? And he's already inviting her up to his hotel room for the night!" She winked at me and laughed. But to my ears her laugh had a somewhat world-weary quality to it. It made me wonder if perhaps it was rooted in some painful experience…

....

Marty Pasetta, the Producer-Director of *The Monte Carlo Show*, didn't like Cher. I have no idea why. It was just a fact. He didn't like her. Knowing Marty, his dislike for her was most likely the result of some previous professional disagreement. As I've stated elsewhere in this book, Marty was famous for being volatile and had a habit of throwing temper tantrums and publicly humiliating both the cast and crew on the set.[*] He was also known to hold a grudge. And for whatever reason, Marty harbored an extreme dislike for Cher.

---

[*] *There's more on this in the chapter devoted to John Rich.*

Now, *The Monte Carlo Show* had a combined French-American crew, with the Americans filling most of the "technical" positions necessary for television (camera operators, audio mixers, etc.), while the French crew was in charge of the "theatrical" side of the physical venue itself (stagehands, carpenters, riggers, lighting, etc.).

On a television show, the stage manager is somewhat of a hybrid. He or she is in charge of "running the stage," making sure that all performers are on their marks when they are supposed to be, and that all scenic cues occur at the right time.

But on a TV show, the stage manager is also connected through a headset to the show's director, who is not on stage but in a control booth elsewhere. According to the Director's Guild of America, one of the main duties of the stage manager is "relaying stage directions of the associate director or director..."* This makes the stage manager the director's "proxy" on the stage.

When we began production on *The Monte Carlo Show*, our stage manager was part of the French crew that had come down to Monaco from Paris. But his grasp of English was weak, and Marty spoke no French, so they began having communication problems from the very onset. To make matters worse, the young man had worked almost exclusively in theater, so he had very little experience in television, even in European broadcasting. And no one had warned him that there would be an extremely demanding, impatient, and volatile director on the other end of his headset barking commands directly into his ear.

And that impatient, volatile director was becoming increasingly frustrated by the lack of precision with which his instructions were being carried out. So, after the second or third time that Marty threw down his headset, walked out onto the stage, and screamed at the poor fellow, humiliating him in front of the entire cast and crew, the stage manager simply threw down *his* headset, packed his bags, and headed back to Paris. *The Monte Carlo Show* now had no stage manager, and we had only completed two episodes out of twenty-four.

Since I had a great deal of previous experience managing the stage during my years on *The Lawrence Welk Show*, Marty immediately pressed me into service as the show's stage manager for the remaining

---
* As per the Directors Guild of America network Stage Managers agreement

twenty-two episodes. From that moment on, I never went back into the director's booth. I was now working out on stage with the talent and the crew in front of the audience.

Now on paper, being reassigned from associate director to stage manager would be considered a step down, but in this case, it was a win-win. Even though I was in reality the show's stage manager, I was still listed in the TV credits as the associate director…win. And I was still being paid at the higher associate director's rate…win-win. Oh, and because it got me out of the director's booth and onto the stage, I no longer had to sit right next to Marty while he was screaming and throwing pencils at the monitors. I was now two hundred feet away in a completely different room and was only connected to Marty by that headset. And I could turn down the volume any time I felt like it! So make that a win-win-win!

Therefore, my new responsibility as the stage manager on *The Monte Carlo Show* was to be Marty's "proxy" and relay all of his instructions to the performers on stage. And on this particular show, the performer on stage was Cher. And because I knew how intensely he disliked her, I couldn't help but wonder how this was all going to play out.

Marty had kept his distance from Cher throughout the talk-through and walk-through that morning. Since we weren't working with the cameras yet, we didn't see him at all before lunch. But the afternoon was devoted to camera rehearsal, so the tech crew were all in position, and Marty was in the director's booth coordinating the camera coverage. Since the director's booth was actually in a truck parked outside of the Salle des Etoiles, Marty could only see us on the stage through the camera monitors in the truck, and he could only hear the performers when the audio mixer in the truck opened their microphones. Other than that, Marty's only link to the stage was through me, via the headsets we each wore.

Cher and I were standing together center stage, and I could see in a TV monitor out on stage that we were both in Marty's camera shot. Marty wasted no time in attempting to "lay down the law" with Cher, and his instructions coming into my headset were "explicit" to put it mildly.

First, he ordered the audio mixer to open Cher's microphone on the stand in front of us, so that he would be able to hear what we both were saying. Then he flipped his headset microphone on and growled into my earpiece, "Doug, I want you to tell that b&%* that I'm not going to take any f#*&ing $&% from her! And I want you to tell her that verbatim! Got it? Her microphone is on, so I can hear everything you're saying! Remember…*verbatim*!"

I looked directly into the camera lens, so that I could address Marty "face to face" and gave him the universal "okay" sign. "Got it," I replied into my headset microphone, "Verbatim." Then I turned to Cher and said very clearly into the open microphone, "Cher, Marty just wanted me to tell you how absolutely delighted he is to be working with you."

Cher cocked an eyebrow, looking at me suspiciously. She knew Marty. "He said that?" she asked.

"Yes, yes, he did," I replied into the open microphone. "And he told me to make sure I relayed it to you verbatim!" I looked back into the camera lens and gave Marty a huge grin and a "thumbs up." My grin came quite naturally. I was simply picturing the look on Marty's face at that moment.

By now, Marty was making the kind of sounds you might imagine someone would make if they were having a coronary. He was no longer just verbally abusing Cher. A great deal of his vitriol was now being directed at me as well. There's no need to go into the particulars here, and I wouldn't use that kind of language in this book anyway. Let's just say that Marty was "less than pleased" with my translation of his instructions to Cher.

And to punctuate his displeasure, Marty was no longer yelling; he was now screaming. As a matter of fact, he was screaming so loudly that his voice was actually "bleeding" out from the earpiece on my headset and onto the stage. So even though Cher might not have been able to make out Marty's exact words, she could certainly tell from his volume and tone that that he was screaming insults at me.

Cher looked at me wide-eyed, knowing that what was going into my ear couldn't possibly be good. However, I just kept nodding my head "yes," as Marty screamed, as if I were understanding some instruction he was giving me over the headset. After a bit, I punched my "talk" switch and suddenly said to Marty, "Okay, I'll tell her." Inside my ear, I could hear Marty yelling, "Tell her what? Tell her what?"

I turned to Cher, smiled, and indicated her wardrobe, "And Marty also wanted me to tell you how stunning he thinks you look in that outfit!" Again my headset exploded with language that would make a sailor blush. And again I turned directly into the TV camera, smiled at Marty and gave the "thumbs up" sign, as if I had been conveying his comments word for word.

Cher knew I was lying. She just shook her head and laughed. Then she put her hand over her microphone to block the sound, leaned in close to me, and said softly, "Doug, you and I both know that's not even close to what he's been screaming at you!"

"Oh, yeah? Well, that's my story, and I'm sticking with it," I replied. I grinned at her. A big, wide goofy grin.

She just laughed and asked, "So how much trouble are you going to be in?"

"Not enough to get me fired," I laughed back. "Marty's already lost one stage manager. He knows he can't afford to lose another. Besides," I added, "Isn't this fun?"

....

The show taping was about to start. I was walking Cher from her dressing room out to her mark in the center of the stage. The curtains in front of us were closed, so we were unseen by the audience out front. On the way out, one of the audio utility operators handed her the wireless microphone she would use for the show. Her hair and makeup were perfect, and she was wearing a form-fitting sequined black body suit and jacket with knee-high black boots. She looked amazing. She looked just like…Cher.

As we hit her mark at center stage, I punched my headset microphone to the "talk" position. "Marty," I said, "I'm with Cher. She's on her opening mark, and she has her microphone. We're standing by." Marty (who had finally calmed down) indicated that we'd be starting the taping momentarily.

I turned to Cher. "We'll be rolling tape in about a minute or so. When the show starts, you'll hear the opening theme music, and our twelve dancers will go into their opening routine. At the end of their routine they'll say, 'The Monte Carlo Show is proud to present…Cher!' I'll cue the stage crew to open the curtain, and then it's all yours." I started to walk to my position just off-stage.

"Wait," she said, stopping me. "Can you stay here?"

"Sure," I said. "Is everything okay? Do I need to tell them to hold?"

"No, no. Everything's fine," she replied. "I'd just feel better if you would, you know, stay out here with me just a bit longer."

I realized at that moment that she was having a case of stage jitters. I had learned from experience that it was not uncommon for even the most seasoned performer to get nervous just before going on. It had just never occurred to me that one of them would be Cher.

"Sure, okay," I said. "I can do that. How about if I stay until the curtain starts to open?"

"That would be perfect," she replied.

So I stood beside her. Just the two of us. Center stage. Cher, the international superstar, and Doug, the kid who dreamed of working in television someday. After a second or two, I felt her right hand reaching for my left hand. I gently took her hand in mine and held it. And there we stood. Holding hands. Doug and Cher.

Out in the production truck, the videotape started rolling and quickly came up to speed. From center stage I announced to the crew, "Tape is rolling…speed on tape! Standby!" Through my headset, I could hear the countdown. At ten seconds before the show was to begin, I called out "ten seconds" to the stage. At five seconds, I counted down with the truck: "In five, four, three, two…" Cher and I were still holding hands.

The house orchestra struck up *The Monte Carlo Show* theme music. On the other side of the curtain in front of us, we could hear the show's dancers, Les Girls, going through their opening routine. Finally, we heard them say, "Ladies and Gentlemen, The Monte Carlo Show is proud to present…Cher!" When she heard her name, Cher let go of my hand.

I cued the off-stage crew to open the curtain, and I started walking off behind it. I looked back towards center stage, and there in the spotlight was Cher, the Cher everybody saw: talented, confident, and sensual, strutting down stage to the cheers of the crowd as she sang.

I have no doubt that Cher will not remember any of this. For her it was just another moment before yet another show, like all the ones that had preceded it and like all the ones that would follow in the years to come.

But for me it was a very special moment. And one that I'll always remember with great fondness. Warm. Sweet. Tender.

Thank you, Cher, for inviting me to share that one moment with you.

JOHN RICH

> *Old joke: "Where does a 900-pound gorilla sit? Anywhere he wants."*

Now, unlike the other names I'm using as chapter titles in this book, the name John Rich probably isn't one that you would recognize. But trust me, among the ranks of television sitcom directors, John Rich was a living legend. His credits go back to the "Golden Age of Television" in the 1950's, directing the enormously popular seminal sitcoms *Our Miss Brooks* with Eve Arden and *I Married Joan* with Joan Davis and Jim Backus.[*] In the 1960's he helmed such iconic sitcoms as *The Dick Van Dyke Show, Hogan's Heroes, Gilligan's Island, Gomer Pyle, USMC, That Girl,* and *The Brady Bunch*.

In the early 1970's, John was the director and producer for the first four seasons of *All in the Family*, which is considered one of the most

---

[*] Backus was also famous as the voice of "Mr. Magoo" and as multi-millionaire Thurston Howell III in *Gilligan's Island*.

influential shows in the history of television.* John also directed the pilot episodes of *All in the Family*'s popular spinoffs: *Maude*, *The Jeffersons*, and *Good Times*. In the mid-1970's, John directed the pilot episode of *Barney Miller*, another iconic sitcom that enjoyed a long successful run.

Now, the director of a successful network TV pilot that is picked up for broadcast will receive residual payments for the entire run of that series, even if he or she never directs another episode. Therefore, as the director of the TV pilots for *Maude*, *Good Times*, *The Jeffersons*, *Barney Miller*†, *Gilligan's Island*, and *The Brady Bunch*, John was earning an *astonishingly* good living just walking from his front door to his mailbox to retrieve all of those residuals checks!‡

John won three Emmy awards for his work in sitcoms. One was for directing *The Dick Van Dyke Show* (Van Dyke once described John as "the best comedy director I ever met") and two more Emmys for his work on *All in the Family*. As if that weren't enough, John was also awarded the Outstanding Television Director award from the Directors Guild of America and received several Golden Globes for *All in the Family*.

John was also a guiding force in the Directors Guild of America, receiving the Robert B. Aldrich Award for Extraordinary Service for his leadership and dedication to the guild. And he was held in very high esteem among his peers in the DGA, many of whom regarded him as a legendary figure in the history of television comedy. Yep, when it came to sitcom directors, John Rich was the personification of the "900-pound gorilla." He could sit anywhere he wanted.

In 1980, John was brought in as the director and executive producer on *Benson*, the Witt-Thomas-Harris Productions spinoff of their hit sitcom *Soap*. And it was on *Benson* that my professional association (and consequently my deep affection and lifetime friendship) with

---

* *It takes a TV show four seasons to produce enough episodes for a lucrative syndicated re-run deal, usually 100 episodes, which is the standard milestone for syndication.*

† *When John heard that Danny Arnold was ending Barney Miller after seven seasons, he stopped our rehearsal, got on the stage phone with Danny, and after a half-hour, had talked him into doing an eighth season so that they both would get another year's worth of residuals checks!*

‡ *From time to time, I would enjoy "poking the bear," teasing John about what I called his "mailbox money." I would ask him what size wheelbarrow he needed in order be able to cart all of his checks back to the house!*

John began. To me, the years we worked together were the equivalent of earning a Master's Degree in Situation Comedy. I learned first-hand about what makes a comedy work from week to week, both in the script and on camera. He was also a master at the craft of working with actors to elicit their best performances, as well as the art of precise comedic timing. He became my last (and toughest) mentor. And I became, in John's own words, his "head schmuck."*

In August of 1980, *Benson* was entering its second season, and Don Richetta, the producer who originally contacted me about the associate director's position, informed me that Witt-Thomas-Harris had been looking for a "900-pound gorilla who would come in and settle the show down," providing some stability at the helm. Don never mentioned what caused the instability in season one, but I can tell you from experience that almost all TV series suffer some sort of "growing pains" during their first season on the air, for a variety of reasons.†

So John wasn't brought in just to direct *Benson*. He also became one of the show's three executive producers, along with Tony Thomas and Paul Junger Witt.‡ At this time, Paul and Tony were stretched pretty thin. They were juggling four shows on ABC: *Soap*, *Benson*, *I'm a Big Girl Now,* and *It's a Living*. They also had a fifth sitcom, *It Takes Two* in development for the network. So it's not too hard to understand why Paul Witt and Tony Thomas would want someone with John's talent, experience and "gravitas" to take charge of the day-to-day production on *Benson*, which would afford them more time to deal with all of their other shows.

There had been several directors and associate directors working on *Benson* during its first season, which is not all that unusual. But once John Rich had signed on for the series, he wanted an associate

---

* *To be clear, "schmuck" is a derogatory term derived from a vulgar Yiddish word referring to male anatomy. But with John, "schmuck" could be a term of endearment (or not, depending on the circumstance!). Quite often on the set, when a minor production issue would come up, John would simply refer the person(s) with the issue to me, saying, "Just talk to Doug. He'll take care of it. He's my Head Schmuck."*
† *I discuss this in greater detail in the Chapter devoted to Empty Nest.*
‡ *As the creator of Benson, Susan Harris rightfully claimed credit as an Executive Producer, but because she was writing every episode of Soap, she was not involved in the "hands on" production responsibilities on Benson.*

director who could work alongside him for the duration of his contract. And that's when Don Richetta, the show's co-producer, contacted me.

Don said, "We're looking for associate director who can work with John Rich, and your name came up. He's never heard of you, so he wants to meet. Consider it a job interview. Afterwards, if John is satisfied that you're a good fit for him, the job is yours." I told Don I'd be happy to meet with John, so he scheduled a time and place for us to meet.

The interview took place at the ABC Television studios on the corner of Prospect Avenue and Talmadge Street in the Los Feliz district of Los Angeles, where *Benson* was being filmed.* I was very familiar with this studio lot because it was where I had worked on *The Lawrence Welk Show* only a few years earlier. This lot was also where I had become eligible for full director status in the DGA, having directed the overnight shift of *Weekend With the Stars*, John Ritter's 21-hour telethon for cerebral palsy the previous year.

Studio 54 at Prospect and Talmadge was also where, as a senior in high school back in 1968, I had appeared as a contestant on *The Dating Game*, ABC's network game show. I suppose *The Dating Game* could be considered a prehistoric ancestor of *The Bachelor* or *The Bachelorette* (although The Dating Game was strictly G-Rated). Oddly enough, in 1969 my rock and roll band, Mass Confusion, wound up right back on that same stage in Studio 54. This time it was for our band's network television debut on the ABC music show *Happening*, Dick Clark's follow-up to his long-running show *American Bandstand*. Within months of that broadcast, Mass Confusion had disbanded, and we all drifted off into rock and roll obscurity. Yes, I was quite familiar with the ABC Television Center at the corner of Prospect and Talmadge.

But I digress…This chapter is about John Rich.

You know the old saying, "Ignorance is bliss?" I believe that it's true. While I knew that John was indeed a "900-pound gorilla," and was well aware of his professional credits, I was blissfully unaware

---

* *Now the Prospect Studios, this film lot was originally the Vitagraph Studio. Parts of "The Jazz Singer," the first feature film to incorporate synchronized sound, were filmed there in 1927. It was acquired by the ABC Network in the late 1940's and served as their west coast production center until the late 1990's, when it became part of the Walt Disney Company. As of this writing, the ABC series "Grey's Anatomy" is still being filmed there.*

that he was also considered by many to be a "bull in a china shop." He had a reputation for being gruff, salty, and short-tempered. On *All in the Family*, he once famously became so aggravated with actress Sally Struthers that he kicked a chair across the rehearsal hall with such force that he broke his foot. John had to wear a cast on his foot until it healed. Unbeknownst to me, there was a pretty lengthy list of people who, having worked with John once, refused to work with him again. Looking back, I believe that Don Richetta had chosen his words carefully: "We're looking for associate director who can work with John Rich." So I walked into my meeting with John blissfully ignorant.

As Executive Producer, John was involved in pre-production for the upcoming season and had arranged to interview me during his lunch break. He suggested we talk outside in one of the studio's courtyards. Having been involved in countless script conferences, casting sessions, and meetings with the heads of the various departments involved in production, I think he was craving a little bit of sunshine and fresh air.

My first impression of John was how closely he resembled what I had imagined a legendary television director to be. He had a thick full head of salt-and-pepper hair that was very neatly (and I guessed expensively) trimmed. He wore a lightweight sweater vest over a tastefully expensive white dress shirt sporting gold cufflinks at each wrist, and a necktie. His high-end designer blue jeans showed no hint of fading, and on his feet were a pair of first-rate running shoes. I quickly made a mental note that, if I got the job, I'd need to get myself a better pair of shoes. I had a feeling that I'd be on my feet and running quite a bit in order to keep up with this guy!

John had a pair of half-frame reading glasses on a strap around his neck, and was smoking a large, aromatic (and again I guessed very expensive) cigar. Upon meeting we shook hands, and then he asked me to walk with him around the small courtyard. He said that after sitting in meetings all morning, he needed to stretch his legs. We'd barely started walking when he asked, "So, tell me. Have you ever worked on a network sitcom before?"

I told him I hadn't, and that *Benson* would be my first. Then I added, "But you already knew that, didn't you?"

He said, "Of course. But I wanted to see if you'd try and BS me. So give me a reason why should I take a chance on you."

"I can give you two, " I replied. "One, I've wanted to work in sitcom ever since I was a little kid, so this wouldn't be just another job to me. It's something I've been working towards my whole life. And two, while it's true that I don't have any sitcom experience on my resume, I know sitcom production. I learned it from Desi Arnaz."*

Yes, I had dropped Desi's name, and I think it caught John off guard a bit. He took a long puff on his cigar and looked at me for a beat, as if he were trying to determine whether or not I was on the up and up. But I'd been straight with him about my sitcom experience, no BS. So he just said one word: "Explain."

I told John about my apprenticeship with Desi my senior year of college and how we had produced a multi-camera sitcom from start to finish in the Desilu style under his tutelage. I also made sure to mention that Desi had chosen me to direct the final sitcom project. John seemed satisfied with my answer, although he had a great poker face.

"I know you're in the guild. But you've never done sitcoms. So what *have* you been doing?" he asked. I told him I had been working in musical-variety and mentioned my years working on *The Lawrence Welk Show*. Then I said, "But for the last two years, I've been working with Marty Pasetta."

I had absolutely no idea how much impact that little sentence would have. Marty Pasetta was a brilliant but extremely difficult director-producer, who was as famous for his tantrums as he was for taking on the biggest and most challenging variety specials on television. Marty's credits included numerous Oscars, Emmys, and Grammys telecasts, as well as live broadcast "spectaculars" such as *Elvis: Aloha From Hawaii*, *Super Night at the Super Bowl*, and *President Carter's Inaugural Gala*, to name just a few. I had done two Oscars telecasts with Marty, as well as a number of network variety specials. Just a month earlier, I had finished shooting twenty-four episodes of *The Monte Carlo Show* with Marty, a musical-variety series for FOX that had been produced on

---

* Refer to the chapter on Desi Arnaz and Lucille Ball.

location in Monaco. It had been a grueling schedule, requiring us to shoot four hourlong episodes each week!*

But Marty was just as famous (or perhaps infamous) for his explosive temper and lack of patience. He also had "no filter," and was known for voicing his displeasure in public. When Marty was upset with someone, everyone on the production knew about it. You couldn't help feeling bad for the person who was the object of his wrath, but you also felt a tinge of dread, knowing that the next time it might be you! This would often put Marty at odds with his crew, his cast, or even the network "suits." Marty's reputation for throwing tantrums was well-known within the industry. And apparently John Rich knew Marty Pasetta very well.

"You really lasted two whole years with Marty?" John asked, shaking his head. "How?"

"Well, I guess I have pretty thick skin," I replied. "And when he chewed me out, I never took it personally. I wrote it off as venting."

"Venting," John repeated, grinning. He took another long puff on his cigar and said, "Listen, kid. If you could put up with Marty Pasetta for two years, then there's nothing I can throw at you that you can't handle. You've got the job. Go tell Don we're good, so you can get your contract done."

And just like that, I was now the new Associate Director on *Benson*! I thanked him, and we shook hands again and parted company. I was off to Don Richetta's office, and John started back in the other direction to his next meeting. I'd only taken a few steps when he called out from behind, turning me back towards him.

"Oh, and kid. The next time you have a job interview, you might want to skip all of that Lawrence Welk-accordion-polka crap and just lead off with Marty Pasetta!" He broke into a huge grin, and put his cigar back into his mouth, still grinning.

I grinned back. "Note taken," I said.

And I *did* take that note. Eight years later, director Hal Cooper, another "900 pound gorilla" was interviewing me for the Associate Director's position on *Empty Nest*, the spinoff of *The Golden Girls*. I had done the pilot of *Empty Nest* with director Jay Sandrich, but Jay didn't want to stay on for the series. So Witt-Thomas-Harris brought

---

* *Refer to the chapter on Cher.*

in Hal Cooper as the show's dedicated director and as one of the executive producers. Since we had also never worked together, Hal wanted to meet with me. And if I didn't meet with his approval, I'd be looking for work elsewhere. Hal was a good friend and contemporary of John's, so when he asked, "What have you been doing?" I just cut to the chase. I said, "Well, for the last seven years I've been working with John Rich." I didn't need to say anything else after that. As far as Hal was concerned, the job was mine.

....

"John," I said, "the stage is ready."

It was a Thursday afternoon, and we were in the director's booth on Stage 57 at ABC, hard at work on the "camera dress rehearsal" for the producers of *Benson*. On a multi-camera sitcom, the first three days of rehearsals are devoted just to the actors, writers, director, and stage and lighting crew. No television cameras are involved during this time. The actors work with the director to focus on their "beats," which motivate their movements within each scene; the writers re-write any dialogue that they feel is not working; and the property, wardrobe, and lighting departments work out all of the details required for that week's script.

Usually by Day Three the director, along with the associate director, begin to "pre-visualize" how they will photograph each scene, deciding which of the four camera angles will best cover the physical action the actors have created. They also decide which shot sizes (i.e. close up, wide shot, etc.) will best complement the blocking and dialogue they've been rehearsing, paying close attention to the "punchlines" in the dialogue, physical bits of business that the actors have created, and the comedic timing of the cast. And by the end of Day Three the director and the associate director will have created and written all of those camera shots into their scripts.[*]

But it's not until Day Four, or "camera blocking" day, that the show is actually rehearsed with the cameras for the first time. The cast and technical crew spend the day running through each individual scene,

---

[*] *I discuss this process in greater detail in the chapter on The Golden Girls.*

working out any issues affecting the camera coverage, and making the necessary adjustments to the actors' movements, the shots, or both.

At the end of Day Four is a "camera dress rehearsal," with the actors in full wardrobe, giving the cast and crew the opportunity to time each of the wardrobe changes with a stopwatch. This lets everyone know how long the studio audience will have to sit and wait between scenes during the actual show the following night. Seeing the rehearsal on camera also gives the producers their first look at the director's vision for the show as it will be seen on the air.

We had finished shooting the first scene of the dress rehearsal and had been waiting for several of our cast members to make a wardrobe change required for scene two. But now the wardrobe change was complete, and we were ready to move on to the next scene. Except that John was otherwise engaged.

During the short break, he had been "holding court," regaling the crew both in the director's booth, and on stage through the headsets, with humorous anecdotes from throughout his career. John was mid-story and had everyone's attention. The problem was, at that moment I needed *his* attention, and he wasn't about to give it to me.

Once again, I said, "John, the stage is ready." But he continued to ignore me and went right on with his story.

When he was finished, he looked at the clock, turned to me and said, "Schmuck, what's taking so long? We should've been ready ages ago. This is unacceptable!" I could hear the displeasure in his voice. He wanted the name of the party responsible for the delay, so he asked his standard question. "For whom or what do we wait?"

"We're waiting for you," I replied.

"No, we're not," he snorted. "We've been waiting for the stage,"

"John, the stage is ready."

"Schmuck, you're supposed to tell me."

"I did. Twice." I grinned at him, and motioned as if to say, "Ask anyone." He looked around the director's booth. Everyone nodded, confirming this to be true. He put his glasses back on and said loud enough for everyone on the headset to hear, "Kid, never underestimate my ability to ignore you!" Then he grinned broadly and said, "Okay, schmuck. Let's go. Unlike you, I have a family to go home to. Count it!"

And with that, I said over the headset, "Standby. In five…four…three…two," counting us down into the next scene of the dress rehearsal.

Driving home that night, I could still hear John's words in my head: "Kid, never underestimate my ability to ignore you!" I decided that I should probably take him at his word. I had an idea. So I stopped on the way home to pick up a few items that I would need.

At 5:00 the next day, we were back in the director's booth, about to start our first show taping.* The members of the studio audience were in their seats, and the warm-up man was introducing the cast. All departments were ready, and everyone was in place. We were just minutes away from starting the show. At that moment, I reached into my briefcase under the console and pulled out two shiny new tin cans that were attached to each other by two feet of heavy duty string. I had printed the name "John" in Magic Marker on a can at one end of the string and had printed "Doug" on the can at the other end. I set John's can down in front of him so hard it made a "thwack!" sound, which got his attention. Then I picked up my can, put it up to my mouth, and said in a loud voice, "Doug to John. Doug to John. Please pick up."

John looked at me and said, "What is all this?" I turned directly to him and repeated, "Doug to John. Please pick up."

John looked at me for a beat, then picked up his end of our tin can telephone. He barked into the can, "Schmuck, what do you want?"

"John," I said into my can, "Yesterday you admonished me never to underestimate your ability to ignore me. Therefore, I have constructed this – " I indicated our two tin cans " – high-tech communication device which, as any fool can plainly see, is a private direct line from me to you."

"I can see that, schmuck," he replied, grinning at me. "Anything else?"

"Yes, John." I grinned back and barked into my can. "The stage is ready!"

The booth crew broke into laughter. I persisted in using our tin can phone line to communicate with John for the rest of the night, much to the delight of the crew. And John went right along with it, using the cans to "page" me just as often as I "paged" him, picking up his can and

---

* *Common practice is for sitcoms to tape two shows per night in front of an audience, then intercut the best scenes from each show. The first taping is at 5:00 p.m., and the second is at 7:30 p.m., with a new audience.*

barking gleefully, "Hello, schmuck. This is John. Come in. Over!" And from that night on, our tin can phones became a permanent fixture in the director's booth.

John and I did almost fifty episodes of *Benson* together, and those silly tin cans were on the console in front of us for every single episode. I had a commemorative plaque made which I gave to John at the end of that season. On the plaque were the words, "Kid, never underestimate my ability to ignore you!" along with his name, and the date he'd first said it to me.

When John brought me with him to do the pilot of *Newhart*, one of the first questions he asked me was, "Schmuck, did you bring the cans?"

I replied, "Do you even have to ask?" and we used them on that show as well. Those tin cans followed us to our next two series, *Condo* and *Mr. Sunshine*, as well as to all of the pilots we did together. After seven years, the cans had acquired more than a few dents, and the string that connected them was badly frayed. But we never did a show without those silly tin can phones sitting on the console in front of us for the remainder of our professional association. To me, they were a tangible, physical manifestation of the bond that had been established between this great director and his head schmuck.

....

We were in the middle of taping a show, and the phone in the Director's Booth was ringing. It was no ordinary phone. It was the special "hotline" from the Producer's booth upstairs. It was a direct line from Tony Thomas down to John Rich. I referred to it as the "Bat Phone."*

The idea was that on show night, as soon as we would finish filming a scene, Tony Thomas and Paul Witt would confer with the writers, who would make changes in the dialogue and offer notes on how the cast might adjust their performances in the scene. Then Tony would simply pick up his end of the "hotline," which would automatically ring

---

* *In the 1960's TV series Batman, Commissioner Gordon had a special phone in his office that was connected directly to the Bat Cave. He simply had to pick it up to talk directly to Batman.*

downstairs to the phone that was sitting directly in front of John. In theory, John would then pick up his end of the phone and get Tony's notes. He would then pass the acting notes and dialogue changes to the stage managers on the set, so that they could instruct the actors. And he would give me any notes that might involve changes to our camera shots, special effects, props, or sound and lighting cues. Then we would re-set the scene from the top and shoot it again.

Like I said…in theory.

In practice, John hated working this way. He was, after all, the "900 pound gorilla" with a string of hit sitcoms and three Emmy awards to his credit. He chafed at the idea of a group of writers, sitting around in a room filled with deli plates and bottles of fizzy water "kibitzing"* while they watched the show on TV monitors. He'd been at this too long to have "the scribes" second-guessing not only the stage directions he'd worked out with the cast but also the way he envisioned each scene playing out on camera. Therefore, John had his own method of dealing with Tony's phone. He simply refused to answer it.

So the phone just kept on ringing.

"John, aren't you going to answer that?" I asked.

"No," he replied. After a beat he said, "You are."

"Me? But it's Tony. He doesn't want to talk to me. He wants to talk to *you*."

John just looked at me and grinned. "I'm sure he does. But I don't want to talk to *him*. And since I'm your boss, and since you're my head schmuck, I'm ordering *you* to answer that phone." His grin widened. He just sat there, watching me to see what I would do next. The phone was still ringing. So I picked it up.

I knew that Tony would be assuming he was talking to John, so I quickly said, "Hi Tony. This is Doug," so he would know he wasn't. It was then I heard…"the sigh."

The sigh spoke volumes. The sigh said, "Doug, I don't want to talk to you. I want to talk to *John*." The sigh also suggested, "And if you think I appreciate your over-zealous attempt to insert yourself into this conversation, you're badly mistaken. Show me your hustle some other way, kid. But for now, stay in your lane."

---

* A term derived from Yiddish meaning "to look on and offer unwelcome advice"

After the sigh came the pause. Then, flatly: "Doug, let me speak to John."

I attempted to pass John the phone, but he simply waved me off. He was having too much fun watching me squirm. What I really wanted to do was hang up. But I couldn't. I had to think fast. So I said, "I'm sorry, Tony. John knows this is important, which is why he gave me explicit instructions to pick up right away whenever he's unavailable."

"John's…unavailable?" Tony asked. "In the middle of a show?" You could hear the disbelief in his voice. "Why is he unavailable?" I looked directly at John, hoping I might prompt him into giving me a reason. He just grinned and motioned for me to continue my verbal tap-dance.

"I honestly don't know, Tony," I replied, still looking directly at John, who continued to grin back at me. "He didn't share that with me. Something about it being above my pay grade. He just called me a 'schmuck' and gave me instructions to pick up the phone." John was trying his best to contain his laughter.

To this day, I have no idea as to what kind of thoughts were going through Tony's mind at that moment (nor do I particularly want to know). But it was clear that he was not happy. After a beat, he simply said, "Doug, have John call me as soon as he's…*available*." I assured him that I would.

I hung up and turned to John, who was still grinning. He said, "Not bad, schmuck." He'd been testing me. Regarding what, I have no idea. But apparently I had passed. After a minute or so, John called Tony back and got his notes. And although he never gave Tony any explanation about *why* he hadn't answered the phone, he at least got me off the hook. He confirmed to Tony that he had indeed called me a "schmuck" and had given me very explicit instructions to answer the phone. Thankfully, from that point on, whenever Tony called, John answered. I only picked it up on those occasions when John actually *was* out of the director's booth, usually on stage working with the actors.

....

Caroline McWilliams, who played Marcy Hill, the Governor's secretary on *Benson*, was getting married to actor Michael Keaton. In addition to their friends and families, Caroline and Michael graciously extended wedding invitations to those of us working with her on the show. I was unable to attend the wedding but sent them a gift from their registry. Caroline and Michael's wedding was a topic of discussion around the set, and without realizing it, I gave John an opportunity to "razz" me in public, which was something he delighted in doing.

We were on a "five," and several members of the cast and crew were getting coffee from the craft service table. John had just filled his cup and was re-lighting his cigar. He turned to me and asked, "So schmuck, are you going to the wedding?"

"No," I said. "I won't be able to. But I found something I could afford on their wedding registry and had it sent."

"Oh," he said, holding a match to his cigar, puffing. "What did you get them?"

"A bud vase," I replied.

He stopped puffing and blew out his match. "A what?" he gasped.

"A bud vase. You know. For a single flower."

He took off his glasses for dramatic effect and let them dangle from the strap around his neck. Then he bellowed for all to hear, "I know what it is, schmuck. What I *can't* believe is that you don't know how to pronounce it!"

"What do you mean?" I asked.

Once John had raised his voice, everyone at the table had stopped and turned to see what was going on. Now he had an audience. "What I mean, you cretin, is that those of us who went to schools where you actually had to wear shoes know that V-A-S-E is not pronounced 'vase.' It's pronounced *vahz*." He was rolling now, so he took it up a notch. "I guess I should expect some accordion-loving, grits-eating hillbilly from South Carolina to pronounce it 'vase.' But this is Hollywood, not Hooterville,* you schmuck. And here, V-A-S-E is pronounced *vahz*."

The group at the table just stood there, not quite knowing what would happen next. As I mentioned earlier, John could be very intimidating. There was an uncomfortable silence. Then, in my thickest, most syrupy aristocratic southern drawl I said, "*Pah-don* me. *Ah* stand corrected, *suh*.

---

* *"Hooterville" is the name of the fictitious rural town which was the setting for the 1960s sitcom Petticoat Junction, a spinoff of The Beverly Hillbillies.*

Ah shall not make that particular mistake again." I took off my baseball cap and bowed in genuflection, grinning at John, who grinned back at me. He put his glasses back on, picked up his coffee, and headed back to the stage. I called out after him, and this time my southern accent was decidedly less aristocratic and much more nasal. "But I ain't givin' up my grits!"

During filming a week or so later, we were in the director's booth between scenes. The cast was changing wardrobe, so we had about five minutes until they were dressed and ready for the next scene. John was passing the time by telling everyone in the booth how well his son Anthony[*] was doing in Little League Baseball. He was very proud of his young son's development as a ball player, and as fathers often do, he was bragging on him a bit. We all had our headsets on, so everyone on stage could hear the conversation as well.

But John was about to present me with a golden opportunity for some payback. He announced to everyone, "Anthony's leading his team in stolen bases." When I heard him say that, I pounced.

"Oh, I don't think that's right, John."

"Of course it's right! Wait. What are you talking about?" he asked.

"I think you mean, 'Anthony leads his team in stolen *bahz-es*!'"

John just sat there, blinking at me, as if to say, "What?"

"After all," I continued, "You made it quite clear to me that **V**-**A**-**S**-**E** is always pronounced 'vahz.' And if that's the case, then **B**-**A**-**S**-**E** *must* be pronounced 'bahz.' Right? Ergo, Anthony leads his team in stolen *bahz-es*." John blinked again. I just grinned and blinked back at him. Everyone on the crew was laughing hysterically.

After a beat, John said, "I stand corrected, you schmuck! My son Anthony leads his team in stolen bahz-es!" Once again, the crew roared with laughter. John laughed with them, and then patted me on the arm as if to say, "good one, kid." And from that moment on, the sport of "bahz-ball" became a not-so-private joke between us. Score one for the schmuck!

---

[*] *Anthony is now fine sitcom director himself. His credits include The Big Bang Theory, Mom, and Man with a Plan.*

John had an appreciation for many of the finer things that life has to offer and the means to be able to enjoy them. He was an avid collector of fine art. He also enjoyed smoking only the finest cigars and considered himself to be a wine connoisseur. He would often chide me for what he regarded as my utter lack of knowledge regarding the finer things in life, such as wine. But his chiding was always done in good humor, supposedly as part of my professional development. Or as John would say, "I'm just trying to prevent you from committing some act of schmuckery that might reflect badly on *me*."

Now to be perfectly honest, John was right. The sum total of my knowledge on the subject of wine had been based upon two standard principles: "red with beef and white with fish," and "if you're asked to bring the wine, make sure the bottle has a cork and not a screw-top." Other than that, I knew nothing about wine. But I *did* know a thing or two about buttons, and in the time I'd spent with John, I was learning which of *his* buttons I could push without going too far. And he unwittingly handed me a button when he said, "I'm just trying to prevent you from committing some act of schmuckery that might reflect badly on *me*." So naturally, that's exactly what I decided to do. Hey, where's the fun in knowing which buttons to push with someone, if you're never going to push them, right?

On Fridays, our first show taping would begin at 5:00 p.m., which is also the time when bars and restaurants traditionally kick off their "Happy Hour" for discount drinks. I had decided on the "Happy Hour" theme because I knew it was something John considered too "bourgeois" for his taste. I bought a gallon jug of the cheapest Rosé I could find (with a screw-top, of course!), and kept it hidden in the refrigerator in the prop room. Then before the 5:00 p.m. show, I left the director's booth, went to the prop room, and poured myself a glass from the jug, then went back to the director's booth, where I set the glass of Rosé down on the console in front of me.

Just moments before we were to begin the first scene, I took a large sip of the Rosé, making ridiculous "yummy" sounds as I sipped. I had my headset on, so that the crew on stage could hear everything. And it didn't take long to get a rise out of John.

"Schmuck, what do you think you're doing?"

"I just thought I'd take your advice," I said with mock innocence. "You know, trying to develop an appreciation for the finer things." I referred to the clock on the wall. "And since it's Happy Hour, I'm having a glass of wine."

"Schmuck, there's nothing remotely fine about Happy Hour. And what's that you're drinking?"

"Oh, it's Rosé. It's really good. Would you like a glass?"

"I most certainly would not, you schmuck!" he snorted. "Rosé? How can you drink that crap? Rosé is not wine!"

"Sure it is. It said 'wine' right on the jug." I took another big sip.

"The jug?" John was practically sputtering. "You're drinking something that came from a jug?"

"Yeah." I was on a roll now. "And on the label, right below the picture of the smiling guy with the moustache holding a bunch of grapes, was the word 'wine.' So…yeah, it is."

"I'm telling you, schmuck! Rosé is not wine! It's…it's what's left between an Italian's toes after he's finished stomping on the grapes!"

The crew listening in burst into laughter. I took another big sip, then smacked my lips loudly and said, "Oh, I wouldn't worry about that, John. This Rosé isn't from Italy. It's from California!" More laughter from the crew.

"I don't care where it's from, you schmuck! I'm telling you, that crap you're drinking is not wine! " John started laughing in mock indignation. "Here I am, trying teach you, to literally pull you up out of the abyss of your own schmuckery, and *this* is the thanks I get? You swill Rosé right in front of me? Good Lord, man! Is it that you *can't* learn, or *won't* learn?"

"Don't worry, John," I replied, putting my hand on his shoulder. "I'm learning more and more from you every single day." And with that, I grinned broadly and waggled my eyebrows at him, *ala* Groucho Marx.

He immediately understood my meaning, and laughed, saying, "You schmuck! You had me going there for a second."

"I know, " I replied. "See how much I've learned from you already?" And I waggled my eyebrows at him a second time, and we laughed again.

It was the first of many "Happy Hour" show tapings John and I did together over the years. I would sip the Rosé, and John would feign irritation, "riffing" on his hopeless schmuck of an associate director, to the utter delight of the crew. It was great fun. I miss those times…

....

As I mentioned, John had a tendency to be gruff, salty, and short-tempered. He loved his craft and had no patience for anyone he believed was just "phoning it in," or who was simply not up to the task. And during our time together, I started to be able to sense those times when John was reaching his boiling point. And I also learned that humor would usually diffuse the situation.

Occasionally I would be working somewhere on stage and from across the room I would hear John yell impatiently, "Shmuck! Get over here! I need you!" And I would simply trot over to him and say, "Yes, John? You growled for me?" which usually provoked a laugh and lightened his mood. Sometimes, when I sensed that John's irritation with someone or something was rising to what I considered a "dangerous" level, all I had to do is bring him a fresh cup of coffee, grin at him and say, "John, am I going to have to hose down your enclosure?"

He would laugh, chew on his cigar and growl, "Get away from me, you schmuck!" Afterwards, he would usually deal with the situation in a calmer, more rational manner.

However, there was an instance during season three of *Benson* when John's temper got the better of him. During one of our show tapings, a network still photographer inadvertently stepped in front of one of our television cameras, completely ruining the scene. John came unglued. He yelled, "Cut!" Then he turned to the show's production manager sitting in the booth and roared, "This is outrageous! Who hired that idiot?"

The production manager meekly responded, "ABC." Wrong answer. You could practically see the steam coming out of John's ears. He exploded.

"ABC?!? ABC!?!" he bellowed. "ABC's not a person! It's a logo! It's a letterhead! I want a name! I want a body! I want a throat I can choke!"

It was bad. No one dared to speak, especially the poor production manager. I grabbed my pencil and a notepad and started writing as fast as I could. Before John could start yelling again, I said, "Hang on, John. I want to make sure I get all this down."

John turned to me, still fuming. "What are you talking about, schmuck?"

"I'm talking about you! What you just said," I replied. "It was really funny! I want to make sure I get it all down."

"What do you mean, 'funny?'" he snorted.

"I'll show you what I mean." I'd finished writing, so I read it all back to him. By the time I got to, "I want a name! I want a body! I want a throat I can choke!" John was laughing as hard as everyone else in the booth (except the poor production manager!).

John said, "Hey, that *is* pretty funny! Did I really say that?" He was still upset, but the situation had been diffused. The photographer came into the booth and apologized to John, vowing never to repeat his mistake. John grudgingly absolved him of his sin, and the rest of the taping went on without a hitch.

As we were packing up to go home, John saw me put the note pad in my briefcase. "What are you going to do with that, schmuck? Make me another plaque?"

"Oh, no," I replied. "But I *am* going to hang on to it. You know, for that book I'm going to write someday!" I was only joking at the time. Who knew?

....

As a director, John always insisted on a "closed set"—no visitors allowed… ever. One day on the set of *Benson*, while we were rehearsing with the cast, a young lady walked onto our set, accompanied by three or four network "suits." The group huddled near the craft service table along the wall of the soundstage.

As we were in the middle of a scene, John and I were standing at our script podiums in the middle of the soundstage, directly in front of the set. Without even looking up from his script, John took his cigar from his mouth and said, "Schmuck, go see who that is and find out what they want." I immediately put my pencil down and trotted over to the group.

I introduced myself, and said, "Excuse me. Can I help you?" Then one of the "suits" introduced me to the young lady. "This is Buffy Thomopoulos," he said. "She's on a break from college back east and wanted to come out to Los Angeles and take a tour of the studios."

Although I'd never met this young lady, her last name instantly rang a familiar bell. At that time, the president of ABC was Tony Thomopoulos. This was obviously his daughter. "Hi, Ms. Thomopoulos," I said. "I'll let the director know you're here." At that point, I trotted back over to John.

"John," I said, "It's Tony Thomopoulos's daughter, Buffy. She's visiting from college."

"Schmuck," he snapped back. "I don't care who she is. Or who her father is. This is a closed set. And who the hell names their daughter Buffy?"

"Perhaps it's a nickname," I countered. "I take it that you had no idea she was coming?"

"None," he growled. "This is very unprofessional. If Tony Thomopoulos wanted his daughter to take a tour of *my* set, then he should've cleared with me first."

"So what do you want to do?" I asked.

"Tell her to leave," he snapped back. There was an awkward pause, then he said, "Why are you still standing there?"

"Oh!" I said, realizing, "You want *me* to tell her!"

"Naturally! That's why you're my head schmuck!" He grinned so wide that his eyes narrowed to slits.

So I trotted back over to the group and told them as politely as I could that we had a strict "closed set" policy and that they would have to leave. "Maybe you didn't understand," the one exec said. "This is Buffy Thomopoulos. Her father is the president of the network!"

"Yes," I countered. "I did understand, and I conveyed that to our director. But we adhere to a strict 'closed set' policy. Visitors are only permitted if they've obtained the prior consent of the director, which apparently was not the case here. So I'm very sorry, but I'll have to ask you all to leave." And with that, they left. But they weren't happy about it. And I was certain that we hadn't heard the end of it.

So I was curious as to what would happen next. However, John didn't seem to be the least bit concerned. Just minutes later, the stage phone rang. John looked at his watch, turned to me and said, "That will be Tony Thomopoulos."

Before I could even ask, "How do you know that?" our page girl on stage said, "John, you have a phone call. It's Tony Thomopoulos." John just gave me a knowing wink and announced, "Take five, everybody. I need to take this call." So while the cast took a break, John walked over to the phone mounted on the wall at the end of the soundstage. I could hear his half of the conversation, which was interesting, to say the least.

"Yes, Tony, I knew it was your daughter…Because I run a 'closed set,' that's why…No, I'm not going to make an exception for her…Then you should've called me first and gotten my permission…What do you mean, you're asking now? That's bush league….Look, Tony, what do you think we are here, some kind of zoo exhibit for your kids to come and visit whenever they're on vacation? For your information, this is where I work! It's my place of business!…Okay, I tell you what. The next time I'm on vacation in New York, I'll just drop by unannounced with my kids and we'll all stand in the corner of your office while *you're* at work. How does that sound? Then I can turn to my sons Anthony and Robert and say, 'Ooh, watch this, boys. Mr. Thomopoulos is about to tell those producers that he's cancelling their show. Wait 'til you see the look on their faces when he gives them the news!' Would that be okay with you?…No, Tony. It's not ridiculous. It's the same thing! This is my office! It's where I conduct business! Only right now I can't do that because I'm on the phone with you!"

There was a brief pause, and then I heard John say, "Nice talking with you as well…You, too…We should do this again sometime!" John hung up the phone, grinning from ear to ear. He announced, "Let's take it from the top," and all got back to work rehearsing the scene. Buffy Thomopoulos and her entourage of "suits" never made a return visit to our set.

And the 900-pound gorilla just sat wherever he wanted…

In the early spring of 1986, John and I were working at Paramount on the ABC sitcom *Mr. Sunshine*. In addition to directing the show, John was Executive Producer along with Henry Winkler. John and Henry were partners in Henry Winkler/John Rich Productions and had two shows on ABC: the half-hour sitcom *Mr. Sunshine* and the hourlong action-adventure series *MacGuyver*.*

One day during rehearsal, the ABC page who answered the phone in our studio walked over to where we were working and said, "Excuse me, but the vice president of comedy development for ABC just called and would like for you to call him back on your next break."

John was used to these types of interruptions. He and Henry had skillfully shepherded both *Mr. Sunshine* and *MacGuyver* through very difficult and often contentious development negotiations prior to production. John turned to the cast and said, "Take five folks. Apparently, I need to go call the network."

The young page looked flustered and said, "Uh no, Mr. Rich. I'm sorry. I guess I wasn't very clear." Then she pointed at me. "He was asking for *Doug* to call him."

I was completely dumbfounded. I said, "Me? Are you sure he asked for me?"

She nodded and handed me the message slip with the callback number.

John closed his script binder, took a couple of hard puffs on his cigar, and said, "Schmuck, why is he calling you? Have you got some kind of deal in the works that I don't know about?"

I replied, "Trust me, John. If I had anything in the works, you'd be the first to know." And with that, I walked over to the stage phone and dialed the extension for ABC Comedy Development.

"Doug, thanks for returning my call," the voice said. It belonged to one of the network's numerous vice presidents. He gave me his name in passing, but I didn't quite catch it, and it didn't really matter. He went on. "It's not public knowledge yet, but ABC has just signed a deal with Lucille Ball for her to return to television in her own brand

---

* *Refer to the chapter on Henry Winkler.*

new sitcom, *Life With Lucy*!" The enthusiasm in his voice reminded me of one of those late-night TV pitchmen, hustling Ginsu knives or the Ronco Veg-O-Matic.

"Oookay," I said. "And you're calling me because—"

"I'm getting to that," the voice interrupted: "ABC has given Lucy complete creative control of her new series. And she's going to be directing each episode—"

It was my turn to interrupt. "Is this new sitcom going to be shot on film or videotape?"

"Tape," he answered.

A tiny alarm bell was going off in my head. I said, "But Lucy's only ever worked on film shows. She's never shot on videotape before. It's a completely different process than anything she's used to, and much more technical. In my opinion, there's no way that she can be onstage starring in the show and at the same time directing the cameras and tech crew."

The voice on the phone chirped back, "Well, even though we haven't met, I can tell I'm talking to the right guy! You just hit the nail on the head!" I was getting "the schmooze." That tiny bell was going off again. "Lucy's aware of that," he continued, "which is why she asked us to find her someone who has just the right skill set. And we think that person is you. We're offering you the chance to be Lucy's co-director for the series! Lucy would direct the actors on stage, and you would be in charge of the camera direction. Just think of it. You would be sharing the directing credit with the legend herself, Lucille Ball!"

And there it was. ABC had just asked me to co-direct a sitcom with Lucille Ball. Even as a little kid, watching *I Love Lucy* and dreaming of working in Hollywood someday, I could never have foreseen this! But then my thoughts flashed back to that day my senior year of college, when Desi had arranged for us to observe Lucille Ball working on the set of *Here's Lucy*. I remembered the feelings of disillusionment, as I watched Lucy's disrespectful treatment of her director.* And on *Here's Lucy* she hadn't "officially" had total control. This time she would. My next thought was that *Life With Lucy* was probably not the life for me!

Whatever I said next was going to require some tact and finesse. "I'm very flattered by your offer," I said. "And I truly appreciate your

---

* *Refer to the chapter on Desi Arnaz and Lucille Ball.*

vote of confidence in my ability to handle the job. But as exciting as it sounds, I'm afraid I'm going have to decline your offer."

"Wait," the voice said in disbelief. "You're turning us down?"

"Yes. That's correct."

"Maybe I didn't make myself clear," he replied. "You'd be sharing a directing credit with Lucille Ball. *The* Lucille Ball. You know, as in *I Love Lucy*?"

"Yes, I understand. You made that very clear," I answered. "And like I said, I truly appreciate your offer. And I wish you all the best with the project. But I'm afraid I'm going to have to pass on it."

The overly cheerful enthusiasm had left his voice. "Okay, kid. But you might have just made the biggest mistake of your life!" Before I could respond, the phone clicked, and the line went dead.

I walked back over to the set. John was still standing at his script podium where I'd left him. He'd lit a match and was rolling the end of his cigar in the small flame. He never took his eyes off his cigar.

"So, what was that all about?" he asked.

"Oh, Lucille Ball's coming to the network to do a new sitcom," I said.

"I know," he replied softly, still working the cigar. "And?..."

"And they've given her total creative control. Apparently, she's going to direct every episode, and they want me to be her co-director for the series."

He still never looked up from the cigar. "Series co-director with Lucy? Wow, that's big! You said 'yes,' right?"

"As a matter of fact, John, I said 'no.'"

His eyes, and just his eyes, moved. He was looking hard at me. "Are you telling me you turned down the chance to co-direct a series with Lucille Ball?"

"Yes, John," I answered. "That's exactly what I'm telling you."

John gave me just the hint of a grin. "You're not as dumb as you look, schmuck." His grin got wider, and he began to puff on his cigar. "Now let's get back to work."

So that's exactly what we did. And we worked well together. John was the mentor, and I was his "head schmuck" during years we worked together, but we were friends for the rest of his life. And I still miss him terribly.

P.S. Life With Lucy premiered on ABC on September 20, 1986, and was cancelled after just eight episodes, due to low ratings and generally negative reviews. Only thirteen episodes were ever produced. Five were never aired. Lucille Ball did not direct any of them.

Desi Arnaz, the sitcom pioneer, co-star of *I Love Lucy*, head of his own studio (Desilu) and former conga drum player. Desi was both my inspiration as a young boy, and my first amazing mentor. What a blessed life I have had!

Yep, that's me on the left, trying to look oh-so-cool in front of Desi in my aviator-style sunglasses and homemade leather visor. I still can't believe he'd ever trust a scruff like me with his huge wad of "Babalu" money!

The "Telecaster" publicity photo that Mae West surprised me with following my appearance on *The Dating Game.*

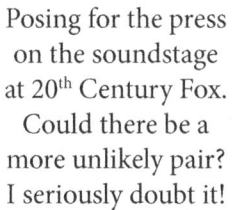

Posing for the press on the soundstage at 20th Century Fox. Could there be a more unlikely pair? I seriously doubt it!

Playing a special "Four Drum Challenge" on *The Lawrence Welk Show*. Left to right are Roger Sullivan, Jack Imel, Johnny Klein and me. Lawrence, of course, is conducting. I am proud to be a member of Lawrence's "Musical Family." And it's a lifetime membership!

Jim Hobson, the Producer and Director of *The Lawrence Welk Show*. Jim was the greatest mentor and the best friend anyone could ever hope to have.

Lawrence agreed to let Jim hire me as a Production Assistant because I could also play the drums. To work on the show you had to "double."

Meeting Henry Winkler for the first time, during the production of *A Gift of Song: The Concert for UNICEF* for NBC.

On the floor of the UN General Assembly with Gilda Radner and Producer/Director Marty Pasetta. I really enjoyed working with Marty, who was brilliant and volatile.

Waiting to be "officially" introduced to Olivia Newton-John. Don't let my smile fool you. I was worried that she would remember our first meeting at *The People's Choice Awards.*

Just "hanging with my homies" screen legend Henry Fonda, and music superstars Maurice and Barry Gibb of the Bee Gees. How's <u>*that*</u> for some world class name-dropping?

On the set of *The Monte Carlo Show*, surrounded by the beautiful "Les Girls." I knew that at this very moment, there were guys my age working in a cubicle somewhere, hunched over a calculator. I, on the other hand, was about to work with Cher.

One day I asked Jim Hobson, "Hey Jim, what would you think about doing the show's closing credits on the side of the Goodyear Blimp?" And then this happened…

The talented cast of *Mr. Sunshine*. From left to right *(bottom row)*: Producer/Director John Rich, Barbara Babcock, Jeffery Tambor, Nan Martin, Producer Henry Winkler.
(top row): David Knell, Leonard Frey, and Ceci Hart.

Being John's "Head Schmuck" (Associate Director) was akin to receiving a Master's Degree in Sitcom Direction. He was both my mentor and my dear friend. And he was definitely a "900-Pound Gorilla" who could sit anywhere he wanted!

John Rich

The talented cast of *Newhart*. From left to right: Tom Poston, Steven Kampmann, Mary Frann, Bob Newhart and Jennifer Holmes. Being a part of this show was one of the most joyful experiences of my life, and was the beginning of my lifelong friendship with Randy Cordray. Plus we got to witness the birth of "Larry, Darryl and Darryl!"

The cast of Empty Nest: wonderfully gifted actors and my "2nd family" for seven years!

Executive Producer/Director Hal Cooper working out a scene with Dave and Richard season one.

Our daily game of "Hearts" backstage. At the table left to right: Richard Mulligan, stage manager Lance Lyon, director Steve Zuckerman and David Leisure. Actress Kristy McNichol looks on.

With Garth Brooks after the show. Definitely *not* Photoshopped!

The "Hold 'Em Hand for Life" Richard gave me the night of our final show. It hangs in my office.

9

JERRY SEINFELD

*One of us is remembering it all wrong.
Or is it both of us?*

"Seinfeld." Just say the name and everyone pretty much assumes that, out of all the other Seinfelds in the world, you're referring to *Jerry* Seinfeld, the comedian. And they would probably be right, since *Seinfeld*, the TV sitcom bearing his name, is considered by many to be the greatest sitcom of all time. *Seinfeld* ran on NBC for nine years (a lifetime for a sitcom), winning ten Emmys and sitting at the top of the Nielsen ratings from 1994 to 1998. *Seinfeld*'s impact on television has earned Jerry "single name" recognition, shared with only a few others, such as Elvis, Oprah, or Cher.*

And Jerry is still at the top of his game, selling out venues with his brilliant stand-up comedy concerts and making regular appearances on late night talk shows. He's also the creator, producer, and star of the very popular *Comedians in Cars Getting Coffee*, currently streaming on Netflix.

---

* *Refer to the chapter on Cher.*

So, it's probably no surprise that this chapter is devoted to the time I spent with *that* Jerry Seinfeld. And I can tell you with absolute certainty that Jerry would never remember me. But the fact remains that we worked together for almost a month.

It was back in 1980, and we were both working on the ABC sitcom, *Benson*, which was beginning its second season on ABC. I was the Associate Director, working alongside John Rich,* who was the both the show's director, and one of its executive producers. Jerry was a brand-new cast member, having been hired in between seasons one and two. John had mentioned to me that during the hiatus between seasons, the creative team behind *Benson*—Paul Witt, Tony Thomas, and Susan Harris—had been very impressed with Jerry's fresh, original stand-up comedy, and regarded him as a "rising star." According to John, Witt-Thomas-Harris Productions had signed Jerry to a "seven of thirteen" contract, so I guess I'd better explain what that is.

In those days, a full season for a prime-time comedy or drama was normally twenty-six episodes. In order to protect themselves financially, the networks would often only commit to thirteen episodes at a time. These were commonly referred to as the "front thirteen." If those thirteen episodes were doing poorly in the Nielsen ratings, then the network could cancel it having only paid for thirteen instead of the full twenty-six. But if those first thirteen did well in the Nielsens, then the network would order a "back thirteen" episodes, which filled out the remainder of the season.

Today, with five hundred or so cable and streaming channels all competing for viewers, *Benson*'s weekly Nielsen ratings would make it the highest-rated show on TV, no contest. But back in 1980, when there were only three commercial networks competing for viewers (ABC, CBS, and NBC), the show was up against highly rated competition, such as *The Dukes of Hazard* or *The Incredible Hulk*. So, while *Benson*'s ratings were certainly respectable by 1980 standards, they weren't as good as those of the competition.

As far as ABC was concerned, it always seemed to be a case of, "Let's see how these thirteen episodes do, and we'll let you know about a pick-up for a back thirteen." As I mentioned in the chapter on Henry

---

* *Refer to the chapter on John Rich.*

Winkler, many of the network execs (or "suits") didn't care about quality program content (nor would they even know it if they saw it). They were only interested in ratings numbers and advertising dollars. During my time working on *Benson*, one ABC exec even chided me, informing me that my job was simply to help provide the "filler" in between their commercials. So, it always felt to me that if ABC had some other "filler" in development that they thought might do better in the ratings than us, they would've replaced us with that show.

Each Wednesday, the industry trade papers *Variety* and the *Hollywood Reporter* would publish the ratings for the previous week, and we'd all stop by the corner magazine stands on our way in to work and pick up a copy to see how we were doing, hoping our ratings were high enough to warrant a pick up. And then, usually around the 8th or 9th episode, ABC would notify us that the show had indeed been picked up (I guess the network still hadn't developed any replacement "filler"). The notification was always a cause for celebration on the set, for it meant we all still had jobs!

But, back to Jerry. This practice of not committing to all of the episodes at once would have a sort of "trickle-down" effect within the production. Rather than hire Jerry for the entire front thirteen, Witt-Thomas-Harris Productions hedged their bet, and signed him to a "seven of thirteen" contract. This meant that Jerry was hired for seven out of the thirteen episodes. However, these types of contracts often stipulated that the company was not actually obligated to *use* him in all seven, for a variety of reasons. As it turned out, Jerry Seinfeld only appeared in three of his seven episodes, and the reason in this case was apparent to everyone, including Jerry. He couldn't act!

As brilliant as he is at stand-up comedy (and I don't think there could be any argument there), back in 1980 Jerry really struggled with playing a character on *Benson*. And it probably didn't help that he was tossed into a talented cast of veteran theater, film, and television actors that included Robert Guillaume, Inga Swenson, Caroline McWilliams, James Noble, Ethan Phillips, and Rene Auberjonois. Compared to these seasoned veterans, "newbie" actor Jerry's lack of experience in portraying someone other than Jerry Seinfeld was painfully obvious.

He was the proverbial "fish out of water." And according to director John Rich, that fish was a lox, which is the Yiddish word for the brined salmon popular on bagels with cream cheese. As you can imagine, to have the director compare your performance to a hunk of dead fish is, well…not good (although he never used the term "lox" in front of Jerry–no, "lox" was a term used in conversations he would save for me!).

Now, the Internet is full of misinformation about Jerry's role on *Benson*, as well as the nature of his departure from the show. A number of bloggers and self-proclaimed gate-keepers of "pop culture literature" have used the Internet to publish their own versions of these events. Much of this ranges from factually incorrect to just plain silly. So, since I was there on set with Jerry through all this, I'll do my best to give you as accurate an account of his brief stint on the show (and his departure from it) as my memory will allow.

Some of these bloggers will tell you that the character Jerry played on *Benson* was named "Freddie." It wasn't. The name of the character he played was "Frankie." Other sites will tell you that Frankie was a speech writer or joke writer for Governor Gatling, the character played by James Noble. This is also incorrect. Jerry's character of Frankie was a courier who *aspired* to be a joke writer, and who was constantly making a pest of himself around the governor's mansion, attempting to "pitch" his jokes (which were crafted by the show's writers to be spectacularly unfunny) to Governor Gatling, but who was thwarted at every turn by Benson.

By way of proof, I offer this exchange of dialogue, taken from the script of one of the episodes in which Jerry appeared:

```
                    FRANKIE
I've got some great jokes the Governor can use.
You want to hear them?

                    BENSON
You're not a joke writer, Frankie. You're a messenger.

                    FRANKIE
Please. I'm a courier.

                    BENSON (annoyed)
Then go courie.
```

So, in just this one brief exchange, Benson not only confirms that Jerry's character is named "Frankie," but Jerry himself clearly identifies Frankie's occupation as a courier. Now, I ask all of you bloggers out there: was that so hard? Do a little research before you go public.

Jerry was usually in only one scene per episode, but by his third episode, that one scene was enough. It was evident to us all that Jerry's lack of experience as an actor was a problem. And Paul Witt, Tony Thomas, and Susan Harris were faced with the decision of what to do about Jerry in regards the next four episodes in his "seven of thirteen" contract.

Now, the typical schedule for a multi-camera sitcom is to shoot one episode per week for three weeks, and then to take a break from production on week four. This "hiatus week" allows the actors to clear their heads and get some must-needed rest. It also gives the writers a break in the production schedule to devote to working on the scripts for future episodes. As clearly as I can recall, it was during this hiatus week following Jerry's first three episodes that the decision was made to let him go. From the company's standpoint, in those three episodes, he'd had three swings at the ball and had struck out (swinging for the fences every time, if his over-the-top delivery was any indication).

So, the decision was made to let Jerry go. The good news was that his "seven of thirteen" contract meant that he would be paid for all seven episodes: the three he'd already taped plus the four in which he would no longer be appearing. The bad news was, of course, that he had been fired. And here is where the story begins to get fuzzy...

In *Seinfeld: How it Began*, the "bonus feature" that accompanies the *Seinfeld Season 1 and 2* DVD set, Jerry recalls that he showed up for work after that first hiatus week having absolutely no idea that he'd been fired. In the interview, Jerry says that he came to the studio that morning for the cast read-through, only to discover there was no script with his name on it.

To further cloud the issue, a blogger who has spent much of her career writing about *Seinfeld*, and touring the country talking about the show, decided to embellish this version of events in her blog. According to her, none of our producers, writers, or cast members bothered to talk to Jerry. She writes that, upon not being able to find his script, Jerry went up to the AD on the set (which was me!), and asked why there wasn't a script for him, and that *I* was the one who told him that he didn't have a script because he'd been fired! Now when, like Shakespeare's Hamlet, my time comes shuffle off this mortal coil, there are a lot of things one might etch into my tombstone. But I can assure you, "Here lies the guy who told Jerry Seinfeld he was fired" is not one of them!

There's one thing I can say with certainty about this particular blogger: she wasn't there, and I was. AD's may be involved in the hiring and firing of extras on a show, but not when it comes to featured cast members. It would never have fallen to me to tell Jerry he'd been fired.

So, even though I was in no way directly involved in telling Jerry he'd been let go, I'm fairly confident that I can give you a reasonable account of how it most likely went down. It may not be exact (and it definitely varies from Jerry's version in the DVD), but it is probably pretty close to the way these things are usually handled.

In Hollywood, there are "white hats" and "black hats." People love wearing the "white hat." The "white hat" is the bearer of good news and is therefore regarded fondly. Conversely, the "black hat" is the bearer of bad news and is regarded far less fondly. And we all know that in television, like in life, sometimes the news is bad.

So, the person who is actually responsible for the bad news usually does whatever they can to avoid wearing the "black hat," and foists that duty off onto someone else. And quite often that someone else is an agent.

In Jerry Seinfeld's case, experience tells me that this is the most likely scenario. Witt-Thomas-Harris productions probably forced Jerry's agent to "earn his paycheck" by having to wear the "black hat." My guess is that during the hiatus week, the company called Jerry's agent and told him they were sorry, but it just wasn't working out (any agent worth his salt would've already known this, having sat in the studio audience during the tapings and observed Jerry's performances).

So, the bad news probably didn't come as any great surprise to the agent. Witt-Thomas-Harris would assure Jerry's agent that he would still be paid for all seven episodes in his contract and probably say again how sorry they were that it didn't work out. And that would be the end of it. The agent would then have to put on his "black hat" and inform Jerry that he was fired and that he no longer needed to show up for work. A more sensitive agent might deliver the bad news in person, perhaps even over a meal. A schmuck agent would simply tell him over the phone. A *really* schmuck agent would force a junior agent to wear the "black hat," and make *that* poor schmuck deliver the news to Jerry. "Let the agent earn his paycheck" is a common way of delivering bad news in Hollywood.

So, while Jerry's version of events makes a cute story on the bonus DVD, the only way that could ever have happened would have been if all three executive producers, Witt, Thomas, and Harris had each assumed that one of the other two had made the call to the agent, meaning that no one had. Either that, or after the call was made, and the agent got cold feet and didn't deliver the bad news to Jerry. Highly unlikely in either case. Even a schmuck agent wouldn't do that to a client. Not if he or she wanted to keep that client.

Also, each week the new scripts are sent by a production PA to the cast members at home a day or so prior to the read-through, to allow them to start familiarizing themselves with the stories and dialogue. This would include Jerry as well since he was part of the cast. If the next episode was to be one the four remaining out of his seven, then a PA would have delivered a script to his apartment a day before the read-through. If the next episode was to be one of the six in which he was not contracted to appear, he would've been notified of that as well, so that he could schedule other work, such as a stand-up gig.

Therefore, even if he hadn't yet been told that he'd been fired, when no fourth script or notification arrived at his apartment, logic dictates that Jerry would simply have called his agent to find out why (at which time his agent would have delivered the bad news). So again, a version of the story that has him simply showing up and unable to find his script seems highly unlikely.

So, I guess it all boils down to two completely different recollections of the same event (which itself is a classic premise for countless movies and television shows. "That's not how it happened. I'll tell you what really happened. I remember that day as if it were yesterday..."). So, while *how* it happened may be somewhat "fuzzy around the edges" for one or the other of us, the fact remains that Jerry was let go after only three episodes.

It would certainly be understandable if getting fired from *Benson* had ended Jerry's hopes of being on a sitcom. But, as we all know, it didn't. Less than ten years later, *Seinfeld* was on the air and became one of the most the beloved, iconic sitcoms in the history of television. And as it turns out, the show, which started out as *The Seinfeld Chronicles*, was filmed at the very same studio where I was working on *Empty Nest* and where we were shooting *The Golden Girls*. Coincidentally, that same studio used to be the home of Desilu, the company that my *original* mentor, Desi Arnaz, founded with Lucille Ball! If you work in the industry long enough, you come to realize what a "small town" Hollywood really is!

Now, I have absolutely no proof to support this theory, but I'd like to think that Jerry turned his negative experience on *Benson* into a positive learning experience while he and Larry David were developing *Seinfeld*. It certainly seems that way, because in *Seinfeld*, Jerry eliminated many of those elements with which he'd struggled on *Benson*.

For example, in *Seinfeld*, Jerry didn't create an unfamiliar character with an equally unfamiliar occupation. He simply played himself; Jerry Seinfeld, stand-up comedian. And since he was still an inexperienced actor, it's much easier when you're playing yourself. One problem solved.

Also, Jerry and co-creator Larry David set the show in New York City, which was their home, as they're both from Brooklyn. This put Jerry and Larry in comfortable, familiar surroundings and allowed them to draw upon their lifelong experiences in the city when coming up with story ideas and with creating characters to inhabit those stories. Another problem solved.

But even more importantly, *Benson* was not Jerry's show. The stories on *Benson* all revolved around the title character, portrayed by Robert Guillaume, who "carried the show." Therefore, in his small recurring role as "Frankie," Jerry was at the mercy of *Benson*'s staff of sitcom writers who wrote what *they* thought he should say (or what *they* thought was funny). Now, however, as the creative force behind *Seinfeld*, Jerry and Larry David could allow Jerry to use his own "authentic" voice as an observational comic.

Related to this, Jerry's role on *Benson* was created and written in such a way that it was crucial for all of his lines to "collect," or result in a laugh, which put tremendous pressure on him to deliver. But in *Seinfeld*, Jerry often had the luxury of playing the straight man to Jason Alexander, Julia Louis-Dreyfus, or Michael Richards, letting them land the big laughs instead. Since he was once again the least-experienced actor in that cast, I'm guessing it was a great relief for him to know that he didn't have to be in every single scene, and that the ensemble would "carry the show."

As I stated above, I have no actual proof that Jerry took his experience from *Benson* and put it to good use while developing *Seinfeld*, but I'd like to think so. I mean, logically it all makes sense. Maybe Jerry will read this and get in touch to let me know if my theory is correct, or not. And if he does, then who knows? Maybe we can put our heads together to finally figure out what really happened back on the set of *Benson* all of those years ago!

10

NEWHART

The ballad of Larry, Darryl, and Darryl...
and Randy

I must confess right up front that the title of this chapter is probably misleading. If I'm being completely honest, it's not really going to be about working with Bob Newhart on his CBS sitcom *Newhart*. But I will tell you that my season on *Newhart* was a special time in my life. MTM was a company I had admired ever since *The Mary Tyler Moore Show* first went on the air when I was still in college.* As a senior at San Diego State, my TV Production class went on a field trip to Hollywood to attend a filming of *The Bob Newhart Show*, and a decade later, there I was at MTM, and working with Bob on the very same soundstage I had visited as a student!

---

* *"MTM" stands for "Mary Tyler Moore" Enterprises, the company she established with then-husband Grant Tinker. MTM produced a number of popular shows including The Mary Tyler Moore Show, The Bob Newhart Show, Lou Grant, WKRP in Cincinnati, St. Elsewhere, Newhart, Hill Street Blues, and Remington Steele.*

And speaking of being a student, working on *Newhart* was akin to being paid to attend a master class in the art of comedy timing and delivery. Bob's sense of timing is as good as it gets, and there is no one better at the art of delivering dialogue, especially in his unique deadpan style. I loved working with him and learning from him the fine art of how to simply "wait and let the laugh happen." The man's a comedy genius, plain and simple.

But rather than relate a number of stories from my time working on *Newhart*, I thought I might use this chapter to tell you a story about a series of events that began during the filming of a single episode very early in that first season. Those events ended up affecting *Newhart* for the remainder of its run on television. Bear with me, however, because getting to that story will require just a little bit of set-up:

I had come to *Newhart* as part of a "package" with director John Rich, with whom I'd been working on the ABC sitcom *Benson*.[*] John had decided to leave *Benson* at the end of season three, and during the ensuing TV pilot season he had signed on to direct the pilot of *Newhart* for MTM and CBS.

In Hollywood it's common practice for directors to bring a trusted associate director with them on a new project. And because of our close working relationship on *Benson*, John had come to rely on me as his trusty "head schmuck." So when John asked me if I would like to go over to MTM and work with him on the *Newhart* pilot, I couldn't say "yes" fast enough. As I said earlier, MTM was a company I had admired for years, not to mention that their studios were so close to my apartment that I could walk to work! If you've never lived in Los Angeles, you have no idea what a rare occurrence that is!

John's deal on *Newhart* was just for the pilot episode. He wasn't interested in staying on to direct the series. His contract specified that if the series went into production, he would receive a residual payment for the run of the series (which turned out to be eight seasons!).[†] Because I was there with John only for the pilot episode, I

---

[*] *I discuss my time working with John on Benson in more detail in the chapter devoted to John Rich.*

[†] *Again, I discuss director's residuals for directing a TV pilot in the chapter devoted to John Rich.*

assumed that once it was completed, I would be returning to *Benson* for its fourth season.

But one day while we were shooting the pilot, *Newhart* creator and executive producer Barry Kemp pulled me aside.* He expressed to me his concern about shooting this new series on videotape. With one notable exception, all of the iconic MTM multi-camera sitcoms had been shot on 35mm film, essentially using the same process that Desi Arnaz had developed for *I Love Lucy* back in 1951.† Only *WKRP in Cincinnati* had been shot on videotape in order to take advantage of a loophole in music licensing at the time.

That loophole allowed programs recorded on videotape to pay a lower licensing fee for the use of copyrighted music than programs shot on film. And because *WKRP in Cincinnati* took place in a radio station, music was an integral part of the show on a weekly basis. As a result, MTM made the decision to shoot the sitcom on videotape.

But the process of capturing a situation comedy on videotape was vastly different from the process used for shooting one on film, and it required a specific skill set from the show's directing team. I could devote pages to describing the differences between the two (which is exactly what I did when I wrote the first draft of this chapter), but they would read more like a television production textbook than a memoir (which is exactly why I deleted those pages for this draft!).

But the important thing to understand is that shooting a sitcom on videotape for the first time could be *extremely* intimidating for a director who had never done it and who didn't understand the process. And at that time very few people at MTM understood the process.

Barry said that when *Newhart* went into production later that year, they would be employing multiple directors over the course of the season. A few of them might have a bit of experience working with tape, but most would not. Therefore, the show would need an experienced veteran associate director in place to "backstop" directors

---

* *Barry Kemp is a prolific writer-producer who created and served as executive producer on the acclaimed sitcoms "Newhart" and "Coach." He also wrote numerous episodes for the series "Taxi." Barry's feature film producing credits include "Patch Adams," "Romy and Michele's High School Reunion," and "Catch Me If You Can."*
† *I discuss Desi's development of the multi-camera film process in greater detail in the chapter devoted to Desi Arnaz and Lucille Ball.*

who might have difficulty coping with the tape process. Then he asked me if I would like to be that "backstop." Once again, I couldn't say "yes" fast enough. It meant leaving *Benson*, but after working on almost fifty episodes of that series, I was ready for a new challenge. And that's how I became the associate director on season one of *Newhart*.

Okay, now that you have the "back story," let me get to the heart of the story I want to tell you. It takes place during the production of just our second episode of that first season, one titled "Mrs. Newton's Body Lies A-Mouldrin' in the Grave."

The series premise of *Newhart* revolves around self-help book author Dick Loudon and his wife Joanna (played by Bob Newhart and Mary Frann), who move from New York to Vermont to pursue their dream of running a quaint New England bed-and-breakfast. In the pilot episode, the couple purchases the Stratford Inn, which dates back to the colonial period prior to the American Revolution, and is need of some repair. Dick and Joanna quickly realize that their purchase of the Stratford Inn is somewhat of a "package deal" when they discover that George Utley, a "legacy" caretaker/handyman (played brilliantly by Tom Poston) has been living on the premises, tending to inn's upkeep. Dick and Joanna decide that George should stay on as the inn's handyman.

In the episode "Mrs. Newton's Body Lies A-Mouldrin' in the Grave," Dick wants George to replace the inn's old furnace down in the basement with a larger, more efficient one. But a problem quickly arises when George informs Dick that the only area in the basement with enough room to accommodate the new furnace is directly on top of the grave of Sarah Newton, the woman who has been buried in the basement of the Stratford Inn for almost 300 years!

Dick and Joanna are shocked and horrified to learn that their newly-acquired inn has a 300-year-old corpse in the basement. But they're also puzzled as to *why* Sarah Newton is buried there, especially since Sarah's husband and children are buried in the local churchyard. So they go to the church where Sarah's family is buried. While going through the old church records, the pastor discovers that Sarah Newton had been denied a church burial because back in the late 1600's the local townspeople believed her to be a witch. The couple appeal to the clergyman on Sarah's behalf, and with a stroke of a pencil, the pastor scratches her name off the "witch list," and gives Dick and Joanna permission to have Sarah Newton's corpse moved to the churchyard to be buried alongside her family. Now all they have to do is get her there...

This proves to be easier said than done. The local mortuary refuses to dig up and re-locate the 300-year-old remains of Sarah Newton. Having failed with the mortuary, Dick's neighbor Kirk Devane, who runs the "Minuteman Café" next door to the inn, says he might know of a local outfit that could help them, and hands their business card to Dick. The business card reads "We'll Do Anything For A Buck."

Having run out of options, Dick goes to the phone and calls "Anything For A Buck," telling them that he needs to have something moved. We can only hear Dick's side of the conversation, but we get the impression that "Anything For A Buck" is too busy to take on more work until sometime the following week. However, when Dick mentions that the object to be moved is "a 300-year-old corpse that's buried in our basement," they inform him that they can be there in five minutes! In closing Dick is heard saying, "Um...we can't wait, either!" And with an uneasy look on his face, he hangs up the phone, unsure of what he's just gotten them into.

A short time later, three very sketchy backwoods characters enter through the front door of The Stratford Inn. The first fellow is thin and is dressed in a dirty long-sleeve shirt buttoned all the way up to the neck. He is wearing equally dirty jeans, and has a blue knit cap over his long, greasy blonde hair. Inexplicably, there is a 25-cent coin tucked comfortably in his ear. He's carrying a shovel and announces their presence, calling out, "Anything for a buck!"

The second fellow has a stockier build and is wearing an unbuttoned yellow plaid shirt over a long sleeve white undershirt with dirty gray work pants. His long brown hair is parted down the middle. His physical presence could be described as a backwoods version of Shemp Howard of the Three Stooges.

The third member of "Anything For A Buck" also has a shovel, which he carries over his shoulder like a rifle. He's wearing an incorrectly-buttoned shirt over a black undershirt, with a dirty brown sport coat over both. His blue jeans are quite dirty as well. He has a pronounced overbite and sports an unkempt shock of thick, curly blonde hair reminiscent of Harpo Marx.

As Dick greets them, the slim fellow in the blue knit cap shakes his hand and with just a hint of a southern drawl says, "Hi. I'm Larry…" He turns and taps the dark-haired fellow on the shoulder. "This is my brother, Darryl…" The dark-haired fellow silently gives Dick a casual two-finger salute. Larry continues, pointing at the third fellow. "And that's my other brother, Darryl." And as the blonde fellow also gives Dick a silent two-finger salute, the studio audience explodes with laughter.

This was the "ground zero" moment in which the characters of "Larry, Darryl, and Darryl" not only made their network television debut but also took their first step towards becoming an iconic part of the cultural landscape for the remainder of the decade.

But, of course, Larry Darryl and Darryl didn't just suddenly appear in front of our studio audience on show night. They had been with us all week, having been previously cast by the producers to appear in the episode. Playing the parts of Larry, Darryl, and Darryl were talented actors William Sanderson (Larry), Tony Papenfuss (Darryl #1) and John Voldstad (Darryl #2).

We also had two other excellent "guest actors" with us that week: Dan Frischman (the kid from the mortuary) and veteran character actor Bill Quinn (the minister). And they had all joined our regular cast members Bob Newhart, Mary Frann, Tom Poston, Jennifer Holmes (Leslie Vanderkellen), and Steven Kampmann (Kirk Devane) that Monday morning as we sat down at the folding banquet table on the *Newhart* soundstage to read through the script of "Mrs. Newton's Body…" with the producers and writers.

The scene in which the characters of Larry, Darryl, and Darryl show up at the Stratford Inn was the last scene in the script. So that Monday morning William, Tony, and John sat quietly together at the table, sipping coffee from the craft service table, and laughing along with the rest of us as Bob and the cast read through the script out loud for the writers, each giving their unique "voice" to the words written for them.

We finally reached the scene in which Dick and Joanna meet the fellows from "Anything For A Buck." All of us sitting at that table had received a copy of the script in advance, so there was no one present who hadn't already read it (or participated in writing it). Everybody knew exactly what was coming next. But when William Sanderson looked over at Bob Newhart and said out loud for the very first time, "Hi. I'm Larry. This is my brother Darryl. And that's my other brother Darryl," no one at the table could contain their laughter.

No one that is, except the show's stage manager Randy Cordray...

I hadn't known Randy prior to working with him on *Newhart*. He had come to Los Angeles in 1975 from Lubbock, Texas, after graduating from Texas Tech University. Not long after his arrival in LA, Randy found work as a stage manager at the television studios of KTLA-Channel 5 on Sunset Blvd in the "heart of Hollywood." KTLA was the first commercially licensed TV station in the western United States, and at that time was owned by the famous "singing cowboy" Gene Autry, who also owned the California Angels baseball team. Randy gained a great deal of experience at KTLA while working on a number of network programs being produced at their studios. Before long, he had worked his way up from the position of second stage manager to that of first stage manager, which meant that he was essentially in charge of "running the stage" for the director.

Here's the thing about the TV and film community in Hollywood. It's a "small club," and it's all about networking. Those who are in charge of production are always looking for the best talent available, and if you're good at what you do, people tend to take notice of you. And the people at MTM took notice of Randy, offering him the position of first stage manager on *Newhart*.

I mention elsewhere in this book that the director on a videotaped show is usually required to work from a control room some distance away from the stage. Therefore, the first stage manager becomes the director's "proxy" on the soundstage, not only responsible for efficiently conveying instructions *from* the director to the cast and crew but also clearly communicating vital information *to* the director concerning conditions on the stage.* And Randy Cordray not only excelled in this area, but he also possessed another quality essential for a great stage

---

* *I discuss the role of the stage manager in a multi-camera videotape program in greater detail in the chapter devoted to Cher.*

manager. He could "think like a director." In this case, however, he just didn't think that Larry, Darryl, and Darryl were funny!

To put it bluntly, Larry, Darryl, and Darryl completely perplexed Randy. He just couldn't make sense of these three sketchy backwoods brothers. And let's face it, the concept really didn't make any sense. Throughout the week as we rehearsed their scene, Randy would pull me aside, whispering, "Doug, this whole thing is just stupid! These three guys are stupid! Two brothers both named Darryl? No one in the audience is going to believe that!"

"They don't have to believe it," I whispered back. "They'll be too busy laughing to notice."

However, Randy was not convinced. "But this is supposed to be Vermont!" he said. "And now we have this guy Larry who comes in with his two idiot brothers and has a southern accent? In Vermont? Are you kidding me?!?"

"Again, it doesn't matter," I countered. "Because it's funny. Take my word for it, Randy: the audience is going to love these guys." Randy just chewed on that for a while, still unconvinced. So I figured I'd go out on a limb. "Randy, I'm telling you Barry's caught lightning in a bottle here. Trust me, the audience is going to love these guys. And if the producers don't bring them back for another episode, I'll eat my hat."

Randy just looked at me for a second and then shook his head and laughed. You know, the way you might laugh if a friend of yours just said something completely ridiculous.

During that week, I had fun with Larry and the two Darryls. During a break in rehearsal, I asked William Sanderson where he'd come up with the idea for Larry to stick a quarter in his ear. He said, "Well, it was just something I came up with for the audition. I thought this guy might always need to have a quarter handy, for whatever. And since he knows his pockets probably have holes in them, he'd carry his money where it would be safe, which would be in his ear. Since it worked in the audition, I just kept it for the show." Nothing I had learned in my theater classes at UCLA had prepared me for that kind of deep dive into a minor character who is only in one scene.

Over lunch one day I made an off-handed remark to Tony Papenfuss and John Voldstad, the two Darryls, saying, "You two guys have the best job in television. You're going to go out there and get a huge laugh from the audience without even having to memorize one word of dialogue! All you have to do is keep from bumping into the furniture!" Tony and John agreed that it was indeed a very good job. But I was surprised when they told me that they were using their time during rehearsals to work up imaginary scenarios between the two of them to represent what each of their "Darryls" might be thinking at various times during the scene. It was very important to both Tony and John that even though they had no dialogue, it would always be clear to the audience that something was going on in their heads at all times. I came away from that lunch with a newfound respect for the two "Darryls."

And as I mentioned earlier, on show night when Larry, Darryl, and Darryl made that historic first appearance, the studio audience instantly fell in love with them. And a month later when the episode aired on CBS, the television viewers fell in love with them as well. And just about two months after "Mrs. Newton's Body..." was broadcast on CBS, Larry, Darryl, and Darryl were indeed back with us, this time appearing in an episode titled "Ricky Nelson Up Your Nose."

During the filming of "Mrs. Newton's Body..." I had boastfully (and quite foolishly) predicted to Randy Cordray that I was convinced that we hadn't seen the last of Larry, Darryl, and Darryl. But at the time I had no idea that Bob Newhart had been so delighted with the trio that he had personally met with Barry Kemp and insisted that they be brought back for another episode. So when Larry, Darryl, and Darryl returned for that second episode, Randy Cordray began to jokingly refer to me as his personal "comedy barometer," and his "official arbiter of what is funny." It instantly became a private joke between us.

In "Ricky Nelson Up Your Nose," Larry, Darryl, and Darryl were more of a presence, as this time the script had been written specifically for their characters, and for the actors who now portrayed them. And once again they delivered, eliciting huge laughs from the audience in that episode as well. This time Randy Cordray didn't need me to be his "comedy barometer." He could sense it as well. Larry, Darryl, and Darryl would be coming back for more. And *Newhart* would never be the same...

I mention elsewhere in the book that the writing staff for a new show is not hired until after the pilot episode has officially been "picked up" for broadcast by a network and given a commitment for multiple episodes. And because these writers were not involved in creating the pilot episode, they face a steep learning curve. During that first season, they will need to figure out what each of the characters from the pilot can and cannot do, how they all interact with each other, and what kind of stories they can tell through these characters from episode to episode that will appeal to a large general audience.

Sometimes characters created for the pilot just don't develop as originally intended when the show goes into weekly production and are written out of the series. The sitcom *Happy Days* is a classic example. When *Happy Days* began its run on television, the main character of Ritchie Cunningham (played by Ron Howard) had an older brother Chuck, who always had a basketball in his hands (even at the dinner table). He appeared in the first few episodes, but his character was deemed superfluous, and Chuck was soon written out of the show, never to be seen again.

Other times, guest characters which are only intended to appear in one episode during that first season may prove to be so popular with the audience that they wind up becoming regular cast members (sometimes at the expense of existing cast members!). In the ABC sitcom *Family Matters*, the character of Steve Urkel was only supposed to appear in one episode. But Urkel proved to be wildly popular with the audience. And it wasn't long before Steve Urkel became a regular on *Family Matters*, which resulted in a "re-tooling" of the show's original premise in order to feature more stories revolving around his character.

And during that first season of *Newhart*, both of these situations occurred...

Part way into season one, Barry Kemp was coming to the painful realization that for *Newhart* to succeed as a series, some of the elements he had developed for the pilot episode needed to be "re-tooled." For the pilot, Barry had created the character of Leslie Vanderkellen, played by the lovely young actress Jennifer Holmes. To paraphrase Mary Poppins, Barry originally envisioned Leslie Vanderkellen as a young woman who was "practically perfect in every way." She was beautiful, smart, gracious, charming, with a heart of gold. In short, Leslie was flawless.

The writing staff quickly discovered, however, that flawless characters aren't funny characters. As that first season went on, the writers had become increasingly frustrated with trying to come up with funny situations for the character of Leslie Vanderkellen. And actress Jennifer Holmes was equally frustrated, seeing her part becoming smaller and smaller each week. Something had to give.

In the back half of season one, in an episode titled "What Is This Thing Called Lust," the audience is introduced to Leslie Vanderkellen's *extremely* flawed cousin Stephanie, brilliantly played by Julia Duffy. Aside from their shared physical beauty, the two characters have nothing in common. Stephanie is the polar opposite of Leslie. She is spoiled, vapid, lazy, and narcissistic, with an overblown sense of entitlement. And for all of the reasons just listed, Stephanie is also outrageously funny (and much easier to write for!).

The studio audience's enthusiastic response to Stephanie told Barry Kemp everything he needed to know. At the end of season one, Leslie Vanderkellen was written out of the show. Season two of *Newhart* began with cousin Stephanie taking her place as the inn's housekeeper. And the first domino in the "re-tooling" of *Newhart* had fallen…

Just like Leslie Vanderkellen in season one, the character of next door neighbor Kirk Devane had remained largely undeveloped since the pilot. During season one, Kirk's continuing "story arc" had been centered around his unrequited romantic pursuit of the lovely but unattainable Leslie.* But once Leslie had been written out of the show, Kirk's whole "raison d'être" had been written out as well. I imagine that actor Steven Kampmann probably suspected that his character had become expendable.

Sure enough, at the end of season two, Kirk was also written out. Larry, Darryl, and Darryl, who had been "recurring characters" in several episodes during season two, replaced Kirk as the new owners of the "Minuteman Café" next door to the Stratford Inn. Over the course of two years Larry, Darryl, and Darryl had vaulted from a single guest appearance to becoming permanent cast members. Newhart had been "re-tooled" yet again, and the third domino had fallen…

---

* In a television series, a "story arc" is a continuing storyline that unfolds over a number of episodes, or even over the run of the show. A well-known example in a sitcom would be the relationship of Ross and Rachel in "Friends."

Now, if you've been paying attention (and I certainly hope that you have), then you probably noticed that I skipped over the second domino, having gone directly from the first to the third. And there's a reason for that...a couple of reasons actually. First, I skipped over it because the first and third domino both involved changes to the cast of *Newhart*. And while the second "re-tooling" domino actually fell in between those two events chronologically, it had nothing to do with the show's cast. But the other reason I skipped over that second domino was because I never saw it coming...

We were getting close to the end of that first season, shooting an episode titled, "A View From the Bench." It was a Wednesday, and we were working on stage, finalizing the blocking with the cast. As *Newhart*'s associate director, I was into my usual Wednesday routine, which was to "pre-visualize" the proper camera angles and shot sizes as the actors moved around the set, making notes in my script as we went through each scene.

After rehearsal on Wednesdays, the director and I would refer to my shot notes to help create our marked "shooting scripts" for the episode. On Thursdays, we would be rehearsing those shots with the camera crew, and on Fridays, we would shoot the show in front of a live audience.*

Sometime Wednesday afternoon, the CBS page who was assigned to answer the phone on stage approached, telling me I had a call. On the phone was Harry Waterson, the executive in charge of production at Witt/Thomas/Harris Productions, with whom I had worked on *Benson*.† Harry was someone I truly liked and admired. He was an affable guy and terrific at his job, but he wasn't the type of person who would call just to say "hello."

And as I expected, as soon as we had exchanged greetings, Harry got right to the point. "Doug," he said. "We're about to go into production on a new sitcom for ABC over here at Witt/Thomas/Harris. The network has given us a 13-week commitment. We just finalized a deal with John Rich to be the show's executive producer and director, and he's already driving

---

* *I discuss this in greater detail in the chapter devoted to The Golden Girls.*
† *Harry and I also both worked for Producer/Director Marty Pasetta, though not at the same time. Harry was Marty's associate producer for the famous "Elvis-Aloha From Hawaii" TV special broadcast live via satellite to 40 countries around the world.*

me crazy, wanting to know why I haven't hired his 'head schmuck' to do the show with him.' Are you interested?"

I couldn't believe my good fortune. We only had a few more episodes of *Newhart* left to shoot, and now I was being offered a 13-week commitment with John Rich which would carry me through the entire "off season" until season two of *Newhart* started back up again in mid-summer. Offers like this just didn't come along that often. "Absolutely!" I said. "I'd love to work with John again. When do you start production?"

"Monday," Harry said.

"Monday," I repeated, not quite sure I'd heard correctly. "*This* Monday?"

"Yes. So what do you say? Can I tell John his 'head schmuck' is on board?"

I remember being a bit nonplussed, unsure of how to react. Even though John Rich was asking for me, it just wasn't like Harry to try and "poach" someone from another show in production. But that seemed to be exactly what he was doing. And he was waiting for my answer.

"I'd love to do it, Harry," I said. "And you know I love working with John. But I can't start Monday. We still have a couple more episodes of *Newhart* left to shoot before we're done for the year. Would it be possible for me to join you when we've finished our season?"

There was an awkward silence at the other end of the phone. Then Harry spoke haltingly, which was also quite out of character. "Oh, um…I'm sorry, Doug. Wow, this is awkward. I, uh…got a call from Barry Kemp. He indicated to me that you were available starting Monday. I was under the impression that he had already discussed this with you."

And that's how I found out that I had been fired from *Newhart*.

I was thirty-two years old, and had already worked with some of the toughest, most demanding producers and directors in the industry in some of the most difficult, intense, and pressure-filled situations. I had earned a reputation as someone who could "stand the heat" and not wilt under pressure.

But at that moment it was all I could do just to keep from crying.

---

* *I discuss my relationship with acclaimed sitcom producer-director John Rich in the chapter devoted to him.*

"Can I call you back, Harry?" I asked, choking back tears. "I need to go and speak with Barry Kemp."

Harry realized he had been the unwitting bearer of very bad news. His voice had a soft, apologetic tone. "Of course," he said. "I'm really sorry, Doug. I had no idea that you two hadn't discussed this. Just let me know what you decide after you and Barry have talked. We'd love to have you with us." I thanked him, left the soundstage, and headed up to the *Newhart* offices to talk to Barry Kemp.

When I told Barry that I'd just spoken to Harry Waterson, his eyes widened, and his expression fell. I didn't have to say anything else. He knew that I knew. And he knew how I'd found out. He immediately apologized for not including me in discussions about the other way in which *Newhart* was being "re-tooled." CBS and MTM had made the decision at the network level that starting in season two, *Newhart* would no longer be shot on videotape, but would instead return to their familiar film format, in keeping with all of MTM's other shows. The decision to switch from videotape to film had been the second domino.

At this point, I could offer up a lengthy explanation as to how and why these decisions were made, but in the end it doesn't really matter. The bottom line is that a TV show which is shot on film has no associate director. The decision to shoot *Newhart* on film meant that just like Jennifer Holmes and Steven Kampmann, I had also become expendable.

Sometimes in life it's not *what* happens to you that really hurts. It's the *way* it happens that breaks your heart. Although it hadn't been intentional, I'd been blind-sided. After he apologized for not telling me about the decision sooner, Barry Kemp said something very nice.

"For what it's worth, Doug, I just feel terrible about this," he said. "During the pilot I asked you to be my back-stop, and you really came through. You helped make *Newhart* a hit. And now, through no fault of yours, I have to let you go. That's why I got in touch with Harry Waterson. I didn't want you to miss out on that job." I knew that Barry was telling me this in the hope it would make me feel better, but somehow it actually made me feel worse.

And that was it. I was already on my way out the door. I had two more days on *Newhart*. I immediately thought of Randy Cordray. "What about Randy?" I asked. "You're keeping him on, right?"

"I hope so," Barry replied. "I haven't spoken to him about this yet. But if he decides to stay on, it won't be as the first assistant. He doesn't have enough experience. I'm bringing in Michael Stanislavsky to be the first. I worked with Michael on *Taxi*. If Randy stays on, he would be Michael's second assistant."

I was concerned for my friend. This would essentially mean a step backward for Randy, from first stage manager down to second assistant director. Michael Stanislavsky would be "running the stage" instead of Randy, who would now be answering to him. "When are you going to talk to him?" I asked. "I want to be able to let him know why I won't be here on Monday."

Barry assured me that he would be talking to Randy before the week was out. He didn't want to make the same mistake with him that he'd made with me. Barry asked me not to say anything to Randy until he'd had the opportunity to talk to him first. For Randy's sake, I agreed to remain silent.

At the dinner break on Friday, Randy was visibly upset. From the expression on his face, I knew that he'd spoken with Barry about the changes for season two. And we both knew he had a huge decision to make. We drifted over to a corner of the soundstage where we could talk a bit more privately.

"This isn't right! It's not fair to either one of us! I've got a good mind to just quit at the end of this season!" he said. "There are plenty of other shows, you know."

"I know," I replied. "And I know you'd have no trouble getting on with one. But let me give you a couple of reasons why I think you should consider staying." I knew he was in no mood to hear what I had to say. But I was going to give him some unsolicited advice anyway. Hey, that's what friends do, right?

"First of all, this show is a hit. It's going to run a number of years. And that's as close to steady employment as we ever get. So you owe it to yourself to really think twice about whether or not to walk away from it." Randy just looked at me thoughtfully. Even though he was angry, he knew I was right. In our business, you walk away from a hit show at your own peril.

"And second, think about what this could mean for your career in the long run. Since they'll be shooting on film, if you just stay with the show for season two, you'll have accrued enough 'film days' to be able to work any show, on film or tape."

Back in the days before digital recording became commonplace, employment opportunities within the Directors Guild of America were divided on the basis of whether or not a program was recorded on film or videotape. The two technologies were vastly different. While director members could work in both, those working below the director in the chain of command were segregated. Shows shot on film utilized first and second assistant directors, while programs shot on videotape used a directing team made up of associate directors, as well as first and second stage managers.

For a first stage manager working in videotape to be able to cross over and work as a first assistant director on a filmed program, he or she would first have to work a required number of days as a second assistant on a film set. And all Randy needed to do to accomplish this would be to "bite the bullet" and continue working on season two of *Newhart* as the second assistant director under Michael Stanislavsky.

Randy decided to stay on for season two. And season three. By that time, he had accrued more than enough "film days" to be able to work as a first assistant or first stage manager on any set, either film or videotape. And after leaving *Newhart*, Randy had no problem finding steady work as a first assistant director.

And because it's a "small club," when Barry Kemp went into production for his ABC sitcom *Coach* in 1989, he asked Randy to join the show, this time as the first assistant director. Before Randy left *Coach* in 1991, he had also become the show's production manager.

In the ensuing years, he became a successful producer on such popular and iconic sitcoms as *Dharma and Greg*, *Still Standing*, and *The Office*. And Randy forever endeared himself with fans of *The Office* when he made a cameo appearance as the captain of the "Maid of the Mist," officiating at the wedding of Jim and Pam (John Krasinski and Jenna Fischer) below Niagara Falls!

When I left the television industry to become a professor, Randy would always take time out his schedule to be available to my students.

Whether it was teaching seminars, hosting visits to the studio, or providing internship opportunities, Randy always went "above and beyond" to provide opportunities for the students to enrich their educational experience.

I have been honored to call Randy my friend for almost forty years now. In a business that at times seems to be overrun with "schmucks," Randy has always been one of the good guys, a person of honesty and integrity whose word means something.

As of this writing Randy and his lovely wife Erin are happily "semi-retired" and living in the Pacific Northwest, where Randy is able to indulge two of his favorite pastimes: rock climbing and mountain biking. From time to time we email, text, or talk on the phone, catching up on life's events and swapping stories.

And every so often we still share a laugh about that first encounter with "Larry, Darryl, and Darryl."

11

THE GOLDEN GIRLS

It's funny how your life can take a turn just by answering your phone...

Looking back on my career in television, I find it interesting that *The Golden Girls* is the one sitcom that I probably spent the least amount of time with, yet it continues to be the one that everybody still wants to know about. It's a real testament as to how popular and iconic *The Golden Girls* has remained through the years.

It was the fall of 1985. I had just finished a freelance job, and I was at home when the phone rang. It was Tony Thomas[*] of Witt-Thomas-Harris Productions, the company that produced *The Golden Girls*, which was not quite halfway into their first season. I knew Tony and his partner Paul Witt[*] quite well, having worked for them on almost fifty episodes of *Benson*, a spinoff of *Soap*, as well as their series *Condo*, and several other series pilots.

During our phone conversation, Tony told me they had just hired a new director for the show and wanted to know if I was available to

---

[*] He also appears in the chapters devoted to John Rich and Danny Thomas.

come and assist him starting the following week, when *The Golden Girls* returned from a scheduled week-long hiatus. Tony said that Gary Shimokawa, the show's very capable regular AD, had been offered the opportunity to direct several episodes of another sitcom, and would return to the show when he completed his directing assignment. Since I had a few weeks before my next assignment, I told Tony I'd be glad to help out on the show for a while.

Half-hour sitcoms usually begin filming the season's episodes about six weeks prior to going on the air. As a result, at the time of Tony's call, only a few episodes of *The Golden Girls* had aired on TV, and I had not yet seen the show. But having worked on a number of both successful and unsuccessful new shows as they tried to navigate through their first season on the air, I couldn't help wondering what challenges Tony's offer would present. And I knew that for a brand-new show to change directors so soon, combined with the last-minute call to me to be the AD for that new director, something serious was going on.

The pilot episode of *The Golden Girls* had been directed by the brilliant Jay Sandrich (with whom I had the privilege of working on the pilot episode of Empty Nest a few years later). Jay is one of the most highly-regarded sitcom directors in the business. His credits include *The Mary Tyler Moore Show, The Bob Newhart Show, Soap, Benson,* and *The Cosby Show*, as well as many successful series pilots, including *WKRP in Cincinnati* and, as I mentioned, *The Golden Girls* and *Empty Nest*.

After directing the pilot, Jay elected not to stay on and do the series. So, Witt-Thomas-Harris brought in Paul Bogart, another very talented and accomplished director, to helm the show for its first season. Paul's credits were equally impressive, going all the way back to the "Golden Age of Television," directing ground-breaking programs such as *The Kraft Theater, CBS Playhouse,* and *Omnibus*. His sitcom credits included such iconic comedy classics as *Get Smart* and *All in the Family*. Paul was also a contemporary of one of my sitcom mentors and good friend, John Rich.[*]

John Rich was the director I had worked with on *Benson*, and as such, we both were quite familiar with W-T-H's production methods. According to John, after just a few episodes, Paul Bogart and Witt-

---

[*] *I discuss John in greater detail in the chapters devoted to him and to Henry Winkler.*

Thomas-Harris Productions had a major falling out. John did not disclose to me the exact nature of the disagreement (nor was it any of my business), but he intimated that Paul Bogart and W-T-H held vastly differing opinions as to how *The Golden Girls* should be run, and apparently neither party was willing to compromise. As a result, Paul either elected to leave the show, or was let go. In any case, the term John used to describe the split was "creative differences," which is probably accurate.

Stability is crucial during that first season, when a brand-new show is trying to find its creative footing. And the director is one of the lynchpins of that stability. The director needs to be effective in working with both the writing staff who are trying to solidify what the show is about, and with the actors who are trying to make sure the brand-new characters they're portraying are fully formed. So, losing a seasoned veteran like Paul Bogart was a major problem, especially for the cast, who depended on him for leadership and guidance. After Paul's departure, several other excellent directors came in but didn't stay, because as Tony Thomas described it, none of them "clicked with the ladies." This was actually Tony's way of saying that they didn't click with Bea Arthur, who could be a *very* tough nut to crack.

Until, that is, Witt-Thomas-Harris found director Terry Hughes. Terry is a dashingly handsome Englishman with an aristocratic air about him. He's tall, with thick silver hair, piercing eyes, a charming smile, and even has a well-placed cleft in the middle of his ruggedly square jaw. The first day we met at the studio for a pre-production meeting, Terry had just come from horseback riding and was dressed in a polo shirt, riding pants and knee-high riding boots. I took one look at him and grinned, "Terry, you look like you just came from Central Casting to audition for the part of Lord of the Manor! The only thing missing is your riding crop!"

He laughed, and in his impeccable English accent, said, "Actually Doug, it's in the car!"

Because Bea Arthur had been unhappy with the previous directors, Tony Thomas and Paul Witt had arranged to have Bea, Rue, Estelle, and Betty[*] meet with Terry before he would actually direct his first

---

[*] *I discuss Betty White in greater detail in the chapter devoted to her.*

episode. They wanted to see if Terry and the ladies (meaning Bea) had the right "chemistry." If not, Tony said they would've had to keep looking for a director.

"I'm guessing that meeting went well," I said to Tony.

He just laughed and said, "Yeah, Bea took one look at Terry, turned to the others, and said breathlessly, 'Oh, my god! He's gorgeous!'"

"And the others?" I asked.

He smiled. "Rue likes whatever Bea likes, and Estelle's afraid of Bea, so she's fine with him. And Betty gets along with everyone."

I said, "Sounds like your problem is solved."

"We think so," Tony answered. "There's just one thing," he added. We don't actually know for certain that Terry knows how to direct an American sitcom."

Tony went on to say that he was "reasonably sure" that Terry knew the sitcom process, and listed his credits, which included *The Two Ronnies*, *Michael Palin's Ripping Yarns*, and *Monty Python Live at the Hollywood Bowl*. "The problem is," Tony said, "Those are all British programs. We're not sure that Terry knows how to shoot a sitcom, you know…*our* way. Which is why you're here."

"I see," I said. "So, you want me to be…"

"…Our insurance policy," he said, finishing my sentence. "We have no idea if Terry knows how we work, but you do. So, we figured that if he can just work with the ladies and keep Bea happy, then you'll be there to make sure it all gets on camera."

"And if it turns out that Terry actually *does* know how to shoot a sitcom your way?" I asked.

"Then so much the better," Tony answered. "But if he doesn't, then it's your job to figure out how make it work. I don't care how you do it. Just make sure it gets done." That was Tony's polite way of saying it was *my* neck on the line.

And just like that, I was the Associate Director of *The Golden Girls*. At least for a while.

As is normal on a multi-camera sitcom taped in front of a live audience, the work week on *The Golden Girls* was divided into two basic parts. The first three days were devoted to blocking and staging the actors, polishing and refining the script, and working out all of the technical issues involved with sets, wardrobe, props, special effects, etc. The work more closely resembled the preparation of a stage play for the studio audience and was done without the four television cameras present.

The last two days were "tech days," used for refining the camera angles and shot sizes with the four camera operators; working out the "choreography" involved in positioning the two boom microphones used to record the dialogue; making last-minute adjustments to the lighting; and rehearsing sound effects, lighting effects, and any special effects that might be required by the script.

Day four would begin with a camera meeting in which I, as the associate director, would sit down with our four camera operators and assign them between 250 and 300 shots that were to be used in the show. As I dictated the shots from my marked script, each of the four camera operators would carefully write down their individual shots on a series of "shot cards" *(usually one card per scene),* which they would fasten on to their cameras, just below their video viewfinders. Each shot had a unique number, from 1 to approximately 300, and as each shot came up on line, I would call out that number into their headsets. That way, as a scene progressed, each camera operator could simply glance at their shot card and know which shot number was currently on the line, and which shot number was coming up next.

Throughout the day, each scene in the show would be rehearsed on camera. This was often done out of order, since we might rehearse all of the scenes taking place in a given set before moving on to the next set. For example, the tech crew might rehearse all of the scenes taking place in the living room before having to move the four cameras and two boom microphones to the kitchen to rehearse all of those scenes, etc.

At the end of day four was a "dress run-through," in which we would run the entire show from top to bottom in the correct order, on camera and with the cast in their wardrobe. This way the producers could see the wardrobe on camera, and we could time each wardrobe change with a stopwatch to make sure the audience wouldn't be kept waiting too long between scenes. Speed was always a factor, since a tired audience that has been sitting too long is not inclined to provide the laughter needed for the show's soundtrack.

The dress run-through was also the first time the producers would see the multi-camera "switch feed," in which the director would cut in, or "switch" shots from all four cameras to indicate his or her vision as to what the show would look like "on TV" to the viewer at home.

As a result, it was quite common after the dress run-through for the director to get notes from the producers regarding camera angles and shot sizes. Occasionally these notes could be thoughtful and reflective, but quite often they could be…well, just plain stupid (during a "hurricane" episode on Empty Nest, I actually had to argue with a producer that the branches on the palm tree he demanded to see swaying in the background were never going to move, because the tree in question was just a *painting* of a palm tree on a scenery drop!).

Note: The "palm tree" argument notwithstanding, many directors quickly learn that if they want to enjoy steady work in episodic television, then quite often the best policy is to not question these notes, or challenge them, but just to graciously accept them. Experienced, self-confident directors will incorporate the few thoughtful notes into their scripts, and simply toss all of the stupid ones in the trash (and FYI, most veteran actors will usually do the same thing).

You would be surprised how many producers, after watching the show taping the very next day, will complement you on how well you'd incorporated some ridiculous note they'd given you that you'd completely ignored and discarded. (We also quickly learn to just smile and say, "Yeah. Hey, thanks for that note," even though we usually have no idea which note they're referring to).

Day five was the day we taped the show in front of the studio audience. This day would start at noon, with the cast and crew going through one more camera rehearsal of each scene, incorporating whichever of the producers' acting notes and camera notes they had deemed "noteworthy" from the previous evening's dress run-through.

Around 3:00 p.m., the cast would go to makeup and hair, and the crew would set up for the first show taping at 5:00 p.m. *The Golden Girls* always shot each episode twice, using two separate audiences, one at 5:00 p.m. and another at 7:30 p.m. Later during the editing process, the producers would select the best elements from both of the two tapings (the ones that generated the biggest laughs) and combine them into one seamless episode for broadcast on the network.

The second show taping would usually end between 9:00 and 9:30 p.m., at which point the audience would go home. The cast and crew would stay and do any "pickup" shots that might have been missed during the tapings or that were required to accommodate a last-minute re-write. The day usually ended sometime around 11:00 p.m., at which point the show was handed over to the post-production crew to be edited for broadcast. The following week the cycle would repeat itself, but with a different script, which would pose a new set of challenges.

Our first Monday and Tuesday on *The Golden Girls* went extremely well. The episode was titled "The Custody Battle." Terry was quite at ease with the ladies, and they were equally at ease with him. And as a director, his skill in working with a group of veteran actors was apparent to us all. He guided the cast smoothly and efficiently as they blocked out each scene, working out their various motivations and movements within those scenes, taking the script "from the page to the stage." The run-through for the writers and producers at the end of the day on Tuesday also went well, and the notes were minimal. All in all, everything was running smoothly, and I was really enjoying my time on stage working with Terry and the ladies.

After the writer's run-through on Tuesday, the writers would do what was considered their final re-write of the script (although in reality, on a sitcom the re-writing often continues right up to and sometimes right through the show taping on Friday!). On Wednesday morning, we all got our fresh scripts and continued to work, accommodating the writers' minor revisions into the scenes we had blocked and rehearsed on Monday and Tuesday. The run-through at the end of the day on Wednesday also went well, and again the notes to the cast were minimal.

At 6:00 p.m., the cast went home, and the lighting crew came in to begin focusing the lights for the camera rehearsal, which would start promptly at 9:00 a.m. on Thursday morning. After the producers' run-through on Wednesday, it would be a common practice for the director and associate director to sit down together and decide how best to cover all of the actors' movements and dialogue on camera. They go through their scripts page by page, designing shot sequences and transcribing them into their scripts. Often this would take quite some time to accomplish. As a result, one of the show's production assistants might order some food for them from a restaurant near the studio so that they could continue working through dinner.

Having worked with a number of directors, I knew that their "shot blocking" process could take anywhere from an hour and a half to four hours to complete, depending on their method and experience. Since the run-through had ended at 6:00 p.m., I reasoned that we might be finished marking our scripts as early as 8:00 p.m., or we might still be writing shots until 10:00 p.m. or so. I was okay with it either way, and if we decided to order dinner, I was prepared to lobby vigorously for Roscoe's Chicken and Waffles, which was right across the street from the studio.

Keeping in mind that Tony had hired me as his "insurance policy" to make sure that we had the proper camera coverage, I asked Terry how he would like to handle planning out the shots. He said, "Doug, this first time out, I think I'd like to just take my script home and work out the shots all on my own. I really need to think it all through, and I'm afraid it would just be too agonizingly slow for you to have to sit there and wait for me."

I could feel the hairs on the back of my neck starting to tingle. And I could hear Tony Thomas's voice in my head: *Just make sure it gets done.* And now here we were, the first time out, and Terry was taking away my chance to familiarize him with the kind of camera coverage Witt-Thomas-Harris would be expecting to see the at the dress run-through the very next day. I was already starting to have real concerns about *that* note session.

So, I made my pitch: "I don't mind waiting for as long as it takes, Terry. It's all part of the job. I'm here to help."

"Thanks," he replied, "But this first time out I really just need to go home and sort it all out in my head before I start writing any shots."

And that was it. I had offered, and Terry had politely declined. He was the director, and I would be crossing a line professionally if I attempted to press the issue any further. "Okay," I said, "But I'll need to have time to copy your shots into my script before the camera meeting tomorrow at 9:00. How will I get them from you? Will you messenger your script to me later tonight?"

"Oh no, it will be too late for you to start on it tonight," he replied. "Tell you what. I'll meet you at 8:00 tomorrow morning in my office and give you my marked script. That should give you an hour to copy my shots into your script, and still get to the camera meeting on time."

At this point, there wasn't really anything else I could do. "Okay," I said, "See you tomorrow at 8:00 sharp," and we both went home: Terry to work on his shots, and me to toss and turn all night.

I was at Terry's office a few minutes before 8:00 a.m. on Thursday morning, ready to go. Unfortunately, Terry didn't show up until twenty minutes later, having underestimated LA's traffic at that hour. So now, instead of an hour, I only had forty minutes to copy all of his camera shots into my script before my meeting with the four camera operators at 9:00 a.m. Things were getting tight, but I told myself that if I worked fast, I just might make it. Then I opened Terry's script…

At first glance it was just kind of surprisingly amusing, as Terry had written all of the shots into his script in the wrong margin. In a television sitcom script, the dialogue is placed in the center of the page, leaving a wide margin on the right-hand side of the page with room for the director to write in the 250 to 300 shots. However, Terry had written all of his shots in the much narrower left-hand margin, where the three-hole punch attaches the pages to the binder. As a matter of fact, he actually had written some of the shots *around* the holes that had been punched into the margin.

"Terry," I said, "You're not in England anymore. You're in America. We drive on the right over here." He looked at me quizzically. I held up his script, pointing with my pencil to the much wider right-hand margin, and repeated, "We drive on the right."

He just laughed and said, "Yes, I'm still not used to everybody driving on the wrong side over here."

But then, as I started going through the first scene, my amusement quickly morphed into concern. I could only find shots for cameras one, two and three. Where were all of the shots for camera four? Was the whole script like this? A quick glance through his script confirmed that it was. I voiced my concern. "Terry, you've only written shots for three cameras. Didn't Tony and Paul tell you we had four?"

"Yes," he replied, "They did mention there were four, but I wasn't sure if that fourth camera was just a back-up in case one of the others broke down, or if they expected me to use it."

And there it was, the disconnect between British and American sitcoms. And I was caught right in the middle of it. While it's true that during the 1950's and 60's multi-camera sitcoms produced in Hollywood commonly employed three cameras on shows like *I Love Lucy* and *The Dick Van Dyke Show*, by the 1970's sitcoms such as *All in the Family* and *Sanford and Son* had begun using a fourth camera. And by the 1980's, all of the multi-camera sitcoms in Hollywood were using four cameras. But apparently in England they were still only using three. Lucky me.

"Oh," I said, "They *definitely* expect you to use the fourth camera!"

To which Terry replied, "Oh, okay." He looked at his watch. "I don't have time to re-work my script right now," he said. "I need to meet with the ladies and give them some notes before we get started. So, I tell you what. Just go through my script and add camera four wherever you think it belongs." And with that, he left.

My heart was pounding. I looked at my watch. Thirty-six minutes until the camera meeting. Thirty-six minutes to figure out from Terry's script notations all of the places in the camera coverage where camera four should be inserted, write the shots in, and then re-arrange all of the shots from the *other* three cameras to accommodate the addition of camera four. And as if that weren't enough, I then needed to copy all 300 of those re-arranged shots into *my* script, all before 9:00 a.m. It simply couldn't be done.

So, I just did what *could* be done. Looking at our rehearsal schedule for the day, I took out the script pages for the first two scenes (out of nine) on the schedule and re-wrote the shots for just those scenes into Terry's script, adding in camera four where I felt it was needed, and re-arranging the shots for cameras one, two and three to accommodate. Then I copied the new shot sequences for those same two scenes into my script. Before I left for the camera meeting at 9:00 o'clock, I removed the remainder of Terry's marked script from his binder, leaving in just the two scenes I had corrected. That way, I had the remainder of his three-camera script with me so that I could work on it throughout the day.

At the camera meeting, I explained the situation to the four camera operators, who immediately understood (although it didn't stop them from howling with laughter at my predicament!). I gave them my corrected shots for the first two scenes, which they copied onto their shot cards. We spent the short amount of time we had left in the meeting working together on the shots for the third scene we would rehearse that day.

So, at 10:00 a.m., when the camera rehearsal officially started, we had corrected scripts and camera shot cards for just three out of nine scenes. Throughout the morning, whenever there was a lull in the action, or a discussion on stage, I would use that time to keep re-arranging the shots for next scene coming up on the rehearsal schedule, re-writing Terry's script and my own. Each time I finished re-working a scene, I would slip those pages back into Terry's script.

And each time we finished rehearsing a scene, I would call a "mini-meeting" with the camera crew on stage and give them the shots I had just re-worked for upcoming scene. And as I dictated the shots, they would again transcribe them onto their individual shot cards. Throughout the morning, I was just trying to stay one scene ahead of where we were in the schedule.

The hour-long lunch break was such a blessing! I now had a whole hour to work alone with the scripts. This gave me enough time to finish re-writing and re-arranging the remaining scenes to be rehearsed that afternoon, and to copy the shots into my script. By the end of lunch, Terry and I at least had matching, corrected scripts. However, because there was no time in the schedule for another camera meeting, I still had to rely on my series of "mini-meetings" for the camera operators, in order to make sure they were able to get the shots onto their cards ahead of the next scene.

One thing I noticed throughout the day was that Terry generally liked what he was seeing on camera and did not appear to have any major issues with either the way I had integrated camera four into the coverage, or the way I had re-arranged the other three cameras to accommodate. I found this to be very encouraging, and the germ of an idea began for form. But more on that later…

We made it to the end of the camera rehearsal, and everyone started setting up for the dress run-through. Thankfully, neither Tony Thomas nor Paul Witt were aware of what it had taken to get us to this point. Like most executive producers, they tended to spend their days away from the stage, working from their offices. As far as they were concerned, as long as no one was calling them from the stage with a problem, then everything was good. And that was just fine with me. After all, Tony had said to me, "I don't care how you do it. Just make sure it gets done," right? Well, it got done.

However, the dress run-through would be the true test, because now Tony and Paul would be watching on their TV monitors, along with all of the other producers, and would be paying close attention to the camera coverage. Afterwards, they would be giving their new director (and his trusty associate director) notes regarding the camera coverage.

But to my relief, the dress run-through went quite smoothly and bore a very close resemblance to any number of previous camera run-throughs I'd done for Witt-Thomas-Harris over the years. There were no glaring errors, missing shots, or awkward camera angles. After the last scene, I thanked the camera crew for their hard work, patience, and willingness to roll with the punches throughout the day. Together we had turned what could have been a bad situation into a very productive day.

After the run-through, Terry and I sat down with the producers to get their camera notes. And again, much to my relief, the notes were minimal. Tony and Paul seemed genuinely pleased with what they'd seen on their monitors during the run-through and suggested only a few minor changes. After the note session broke up, Tony quietly pulled me aside. He basically wanted a "report card" regarding Terry's technical proficiency, and I knew I needed to have an answer that would satisfy him. "The camera coverage looked pretty solid," he said. "Is there anything I should be concerned about?"

"No, not really," I grinned, "I *did* have to point out to him that we drive on the right over here." Then I related to Tony that Terry had written his shots into the left-hand margin of his script, and that I'd spent the day re-writing all of the shots in his script into the right-hand margin. Both of those things were true. But that was all I told him. The rest I kept to myself. Tony seemed satisfied with my report, and we both called it a day. I was exhausted, physically and mentally. I went home Thursday night and crashed.

The two tapings on Friday went smoothly as well, and both the cast and the company seemed pleased with the results. Terry's first episode was "in the can." That Friday night everyone went home happy, especially me. But as happy as I was that it had all worked out, I knew we couldn't go through the same chaos the following week. Something had to change. Fortunately, that germ of an idea that had formed during the camera rehearsal on Thursday would begin to take shape over the weekend…

By the following Monday morning, that idea had blossomed into a fully-formed plan. However, Terry and I were still getting to know each other, so I wasn't sure how receptive he would be. Again, as an associate director, there's a professional line that you don't want to cross with your director, and the plan I wanted to pitch to him was tiptoeing close to that line. But I felt it was worth a shot. So, after the cast had finished their table read of the script, I approached Terry and made my pitch: "Terry, I've been thinking about a way that we might make camera blocking on Wednesdays more efficient."

Whatever anxiety I'd had regarding Terry's willingness to hear my pitch quickly evaporated. "Great!" he said, enthusiastically. "What's your idea?"

Bolstered by his initial positive response, I elaborated. "Well, I came up with an idea over the weekend that would allow us both to go home on Wednesday at the end of the run-through, with our scripts completely marked and ready for Thursday." His reaction was instantaneous.

"Marvelous!" he said with delight. "Because last Wednesday night was bloody awful! I was up way too late working out those shots and paid for it on Thursday. I'd rather not repeat that." It was the best reaction I could have hoped for. Terry was on board with the concept. Now I just needed for him to approve the process.

The plan that I pitched to him was as follows: by Wednesday, Terry and the cast would have the blocking and movement that occurs in each scene pretty well locked-in, with only minor changes. Therefore, I suggested to him that on Wednesday, as we went through each scene, I could write down what I felt might be the appropriate camera angles and shot sizes in my script, based on my observations of what he was doing with the actors.

And then as soon as Terry and the cast finished rehearsing a scene, I would bring my marked script over to him for review. He would look at my suggested shots and make whatever changes he deemed necessary, and I'd make those changes in my script. Then once he was satisfied with the shots for the scene, he could either copy them into his script, or simply give me his script pages so that I could write the shots in for him while he worked on the next scene.

Following the plan, we would simply repeat the process scene by scene throughout the day until all of the scenes had been rehearsed. And by the end of rehearsal on Wednesday both of our scripts would be identically marked with matching shots.

I also told Terry that having the shots already written in our scripts would give us a huge advantage during the producers' run-through at the end of Wednesday, since we would now be able to "double check" them against what we were seeing in the run-through. This would allow us to make any little minor adjustments we deemed necessary. And when the run-through was over, we could go home 6:00 p.m., along with the cast.

When I finished the pitch, Terry just smiled and said, "I like it. Let's try it." So, that Wednesday, Terry and I put "the plan" into action, exactly as I had pitched it.

Throughout the day, as we rehearsed each scene, I would mark my script with what I felt were the appropriate shots to cover both the action on stage and the dialogue. When we finished a scene, Terry would tell the girls to "take five," and I would bring my marked script over to Terry's podium. He would look at my shots and make his changes, which were along the lines of, "Okay…good…oh here, change this over-the-shoulder shot of Rue and Betty on camera one to just a close-up of Betty instead…good… good…here, let's move that four-shot of the ladies at the kitchen table from camera two to camera three so I can have a single of Bea on camera two for her reaction to Estelle's line…"

And that would be it. Then I would make the changes he requested in my script, after which he would simply write those same shots into his script, using his own familiar shorthand. The whole process only took about five minutes. Then we would move on to the next scene.

And at the run-through Wednesday afternoon, as the actors went through each scene, we were able to follow along and track the shots we'd written into our scripts earlier in the day, to make sure that they worked as we had "pre-visualized" them. Afterwards we only needed to make a few minor adjustments, if any. And, just like in my pitch, Terry and I were able to go home at 6:00 p.m., and get a good night's rest. That Wednesday night I hardly knew what to do with myself, as I'd never been able to go home that early on a camera blocking night before!

Thursday's camera rehearsal went smoothly, with just a minimum of adjustments as we were now able to see on camera what we had previously only visualized in our "mind's eye" the day before. And again, after the dress run-through on Thursday, the camera notes from Tony and Paul were minor. Terry and I were easily able to make those few changes with the camera crew during Friday's rehearsal prior to the two show tapings that evening. And since there were few changes during the rehearsals, the tapings in front of the audiences were smooth and efficient. "The plan" was working!

I was pleasantly surprised at how quickly and effortlessly we had adopted this system. What I was learning about Terry was that, even though he'd mistakenly only blocked shots for three cameras that first week, there was absolutely no doubt that he had a multi-cam director's innate ability to be able to pre-visualize all four of the camera angles, and he knew exactly what shot sizes were needed to successfully capture the show on video. And I hope that in me he found an associate director who shared his pre-visualization, and who could anticipate during rehearsal what he eventually wanted to see on the air. At any rate, we continued to use "the plan" for the rest of my brief stint on *The Golden Girls*.

Gary Shimokawa returned from his directing assignment, which meant it was time for me to leave the show and move on to my next assignment. Since he had not yet worked with Terry Hughes, I briefed him about the camera blocking plan we'd developed in his absence. Gary was enthusiastically on board with "the plan" as well. I don't think he'd ever gone home early on a camera blocking night, either! He and

Terry continued employing "the plan" until Gary left the show after the second season. It's my understanding that Gary then passed "the plan" along to *his* replacement, Lex Passaris, who became the show's associate director until 1991, when Lex would become the director of *The Golden Girls* following Terry Hughes' departure to pursue other projects.

In the years that followed, Terry and I worked together on a number of television pilots and used "the plan" each time. Since leaving *The Golden Girls*, Terry Hughes has continued his career as a very successful sitcom director, helming hit shows such as *Third Rock from the Sun*, *8 Simple Rules*, and *Friends*. As of this writing, Terry is currently a director on *Man with a Plan*, starring Matt LeBlanc. I wonder if on *Man with a Plan*, Terry's still using "the plan?"

12

GEORGE CLOONEY

Who forgets spending a week with George Clooney?
Me, apparently...

Back in the late 90's, when I was teaching at Southern Illinois University in Carbondale (go Salukis!), I agreed to help out a colleague with a research project. He wanted to find out if television viewers could remember a specific product brand and message in a commercial that was "clustered" among other commercials. His goal was to determine if the commercial's position *within* the cluster factored into the viewers' ability to remember the product and brand.

My contribution to the project involved creating an original program which would become the vehicle in which to insert the commercial clusters. The program (and commercials) would then be screened by research subjects for data gathering and analysis. Therefore, I put together a one-hour sketch comedy program in which to insert the commercial clusters. For expediency, I decided to base the show on those jokes that seem to constantly float around the Internet, with no known origin. So, I gathered up hundreds of jokes from around the web and turned the best of them into little comedy sketches: just a quick set up, then the punchline, and that was it.

So, kids, right about now you're probably thinking to yourselves, "Paw-Paw Doug, I thought this book was supposed to be about your life *before* you became a college professor, not after. What does this story have to do with George Clooney?" Not much, except that one of the sketches I included in the program was as follows:

```
A MAN ENTERS, STOPS, AND TURNS DIRECTLY INTO THE CAMERA:

            MAN (to Camera)
    L.A. is a place where that fellow you see
    coming out of Starbucks who looks just like
    George Clooney…is George Clooney!

THE MAN TURNS AND EXITS.
```

It's a cute joke. Nothing special. But just tuck it away for now. We'll come back to it later.

Kids, as you know, the full title of this book is *Name-Dropping: My Life in Hollywood Among Celebrities Who Won't Remember Me!*, and I have no doubt that this is true of George Clooney. I can't imagine that he would remember our time working together. But, what gives this chapter an unusual twist is that, in this particular instance, I didn't remember working with him, either!

As I mention elsewhere in the book, my time working on *The Golden Girls* was brief, since I was essentially just helping out at Witt-Thomas-Harris Productions in between other jobs. So, I don't remember a great deal about the actual episodes themselves. I can recall that, in one of the episodes I worked on, the girls were attempting to install a new toilet in their bathroom. But other than that, I don't remember much else about the episode storylines.

However, I do still receive (tiny) residuals checks from the show, and included with each (tiny) check is a ledger sheet listing each episode I worked on by its title. So, even though I don't remember too much about the episodes, I get these periodic reminders of their titles, and one of those episodes is titled, "To Catch a Neighbor."

A few months ago, I was watching TV, just channel surfing, when I scrolled to one of the cable channels that still carries the re-runs of *The Golden Girls*. The episode that was coming on next was listed by title: "To Catch a Neighbor." The guide channel also gave a brief description of the episode, which involved two police officers using the ladies' home as a base of operations to stake out some dealers of stolen gems who were passing themselves off as the "nice couple next door."

I recognized the title of the episode from one of my (tiny) residuals checks, and the brief episode description seemed to ring a familiar bell, so I thought, "Hey, why not? It'll be fun to watch. And since I don't really remember it, it will all be new to me."

So, I settled in to the couch to watch the show. A few minutes into the episode, the two police detectives made their first appearance on screen. Imagine my surprise when I realized that one of those detectives was George Clooney! I mean, how could I have forgotten spending a week with George Clooney? Granted, this was before "E.R." and before he became an international celebrity, but still! It's George Clooney!

George and veteran actor Joe Campanella played the detectives, with George in the role of Bobby Hopkins, the gung-ho junior partner to Joe's more experienced senior detective, Al Mullins. Bea Arthur[*] had a great time verbally sparring with Joe throughout the episode, as Dorothy develops a crush on Al, despite all of her denials and protestations to the other ladies. And Rue McClanahan[*] got a chance to display Blanche's rarely-seen maternal side with George's character of Bobby, worrying about the safety of the brash young detective from a mother's perspective.

As I watched the episode, everything did indeed begin to have a familiarity about it. Although I hadn't remembered any of the dialogue or the jokes, I did start to have recollections related to the work we all put in rehearsing and taping that episode: the cast and crew, the sets, the rehearsals and run-throughs for the producers, camera blocking, and finally taping in front of the audience. It all felt familiar as the episode played out. And sure enough, as the closing credits rolled,

---

[*] Bea Arthur and Rue McClanahan appear in the chapter devoted to *The Golden Girls*.

there was my name on the screen. It was "official." I'd spent a week with George Clooney!

Which brings me back to the story I related at the beginning of this chapter. About a year after I produced that sketch comedy show for my colleague's research study at Southern Illinois University, I was spending the summer in Los Angeles with some of my students. As the on-site intern coordinator for SIUC's "Hollywood Studies" internship program, each summer I would take between thirty and fifty students out to LA to work as interns within the industry. The students and I all lived in an apartment complex in Burbank, on a hill overlooking the Warner Brothers studio lot.

Because I was in LA for the summer, I had made arrangements to have lunch with a former colleague from SIUC who was now teaching at Pepperdine University in Malibu, where I had lived as a teen-ager.* Since I was lunching in Malibu, I thought I'd make a day of it, and drive out to visit the house in which I'd lived back in the 1960's and see if much had changed. Not much had.

So, after spending the morning out at Zuma Beach and Trancas Canyon, I drove back down the Pacific Coast Highway towards the Pepperdine campus and the famous "Malibu Colony," where many of the celebrities have homes. My buddy and I had arranged to meet at a restaurant in a shopping area on Cross Creek Road, near Pepperdine's campus. The enclave contained a number of restaurants and shops, and because I was about forty-five minutes early, I thought I'd pop into their Starbucks for a latte while I passed the time.

As I walked up to the Starbucks, I couldn't help but notice five brand new Indian motorcycles parked out front. Now, today, it's not uncommon to see people riding Indians. Polaris Industries, the company that makes snowmobiles and ATV's, obtained the rights to the brand, and has been successfully manufacturing and selling Indian motorcycles for a number of years now. But back around the turn of the century, an Indian motorcycle was 1) very hard to come by, and 2) prohibitively expensive. As a result, you were lucky if you saw one Indian motorcycle on the street, much less five of them all together in one place! The Indian motorcycle dealerships didn't even have that many on display in their

---

* *I discuss this in greater detail in the chapter devoted to Desi Arnaz and Lucille Ball.*

showrooms! And those five Indian motorcycles parked in front of Starbucks probably represented an investment of somewhere between $100,000 and $150,000 dollars!

As I stood next to the bikes, I asked myself, "Who on earth can afford these, and how on earth were they even able to get them?" As if on cue, the door of the Starbucks opened, and out walked George Clooney, accompanied by four of his buddies. They were all decked out in riding leathers and carrying helmets. As he approached, we made eye contact, and I just shrugged, grinned, and said to him, "Well, George, I just got the answer to my question about who on earth could manage to score five brand new Indian motorcycles!" He just laughed out loud, understanding my inference, straddled his bike, and buckled his helmet. "Have a nice ride," I said, and waved.

He waved back and said, "Thanks." And with that, they all fired up their bikes and rode off towards the Pacific Coast Highway.

And as I turned to go in and get my coffee, it suddenly hit me: that silly little comedy sketch I'd created back at the university! Who could have guessed that it would turn out to be so prophetic?! I was in Los Angeles, the place where the fellow coming out of the Starbucks who looked just like George Clooney really *was* George Clooney!

SUZANNE SOMERS
AND *SHE'S THE SHERIFF*

Doing a show with chimps in it?
Call Doug. He's your guy!...

I first encountered Suzanne Somers in 1980, on the set of the hit ABC sitcom *Three's Company*, in which she had been co-starring with John Ritter and Joyce DeWitt. Even though the show was broadcast on the ABC network, it was taped in front of a studio audience at CBS Television City. Back in 1978, *The Lawrence Welk Show* had also been taping at Television City, and during that time, I had made the acquaintance of Dave Powers, who was then directing *The Carol Burnett Show*. Dave was now the series director on *Three's Company*, and knowing that my ultimate career goal was to direct sitcoms, he graciously invited me to sit in on a camera rehearsal and show taping. And this is why I refer that first instance with Suzanne as an "encounter," because we never actually met face to face. She was down on stage, and I was merely observing from up in the TV control room.

At the time, Suzanne was in the middle of a nasty and very public salary dispute with the network. Four years into her five year contract, she was demanding that ABC renegotiate and increase her salary from $30,000 per episode to $150,000 per episode, plus ten percent ownership of the show's profits.* Despite Suzanne's popularity, ABC recognized that John Ritter was really the glue that held *Three's Company* together. Week in and week out, John "carried" the show with his charm, his impeccable timing, and his mastery of physical comedy. And Suzanne would never be able to shoulder that responsibility in her role as John's "bubble-headed blonde roommate."† So while Suzanne may have been the "media darling" at the time, she was not the star of *Three's Company*. That role clearly belonged to John Ritter.

As a negotiation tactic, Suzanne staged a "walkout," refusing to work with the rest of the cast. However, she was still contractually obligated to appear on the show. As a result, for the remainder of her contract, Suzanne's role on *Three's Company* was reduced to one minute per episode, and when the contract expired, she was fired from the show.

As I mentioned above, the ugly negotiations between Suzanne and ABC had been reported extensively on television, in magazines, and in newspapers, and had placed Suzanne in what appeared to be a tenuous position. Realizing that she was going to be let go from *Three's Company*, Suzanne had struck a tentative deal with CBS to star in a new sitcom pilot for them when her contract with ABC expired. But between all of the negative publicity surrounding her exit from *Three's Company* and executive changes at CBS, that pilot project was scrapped.

When she was co-starring on *Three's Company*, Suzanne Somers seemed to be everywhere. But the massive cloud of media coverage that she had built up through her exposure on the sitcom all but evaporated once she walked off the show. It certainly appeared as though the television industry wanted nothing more to do with her. No new series

---

* *Accounting for inflation, her salary demand would be the equivalent of insisting on a raise from $93,000 dollars per episode to $466,000 dollars per episode today.*
† *For comedic contrast to Suzanne's character, actress Joyce DeWitt played the "smart brunette" roommate.*

offers. Not even any "guest star" roles on other shows such as *Knight Rider*, *Magnum, P.I.*, or *The Fall Guy*. She'd simply disappeared from the TV landscape.

By 1982, it appeared as though Suzanne Somers was done with television, and television was done with her. After several years, she re-emerged in Las Vegas with a nightclub act.

Flash forward five years to 1987:

I was once again working for Tony Thomas of Witt-Thomas-Harris on the TV sitcom *One Big Family*, and we were nearing the end of production of our first (and what would turn out to be our only) season. *One Big Family* was what was known as a "first run syndication" TV sitcom. During the 1980's, the FCC had begun to relax some of its rules regarding program ownership and syndication. It's all fairly complicated, and the explanation would read like a textbook, so there's no reason to bore you with the details. The upshot is that as a result of this relaxation of the rules, new networks such as FOX, the WB, and UPN were being created, along with the production of new "first run syndication" programs.

Because the rules were changing, networks and production companies were betting that there could be a lucrative market for new original sitcoms in the daily time slot known as "fringe time." Basically "fringe time" refers to the block of time that falls after the evening news but before prime time. Usually "fringe time" is between 7:00-8:00 p.m. EST *(6:00-7:00 p.m. CST)*. For years, this time slot had been the province of game shows, TV news magazines, and network re-runs.

Historically "fringe time" has been an absolute gold mine for syndicated re-runs of network sitcoms such as *The Brady Bunch*, *Gilligan's Island*, *The Cosby Show*, *Friends*, and *Seinfeld*. Re-runs of network sitcoms can trace their roots all the way back to *I Love Lucy*.* But the mid 1980's gave rise to "first run syndication" sitcoms that were not re-runs, but were instead new original programs, such as *Small Wonder*, *Out of This World*, and *Harry and the Hendersons*. These sitcoms were created specifically to be sold through syndication to TV stations and affiliates around the country to be aired in "fringe time." *One Big Family* was just such a program.

---

* *Refer to the chapter on Desi Arnaz and Lucille Ball.*

And because these shows weren't broadcast in prime time, their budgets were substantially lower than their network counterparts. But production of these low-budget shows still meant a lot of new jobs, and the professional guilds within the industry wanted to make sure that those jobs went to their union members. Therefore, The Screen Actors Guild, The Writers Guild of America, and The Directors Guild of America all came up with a "first run syndication" pay scale that was much lower than their network prime-time rates to ensure that the producers of these programs would hire union talent.

Now by this point in my career, I had years of sitcom experience under my belt, but it was mostly as an associate director. When it came to actually directing sitcoms, I was still basically a "newbie." When the Directors Guild of America offered producers a reduced "first run syndication" rate for directors, it turned out to be a real blessing for me.

The rate for directing a half-hour sitcom for syndication in "fringe time" was only one third of the standard network rate for directing a prime-time sitcom. But no matter whether it airs in "fringe time" or prime-time, the amount of effort and skill that is required to direct a half-hour sitcom is the same.* As a result, most of the established sitcom directors were unwilling to work for two-thirds less than what they were currently earning. And that created opportunities for "newbies" such as me. I was only too happy to work for a third of what an established director would make to gain some much needed experience and to start establishing myself as a sitcom director.

As I mentioned earlier, Witt-Thomas-Harris Productions was producing *One Big Family,* and I had worked for Tony Thomas and his partner Paul Witt as the associate director on *Benson, Condo, The Golden Girls,* and a number of TV pilots. The star of *One Big Family* was Danny Thomas, who was himself a ground-breaking pioneer of television sitcoms.† He was also Tony's father. Now I'd like to think that Tony asked me to work with his dad because I had earned his trust and respect through our long professional association. That's what I'd *like* to think. However, I do recall a production meeting with Tony at his

---

* *Syndicated sitcoms sometimes require more effort and skill, since you're usually working with far less experienced writers, cast and crew members.*
† *Refer to the chapter on Danny Thomas.*

office just prior to the start of work on *One Big Family*. At one point during the meeting, Tony put his arm around my shoulder, grinned, and said, "Doug, this is my dad we're talking about here. So don't f*#@ it up." So there's a very good chance that the reduced director's rate from the union played a major part in his decision to hire me.

During one of the episodes I was directing, Tony came down to the set with an old friend of his, a producer named David Goldsmith. After introducing us, Tony said that David was producing his own first-run syndication sitcom titled *She's the Sheriff* over at MGM. Tony asked me if I would mind if David spent some time with us observing how we put our show together.*

So David hung out with us on the set, observing me as we rehearsed the various scenes in the show. He came back later for our camera rehearsal and sat in the control room as we put each scene on camera. I guess he liked my work, because towards the end of the camera rehearsal David offered me a "three episode deal" to direct three episodes of *She's the Sheriff*.

I immediately jumped at his offer with an enthusiastic "Yes!" During our very brief "handshake negotiations," David mentioned that the star of the show was Suzanne Somers. "She's pretty anxious about it," he confided. "She's been out of television for years, and she's hoping that this will be her way back in." And so almost ten years after observing her on the set of *Three's Company*, I was about to be directing a television series starring Suzanne Somers.

Interestingly enough, it turns out that Suzanne Somers was not the first choice to star in *She's the Sheriff*. Nor was she the second. Or the third. She was actually the fourth choice. It took *She's the Sheriff* five years from the time the pilot script had first been commissioned to finally receive the "green light" for broadcast. And during that time, three other actresses would be cast in the lead role of the sheriff before the part finally went to Suzanne.

The program originally began in 1982 as a pilot project for CBS (just one year after Suzanne left Three's Company), but under the title

---

* It is standard industry etiquette to obtain the director's permission to bring a visitor onto the set.

Cass Malloy. The pilot told the story of Cass Malloy, the widow of a recently-deceased sheriff who assumed her late husband's official duties for the remainder of his term, and the challenges she faced as a woman in a predominantly male environment. The creators of the show, Dan Guntzelman and Steve Marshall, originally cast Annie Potts in the leading role of Sheriff Cass Malloy.[*] But Annie departed from the project early in the development process.

Annie Potts' replacement was Caroline McWilliams, the lovely and talented actress I'd gotten to know when we worked together on the ABC sitcom *Benson*.[†] CBS actually commissioned a pilot of *Cass Malloy* with Caroline playing the title character, but the pilot episode didn't perform up to the network's expectations during audience testing, so they decided not to pick it up as a series. At this point Marshall and Guntzelman moved on with their careers, finding success as producers of the sitcom *Growing Pains* for ABC.

But with an ever-increasing market for "fringe time" programs, the two creators decided to revive their *Cass Malloy* project with a new title, *She's the Sheriff*. Lorimar-Telepictures liked the concept and offered them a series deal. The character of Cass Malloy was re-named Hildy Granger, and the setting of the show was moved from Burr County, Indiana, to Lakes County, Nevada. But other than a few minor changes, it was essentially the same show that Marshall and Guntzelman had developed for CBS five years earlier.

This time around, Priscilla Barnes was cast in the lead role, which would turn out to be somewhat ironic. Barnes had originally auditioned for the part of Chrissy Snow on *Three's Company* but lost out to Suzanne Somers. But when Suzanne left *Three's Company*, the producers cast Barnes as a new third roommate Teri Alden, thereby filling the void created by Suzanne's departure. Barnes would remain with *Three's Company* for the rest of its successful run, while Suzanne essentially disappeared from television.

---

[*] *Annie would have great success in the film Ghostbusters and in the hit TV sitcom Designing Women. She is currently starring as Sheldon Cooper's "Meemaw" in the Big Bang Theory spinoff Young Sheldon.*

[†] *More on Caroline McWilliams in the chapter on John Rich.*

But at some point, and for reasons that are unknown to me, Priscilla Barnes and *She's the Sheriff* parted ways. And in another ironic twist, Suzanne Somers, the actress who beat out Barnes for the part of Chrissy Snow, only to have Barnes replace her on *Three's Company*, was now replacing Barnes as Hildy Granger in *She's the Sheriff*. It was a classic example of the "Hollywood Merry-Go-Round!"

....

It was a Friday afternoon, and I was walking across the studio lot at MGM in Culver City to meet with the producers of *She's the Sheriff*. I was to begin my first episode on the following Monday. On Thursday, I had received a copy of my first script and the set design blueprints so that I could create a workable plan to coordinate all of the various production elements that the script required. It's a pretty standard practice for the director to meet with the producers a day or so prior to the week of production, and this is usually where a number of production issues are ironed out. The title of my first episode was "Monkey Business," which turned out to be both prophetic and a major understatement.

In the script, written by Mark Miller and Executive Producer Mark Rothman, a second-rate chimp trainer named Frankie Fontaine is driving with his chimp act to perform at a Lake Tahoe casino. However, one of the deputies pulls Frankie over for drunk driving, and he and his chimps are brought into the sheriff's office. Frankie is placed in a holding cell to await arraignment, but the local animal shelter informs the deputies that they have no room in which to house all of Frankie's chimps. Therefore, the decision is made to keep the chimps at the jail. The five chimpanzees quickly run amok, with hilarious mayhem to ensue (at least in the minds of the two writers!).

I knew that executive producer Mark Rothman and co-producer Marty Nadler had both worked on *Laverne and Shirley*, and therefore were very experienced in broad, physical comedy. But this script would be a real challenge, because almost all of the physical comedy in the episode had been written for the chimps rather than the actors. On practically every page of the script, Suzanne and the rest of the cast were simply reacting to something that the chimps were doing. So while I may have been a "newbie" at directing, the years I'd spent working on variety shows had provided me with a significant amount of experience in the potential pitfalls that can occur when dealing with performing animals.

Our meeting took place in the writer's room in the show's suite of offices. Sitting down at the writer's table with Mark Miller, Mark Rothman, David Goldsmith, and Marty Nadler, I pulled out my script. I had "dog eared" the pages on which I had questions, which in this case was practically every page.

"Okay," I said. "Let's just jump right in. By my count, there are five chimps. Is this correct?" They confirmed that it was. "Now, are these five chimps a self-contained act? In other words, are they used to being around each other and working as a unit?"

"Uh…no," Mark Rothman said. "We booked five separate chimps that work with five different trainers."

This was not what I'd been hoping to hear. "Sightlines" are crucial when working with animals on a set. The trainer must be directly within the animal's line of sight at all times in order to maintain control, and to cue the animal to perform the learned behavior at the appropriate time in the scene. So the trainer must be positioned on the stage so that he or she is standing directly behind the actor, over his shoulder and just out of the camera shot. That way when the animal looks at the trainer, it will appear on camera that he's looking directly at the actor he's supposed to be interacting with. And with four television cameras, two boom microphones and a stage crew all sharing space with the actors, it's hard enough to find a place for *one* trainer, much less five.

"Are you aware," I went on, "that when grouped together, chimps often try to create a hierarchy, and that sometimes one chimp may try to physically assert his dominance over another if he perceives that other chimp as a threat?"

Marty Nadler just looked at me for a beat, blinking. Finally, he said, "And by 'physically assert' you mean…?"

"Attack," I replied. "And I wouldn't want to be the actor standing in between them if it happens," I added, letting it sink in for a second or two. "Okay, so you have these five chimps doing all kinds of behaviors such as typing on a typewriter, answering phones, handing Suzanne her hat, and hog-tying the deputy in a cell. Did you write these gags into the script after talking to the trainers? In other words, are these behaviors ones that the chimps already know how to perform?"

"Oh, no," Mark Miller said. "We just wrote a bunch of stuff for the chimps that we thought would be funny. We have no idea if they can actually do any of it."

"But we *have* spoken to the trainers," Rothman quickly added, as if to try and reassure me. "And we decided to give each trainer one specific thing for his chimp to do. So you know, chimp A types on the typewriter, chimp B answers the phone, chimp C ties up the deputy, etc."

I also wanted to know if Suzanne had read the script, and if she was okay with it. Some actors are very uncomfortable working around animals, especially "non-domestic" animals that are quite strong and potentially dangerous. However, the four of them assured me that Suzanne had read the script and was not concerned about working with the chimps. Then David Goldsmith added, "And Bobby Costanzo, who we've cast to play Frankie Fontaine, is okay with it as well."

David's remark brought up my next question. When a director is hired to work on an episode of a series, he or she is supposed to be brought in to help cast the guest actors who will be appearing in that particular episode. But veteran character actor Bob Costanzo had already been cast as Frankie Fontaine before I was even signed to direct the episode. I'd never worked with Bob on a show, but I was familiar with his work, and I had no doubts that he fit the part of the somewhat shabby, badly hungover chimp trainer. But still the question still lingered regarding why he had already been cast without my input.

"Bob's a great choice," I said to David. "And he'll make an excellent Frankie Fontaine. But I'm curious as to how I 'inherited' him as a guest actor."

At that point, the four of them exchanged sideways glances. "Well, you see, Doug," David said, "it's like this. Um…someone else was originally supposed to direct this episode, and he was the one who cast Bob."

"I see. And this director is no longer available?"

"Uh, no," Mark Rothman said. "He, uh…he left."

"Rather abruptly," Marty Nadler added.

I looked at the four of them, just sitting there. In that awkward silence, I began to understand just how deep the hole was that I had so eagerly jumped into. "I see," I said finally. "So I'm replacing this other fellow. Would I be safe in assuming that you looked at other directors before offering the episode to me?"

"Oh, yes!" Marty Nadler said cheerfully. "We probably sent this script to a dozen directors we knew!"

I already knew the answer to my next question, but I asked it anyway. "So I got the job because…"

"…They all turned us down!" Mark Rothman chimed in. "You're the only one who was willing to take on a show with Suzanne Somers and a bunch of chimps!"

Well, I wanted to establish myself as a director and gain some much-needed experience, right? Be careful what you wish for…

"Are you going to yell and scream at us?" The question had come from actor Lou Richards. I was at the craft service table on the set of *She's the Sheriff*, getting a cup of coffee with several of the cast members before starting my first day of work. Lou played the lovable but not-too-bright Deputy Putnam in the series.

"Absolutely not," I replied. "Why would you ask that?"

Actor Guich Koock, who played Deputy Mulcahy, grabbed a donut from the box on the table and said, "Because the last guy yelled at us. A lot! And he threw stuff at us!"

"Yeah," added Leonard Lightfoot, who played Deputy Wiggins. "The guy chucked a metal wastebasket at my head!" Veteran actor George Wyner, who played the scheming deputy Max Rubin, had drifted over to our little "coffee klatch." He confirmed that for the past few weeks, the mood on set of *She's the Sheriff* had been uneasy and tense. And since I was the "new guy" coming in to direct, coupled with the fact that no one in the cast had ever even heard of me, they were all understandably apprehensive.

I looked over across the stage at Suzanne, who was standing with the producers. She was smiling, laughing, and making small talk with them about what they'd done over the weekend. I was guessing that my predecessor had most likely never chucked a wastebasket at *her* head. Then again, maybe he had. Perhaps that's why he had departed "rather abruptly" to use Marty Nadler's words.

When I had walked onto the *She's the Sheriff* soundstage five minutes earlier, I'd been thinking that my biggest problem would be the chimps. It's funny how sometimes it only takes a few minutes to discover just how wrong you can be.

Usually, the first item of business is the "table read," in which the cast will sit around a portable banquet table in front of the set and read through the script along with the director, producers, and writers. However, in light of the concerns voiced by the cast, I informed the producers that I needed a few moments for a quick "huddle" with the regular cast members prior to beginning the day's work.

I gathered the cast into the sheriff's office set and quietly said to them, "It's come to my attention that some of you have been treated in a very disrespectful and unprofessional manner. And if that is the case, I apologize for what another director has put you through. Any kind of abusive behavior is inexcusable. And I know we've just met, but I promise you I don't work that way. I don't yell, I don't scream, and I certainly don't throw things. You can't do your best work if there's fear or tension in the air. You don't even know me, so it's understandable that you would have no reason to trust me. I get that. All I'm asking is that you keep an open mind, give me the benefit of the doubt, and hopefully I'll earn your trust." Thankfully, they agreed that they would.

As the "huddle" broke, and we all began to walk back over to the table for the read through, Suzanne pulled me aside and escorted me to a more private area of the set. She thanked me for my efforts to put the cast at ease, and then said, "Oh, and Doug, I do have one small request."

"Okay," I said. "What is it?"

"When you're blocking us in the scenes, I'd appreciate it if you would arrange it so that I am on the stage left side of the set whenever possible."

Before I could ask her why, she pre-empted my question.

"The left side of my face is my 'good' side. I photograph much better from that side. So when you're staging the scenes, see if you can work out the blocking so that I'm standing stage left. Then my 'good' side will be facing the audience and the cameras."

"I'll do my best," I said. "But you know—" Again she pre-empted me.

"Oh, I know you won't always be able to. But I'd prefer to be stage left whenever possible, okay? Oh, and try to do it a way that's not too obvious in front of the rest of the cast. It's a 'vanity' thing, I know. But I'd appreciate it." And with that, she flashed me her big, toothy Suzanne Somers grin and headed over to the table for the read through.

Standing in the middle of the sheriff's office set, I took a quick look around as if to get my bearings. I had five chimpanzees of various sizes and ages sitting in caged enclosures scattered around the soundstage, each chimp strategically spaced a safe distance from the others. I had five chimp trainers huddled in a far corner, discussing traffic patterns, "sight lines" and safety. At the read through table, I had a cast that was on edge, having suffered a fair amount of abuse from a director who preceded me. And I had a star that wanted me to position the rest of the cast (including the chimps) in such a way that I would be photographing her from her "good" side. And this was all in the first twenty minutes! It was going to be an interesting week...

The first day of rehearsal was a series of small successes surrounded by major setbacks. On the plus side of things, the cast and I were getting along quite well. The morning's rehearsal had been difficult, to say the least. But I think the cast members were starting to realize that I was doing my best to be a facilitator and help them work through all of the problems with humor and understanding. When something would go wrong on the set, rather than lose my temper, I would just laugh at the situation and make a wisecrack along the lines of, "Well I certainly didn't see *that* coming!" And gradually I could sense the mood on the set was beginning to lighten up. The cast began to relax and enjoy the process, no longer worried about being verbally (or physically) attacked for some mistake or miscue. I was encouraged by the growing sense of camaraderie.

On the minus side, however...were the chimps. My earlier concerns about placing five strange chimps in a set together were proving to be valid. If I had to describe that morning's rehearsal in one word, that word would be "mayhem." Each chimp was nervous around the others, making it difficult for them to stay focused on their individual trainers. The trainers were having their own issues, each trying to find a suitable spot from which they could maintain proper sight lines with their chimps.

At one point, there was a clash for domination between two of the chimps. Fortunately, no actors had been standing near them when it happened, and I immediately called for the cast to clear the set. As the actors ran *off* the set, the trainers ran *onto* it. As they ran in, the trainer of the larger, more aggressive chimp unclipped a large key ring from his belt and hurled it just as hard as he could directly at his chimp's head. There had to have been at least twenty-five keys on that keyring, making it quite heavy.

The large chimp yelped as that ring full of keys bounced off his skull, and he quickly retreated back to his original position, cowering as his trainer approached. The trainer turned to me, smiled, and said, "First you have to get his attention." I was shocked by this, but he assured me that the chimp had not been harmed in any way. I wasn't altogether sure I believed him. But I noticed later that any time his chimp lost focus, all that trainer had to do was rattle his keyring and the chimp would snap to attention, taking a submissive posture.

After lunch it was more of the same. The trainers did their best to coax the behaviors from their chimps, with mixed results at best. And I did my best to choreograph the insanity so that it made some kind of sense, all the while trying to place Suzanne Somers on the stage left side of the set so that the cameras would shoot her good side, also with mixed results. Sometimes it was easy to maneuver her to stage left. Other times it was a bit of a stretch to figure out how to get her there and still make sense of the scene. But at the end of the day, Suzanne seemed satisfied, and if the other cast members were aware of what I was doing, they were gracious enough to keep it to themselves.

But working with the chimps was like trying to wade through knee-deep mud. At the end of rehearsal on Monday, we had only accomplished about half of what was needed to stay on schedule. And I was very concerned about the possibility of a repeat of the "keyring discipline" taking place in front of a shocked studio audience. By and large, the cast had spent the day making small adjustments to what they were doing to try and accommodate the chimps. But our attempts to coax the scripted behaviors from the chimps was inconsistent at best. And when they *did* manage to perform the correct behavior, it would often be at the wrong time, making it all but impossible for the actors to play out the scenes as written. By the end of Monday's rehearsal, it was obvious to me that the normal production approach for a multi-camera sitcom was simply not going to work.

I had a plan, but it would require a major concession from the producers. So after the rehearsal I went up to their office. Mark Rothman was there, along with Marty Nadler and David Goldsmith. I told them, "If we're going to pull this off, we need to shoot it film-style, without an audience."

Multi-camera sitcoms spend three days rehearsing, one day camera blocking and one day shooting with an audience.* And they shoot in chronological order like a play, so that the studio audience is able to follow the story from beginning to end. But if we were to cancel the audience, then instead of simply rehearsing with the cameras on day four, we could actually start filming with them, which would give us all of day four and day five to film the entire show. And since the full crew would be there on days four and five anyway, no significant extra expense would be incurred. That was my plan.

"That's your f*&%ing plan?" Mark Rothman sputtered. "Tell the audience to stay home?" Okay, I'll admit his response wasn't as supportive as I might have hoped, but to be fair I did just kind of spring it on him. He was still sputtering. "Just who do you think you are, kid? You're here for one day, and you have the nerve to come into my office and tell us how we should shoot our show?"

"Just this episode," I countered. I gave them a quick synopsis as to how difficult Monday's rehearsal had been. Then I laid out my plan. "We'll use the 'block and tape' method. It's our only shot at getting what you want from the chimps. We'll rehearse a scene with the cast in full makeup and wardrobe, and as soon as the chimps master the behaviors for that scene, we'll immediately videotape it. Then we'll move on to the next scene, and the next, rehearsing and taping until

---

* This process is described in greater detail in the chapter on *The Golden Girls*.

we have them all. I've done it dozens of times on other shows, so I know it will work."

After that, I stressed that because we already had a full crew scheduled for Thursday and Friday, the cost would be the same. The only major difference is that we would need to bring in a "sweetener" to add a laugh track to the show during post-production to make up for the lack of a live audience.* "Trust me," I added. "If you make an audience sit through what we just went through, they won't be laughing anyway, and you'll still have to add a laugh track."

Nobody was saying anything. So I figured I might as well keep going. "Look, I realize I'm only here because everybody else turned you down. I get that. I'm the schmuck. But in this case, I'm a schmuck who knows what he's doing. And I'm telling you, if you want this show completed on schedule, this is how we do it."

"Well, if you think I'm going to cancel the audience on your word alone, you're crazy!" Mark Rothman growled. "It'll take a lot more than that to convince me."

"Okay," I replied. "How about this? Just come down to the stage tomorrow morning during rehearsal and see for yourself. And if you're not convinced that I'm right, then you can call me the schmuck who cried 'wolf' in front of the entire cast." Mark was still fuming but agreed to leave it at that. It only took one day on *She's the Sheriff* for me to put my neck on the chopping block.

We'd been rehearsing for about an hour on Tuesday morning when Mark Rothman, David Goldsmith, Marty Nadler, and Mark Miller showed up on the set to observe the rehearsal. We were just about to rehearse a bit of business involving one of the younger chimps sitting by the front door of the sheriff's station. The script called for the chimp to hand Suzanne her hat on her way out the door then attempt to "escape" by taking her hand and escorting her out. Suzanne would then escort the chimp right back inside with the admonition, "Nice try, shorty." It was one of the simplest of the gags they had written for the chimps and would comprise only about fifteen seconds of the thirty-minute episode.

---

* *The most famous of these was Charley Douglass, an audio engineer and pioneering "sweetener" who invented his own proprietary and technically sophisticated "laff box."*

The cast took their places in the scene, and the trainers placed the chimpanzees on their marks. I told the producers, "We're not going to run the entire scene for you. We're just going to do the bit with Suzanne's exit." And with that I called, "Action."

Suzanne crossed over to the door, but the chimp failed to pick up her cap. We stopped and re-set. On my cue, Suzanne crossed over to the door once again. This time the chimp picked up the cap but dropped it on the floor before Suzanne had reached him. So again, we stopped and re-set. Another miscue. We stopped and re-set. Another miscue. And another. And another. It went on like that for over a half hour. All for just fifteen seconds of the show. We never did get it right. The chimp's trainer was both frustrated and apologetic. Suzanne was just frustrated.

I turned to the producers and noticed that the color had drained from Mark Rothman's face. "Would you like me to re-set and try it one more time?" I asked.

"No," he replied. "That's the scariest thing I've ever seen. Doug, I'm sorry I doubted you. We'll cancel the audience immediately." And with that, they left.

So we shot "Monkey Business" without a studio audience. Since we were no longer obligated to shoot the show in chronological order, we determined that it would be best to videotape all of the scenes involving the chimpanzees on Thursday. This would make Friday a much easier day, since the stress of working with the chimps would be behind us. The plan worked, and by shooting the chimpanzees' behaviors immediately after rehearsing them, we were able to successfully capture all of the "chimp gags" that had been written into the script on Thursday.

With the chimps no longer on the set, shooting the remaining scenes on Friday was like a breath of fresh air. As a result, we finished "Monkey Business" on schedule and within the budget. My first episode of *She's the Sheriff* was "in the can." Chalk one up for the newbie!

The following week, I spent Monday through Thursday on the soundstage rehearsing my second episode of *She's the Sheriff*. But at the end of rehearsal each day, I would hustle across the MGM lot to the post-production department to work on my "director's cut" edit of "Monkey Business." Each day while I was on the set rehearsing, the editors would work diligently to try to make sense of all of the scenes we had recorded out of order a week earlier. And after rehearsal on Monday through Thursday, I would join them in the edit suite to screen their day's work, make notes and offer suggestions for ways to make improvements.

Editors in Hollywood have a saying…"polishing the turd." The phrase is a cynically humorous euphemism to describe the process of applying all of your editorial skills to put a slick veneer on a movie or television show that is an absolute stinker. The idea behind it is that if a show looks slick and polished visually, then maybe people won't notice the poor quality of its content. And on "Monkey Business," we employed all of our combined skills and expertise to make that episode gleam and shine. But the fact remains that no matter how much polish you apply to a turd, underneath that shine is something that is a stinker. And "Monkey Business" was a stinker.

The producers held a regularly scheduled screening every Friday morning, at which they would get their first look at the edited version of the episode shot the previous week. So at 9:00 a.m. on Friday morning, I met Mark Rothman, Marty Nadler, David Goldsmith, and Mark Miller in the show's edit suite to screen the edited version of "Monkey Business." They had not been on the set during the filming, using that time instead to work on future episodes. The producers usually attended the audience taping on Friday nights. But since we had cancelled the audience taping, they were literally seeing the assembled show for the very first time. Therefore, they basically had no knowledge of what we had actually been able to capture on videotape. I was apprehensive to say the least, although I tried not to let it show.

Once they had all taken their seats, I asked the editor to play our assembled version, displaying it on the large "program" monitor screen in the edit suite. As the show played out on the screen, it was as if there were two alternate realities existing in that room. The things I saw that made me cringe were actually making them laugh! The four of them chuckled, hooted, and guffawed all the way through the episode! What was happening here?

A half-hour later, as the closing credits rolled, Mark Miller said, "Doug, I can't believe it! You managed to get the chimps to do everything we'd asked for in the script!" Mark Rothman chimed in enthusiastically. "I'd have been thrilled if you'd only gotten half! This episode has turned out *way* better than I ever thought it would! This is great! I wouldn't change a thing!"

David Goldsmith patted me on the shoulder and said, "I guess we got the right guy to work with the chimps after all!" To me it was just confirmation that people really do see what they want to see. Apparently, they all saw a well-crafted, well-executed, hilarious episode of *She's the Sheriff*. I saw a very shiny turd.

Later that Friday, I shot my second episode of *She's the Sheriff* in front of a live audience, and it went off without a hitch. The cast, crew, and production staff went home happy. But to be perfectly honest, I can't even remember the episode. I had been so focused on trying to make "Monkey Business" work, that the details of that second episode elude me to this day. From a production standpoint, it was far less challenging than working with the chimpanzees. I just kept making sure that Suzanne was stage left, that the rest of the blocking all worked, and that all of the camera shots came up on time and in focus.

My third episode was titled "Max Moves In," and I have to admit, I was enjoying this episode. The story involved George Wyner's character, Deputy Max Rubin, falling victim to a con man and losing everything, including his home. To win a bet with the other deputies that she can get the ungrateful and self-centered Max to say "thank you," Sheriff Hildy offers to let him move into her home until he's back on his feet. To Hildy's dismay, not only does Max never say "thank you," but also he becomes a demanding and obnoxious houseguest she can't get rid of.

Rehearsals for the episode had been going smoothly. The apprehension I had originally encountered from the cast had seemed to have completely dissipated during the two weeks that we had been working together. It appeared to me that the actors were finally beginning to have fun with the process. And I was having a lot of fun with George Wyner as we worked through the various physical gags that he would be required to perform in the episode.

At noon on Wednesday, I was having lunch with Suzanne, along with several other members of the cast and some of the stage crew. It was very informal, and we were all just sitting around the folding banquet table on the set that was used for the cast read-throughs. Everyone was laughing and joking, and we were discussing a wide range of subjects. Suzanne regaled us with a story about a time she'd been trying to sell her house, but the potential buyer didn't just want the usual home inspection. Suzanne said the buyer wouldn't close on the house unless he would be allowed to bring in a "ghostbuster" to scan her home to certify that it wasn't haunted. It definitely was the kind of story that you usually only hear in southern California.

A few minutes later, someone at the table began to nostalgically reminisce about the drugs they had taken back in the 1960's, recounting some of the funny and embarrassing situations that had arisen as a result. Suzanne joined in enthusiastically, recalling some of the silly things she had done "under the influence" of various substances when she was younger. Then she turned to me and casually asked, "So Doug, what drugs did you do back in the 60's?"

"Oh, I've never done drugs, Suzanne," I replied.

She just looked at me for a beat, blinked, and then flashed that big toothy grin. "Oh, come on, Doug. It was the 1960's! And you were in a rock and roll band!" she laughed. "Are you really going to sit there and try to convince me that you've never done drugs?"

"It's the truth," I said. "I've never done drugs, Suzanne."

"Okay, maybe not hard drugs," she countered. "But you've smoked pot, right?"

"No," I replied. "Not even pot. I've never done any drugs."

She looked at me and blinked again. Then she laughed. "Wow! You're either putting one over on me, or you're just plain weird! Either way, I don't know if I'll ever be able to trust you again!" She laughed again, a loud and hearty laugh. Everyone else laughed as well, including me. I thought she was joking, and quickly forgot all about it. Big mistake.

At the end of rehearsal on Wednesday, I got a message from the stage PA saying that the producers wanted to meet with me before I left for the day. I was encouraged by this because I was in the process of successfully completing the third episode of my "three episode deal." I knew the producers had been happy with my work, so I was hoping that they were calling me up to their office to offer me more episodes to direct. I couldn't have been more wrong.

When I entered the office, there was no greeting or small talk. Mark Rothman simply said, "Doug, what the hell did you say to Suzanne?"

I was at a loss. "What are you talking about?" I asked.

"I got a call from Suzanne's husband this afternoon.* He told me that she's suddenly having some kind of 'crisis of confidence' with you as her director. For some reason she's decided that she can't trust you. What the hell happened between you two on the set today?"

"Nothing," I said. "It's been a great day. Rehearsals went smoothly, and we're all set for camera blocking."

"Did you and Suzanne get into some king of argument or disagreement?" David Goldsmith asked.

"No," I replied. "Like I said, it was a very good day. Everyone worked hard, but we were all having fun with it. There were no incidents, and I was under the impression that everyone went home happy."

"Well, Suzanne's not happy," Mark Rothman said.

Then suddenly it hit me. "Lunch!"

"Lunch?" David asked. "What are you talking about?"

I told them about our conversation at lunch, when Suzanne had asked me what drugs I'd used during the 60's, and that I had told her I'd never used drugs.

"You told Suzanne you never used drugs?" Marty Nadler said. "Why would you tell her that?"

"Uh, because it's the truth?" I countered. "Anyhow, when I told her I'd never done drugs, she just laughed and said she didn't think she could ever trust me again. I didn't think anything of it because I thought she was just joking."

"Apparently she wasn't," Mark Rothman said. "And as a result, we've decided not to pick up your option for additional episodes. I'm sorry, but you'll just finish out this week and that will be it."

And just like that, I was fired from *She's the Sheriff*. It hurt to be fired, even from a show that made TV Guide's list of the "Fifty Worst TV Shows of All Time." I called my agent and told him there wouldn't be any more episodes on *She's the Sheriff*. To my surprise, he said,

---

* *Suzanne Somers fired her first manager Jay Bernstein, who had made her a star. Her husband Alan Hamel, a former game show host and TV pitchman, took over the position of her full-time manager and remains so to this day*

"Good, because I just got you a multi-episode deal on the sitcom *It's A Living*." Welcome news indeed!

My last two days on the show were uneventful. Camera rehearsal went smoothly on Thursday, and the show taping on Friday drew big laughs from the studio audience. The way Suzanne treated me those last two days, you'd have thought I was her best friend. That's the way it works in Hollywood. You never see it coming. To your face it's all sweetness and smiles. But behind your back, they have a "black hat" operative doing their dirty work for them.* In this case, Suzanne's "black hat" was her husband/manager, Alan Hamel.

When we wrapped the show that Friday night, I thanked the crew and then gathered the cast, including Suzanne. I told them how much I had enjoyed working with them all and wished them well. And that was the last time I saw Suzanne Somers in person. To this day I have no idea if she had me fired because I told her I'd never done drugs, or if she had me fired for some other reason and was just using that as the convenient excuse. At the end of the day, it didn't really matter. My time on the show was at an end.

She's the Sheriff ran for two seasons and employed a number of different directors.

....

A few years later, just before Christmas, I ran into David Goldsmith while I was working at the Desilu Studios on Cahuenga Blvd in Hollywood.† Witt-Thomas-Harris Productions produced *Empty Nest*, *The Golden Girls* and *Blossom* at Desilu Cahuenga, and had thrown a combined Christmas party for all three shows on the studio lot.

It was fun for the casts and crews of the three sitcoms to have the chance to mix and mingle. Even though we all worked on the same lot,

---

* *For a more detailed explanation of the "black hat," please refer to the chapter devoted to Jerry Seinfeld.*
† *At that time, the Desilu Studios on Cahuenga Blvd in Hollywood had been sold and renamed the Ren-Mar Studios. In 2010, the studio was purchased by the Red Digital Cinema Camera Company, and renamed Red Studios Hollywood.*

our rigorous production schedules didn't allow much time for socializing, so we were all enjoying swapping "war stories" over holiday refreshments.

I was talking with several of my friends from *The Golden Girls* when David approached our group. He appeared to be genuinely happy to see me. He also appeared to be drunk. We shook hands and exchanged warm "hellos." Then he suddenly apologized to me for the way I'd been let go from *She's the Sheriff*. I didn't know if that was something he'd been carrying around all this time, or if it was just the liquor talking. Either way, it was a kind gesture.

He went on, as if he were trying to make up for the way I'd been treated by Suzanne. He turned to my friends, and patted me on the shoulder. "This guy here," he said, pointing at me with the drink in his hand, "This guy is the best chimp director in Hollywood…hands down." My friends just looked at me, trying not to laugh as David went on. "You got a show with chimps? Doug's your guy. Best chimp director in Hollywood."

I thanked David for his kind words and shook his hand once again. He patted me on the cheek, turned, and walked off, presumably in search of another drink. I turned back to my friends, one of whom just looked at me and said, "Wow!"

"I know," I replied. "Maybe I should have business cards made. Doug Smart – Best chimp director in Hollywood!" I never actually had those cards printed. Perhaps I'll save it for my tombstone…

14

JAMES EARL JONES

The night Darth Vader met the psychotic rabbit...

In late March of 1989, I had just finished my first season as the associate director on the *Golden Girls* spinoff series *Empty Nest*. I have been blessed to have had the opportunity to work with some of the legendary pioneers of the genre, from producers such as Desi Arnaz and Danny Thomas who helped create the multi-camera TV sitcom and give it form, to directors Jay Sandrich and John Rich, who skillfully brought it to life on the screen. And my first season on *Empty Nest* was no exception, as I had been given the opportunity to work alongside yet another "900 pound gorilla" and legendary sitcom director, Hal Cooper.*

As *Empty Nest* was winding down, the new TV pilot season was starting up, and it was then that I received a call from Henry Winkler's office. Henry and his partner Ann Daniel were producing a new sitcom

---

* *Hal Cooper's directing credits include such iconic sitcoms as Gilligan's Island, I Dream of Jeanie, The Mary Tyler Moore Show, The Brady Bunch, The Odd Couple, All in the Family, Sanford and Son, Maude, and many more.*

pilot for CBS starring the very talented young actress Ricki Lake, who was just coming off her starring role in the film *Hairspray*, and their company had signed Hal Cooper to direct the pilot. Coincidentally, it was going to be filmed on the very same soundstage at Paramount where I had worked for Henry a few years earlier as the associate director on *Mr. Sunshine*.[*] I had a good working relationship with Henry, and since I had also just finished a season working with Hal Cooper, I was offered the position of associate director on the pilot. As you might imagine, I immediately jumped at the chance to be able to work for Henry Winkler again!

The pilot was titled *Starting Now*. In the sitcom, Ricki Lake plays Ricki Ross, a young aspiring actress who is hoping for her big break while working behind-the-scenes as a production assistant on a children's TV show "Gossimer Glen." The star of "Gossimer Glen" is the diva actress Felicia Kent, a pixie-ish fairy godmother complete with a magic wand; her on-camera persona is reminiscent of "Glenda the Good Witch" from *The Wizard of Oz*. But whenever the director of "Gossimer Glen" yells "cut" and the cameras stop rolling, Felicia's *real* personality emerges, and "Glenda the Good Witch" suddenly morphs into the "Wicked Witch of the West."

Playing the part of the lovely but duplicitous Felicia Kent was Cecilia "Ceci" Hart. Ceci was a very talented award-winning Broadway actress who had worked for Henry previously as one of the co-stars of *Mr. Sunshine*. With her small, slight stature, light blonde hair, and big blue eyes, Ceci was the physical embodiment of a sweet, charming little pixie or fairy godmother. But whenever the script called for it, Ceci could "flip the switch" and play the self-absorbed, egotistical diva Felicia Kent with a delightfully wicked relish that was a joy to behold.

Ceci was also married to James Earl Jones. Yes, *that* James Earl Jones, the actor who has won Tony, Grammy, and Emmy awards; who has been awarded with an honorary Academy Award; and who received the Kennedy Center Honors. He has starred in iconic American films, such as *Dr. Strangelove*, *The Great White Hope*, *Coming to America*, *The Hunt for Red October*, and *Field of Dreams*. He was the voice of Mufasa in *The Lion King*. And although David Prowse may have worn the costume, for

---

[*] I discuss the ABC sitcom Mr. Sunshine in greater detail in the chapter dedicated to Henry Winkler.

generations of *Star Wars* fans around the world (myself included), James Earl Jones is, and always will be, Darth Vader. The media calls James Earl Jones "one of the greatest actors in American history."*

Ceci just called him "Jimmy."

One of the "running gags" that Pamela Ellis, Sally Lapiduss, and Sandy Veith, the creators of *Starting Now,* had come up with for their fictional children's show "Gossimer Glen" revolved around a bunny rabbit. In the script, the rabbit was an "animal actor" who was part of the regular cast of "Gossimer Glen." But the running gag was that this bunny was completely psychotic, and everyone who worked on "Gossimer Glen" was terrified of him.

The bunny character had been conceived and written so that the audience would never actually see it. The writers believed that if the studio audience couldn't *see* the rabbit, but could only *hear* it, then the mental images they would conjure up of this psychotic bunny would be much funnier than watching a real rabbit or rabbit puppet. The scene with the bunny was written so that it gave the studio audience the impression that the actors could actually see the rabbit through the open door of his "bunny house" on the set of "Gossimer Glen." The sounds coming from inside the bunny house, combined with the terrified reactions from the actors who could "see" the bunny, would produce a very funny mental image for the members of the studio audience.

The plan from the onset was to hire an actor to "voice" the rabbit. Now, it usually takes around eight days to rehearse and film a half-hour multi-camera sitcom pilot. And Henry, Ann, and producer George Sunga knew that there was no need to hire an actor for eight days just to sit around the set waiting to eventually stand at a microphone backstage and do "crazy rabbit voices" for a few seconds. Therefore, the decision was made to wait and hire an actor to "voice the rabbit" for just the last two days: camera rehearsal day and the actual show day with the studio audience present.

In the meantime, Henry Winkler asked me if I would be willing to voice the rabbit during rehearsals, so that the actors could work out the timing of the jokes, and so that the producers and writers could see how the bits that they'd conceived with the rabbit would actually

---

* *From an article in the Los Angeles Times newspaper.*

work in the show. I had subbed for "day players" during rehearsals and run-throughs dozens of times in the past, including on *Mr. Sunshine*. It was no big deal. I was merely providing the cast members someone to run their dialogue with until the real actor showed up. I told Henry, "Sure, no problem." So until camera rehearsal day, I was to play the part of the psychotic bunny.

In one of the scenes, Felicia Kent tells her crew on "Gossimer Glen" that the bunny's timing is off. Apparently, his blood sugar is low because he hasn't had his carrot, and she insists that he be fed immediately. Because everyone on the crew is terrified of the rabbit, the job of feeding the carrot to the bunny naturally falls to Ricki Ross, the lowly production assistant.

When it came time to rehearse that bit, I took my place at the "bunny microphone" behind the "Gossimer Glen" set. Our prop department had given me an actual carrot to chew at the microphone, so that the audience out front could hear the bunny devouring his carrot. The set had been constructed so that from my position behind it, I could see the actors through the small open door of the "bunny house."

The script called for Ricki to cautiously open the outer cage, and with great fear and trembling, extend the carrot into the open door of the bunny house. As the bunny, I would then take the carrot from her and pull it into the bunny house, while chewing on the other carrot very loudly directly into my microphone.

Everyone got set from the top of the scene, and Hal Cooper called "action." From my position behind the set, I could hear Ricki, Ceci, and the rest of the cast going through their dialogue in the scene. Eventually the moment arrived when Ricki was to open the cage to feed the rabbit. I could see her through the bunny door as she opened the outer cage and carefully extended the carrot towards me through the open door.

I grabbed the carrot violently, snarling into the microphone as I did. But rather than just pull the carrot into the house, I banged it against the sides, top, and bottom of the doorway, snarling some more. The green leafy top of the carrot was flapping around in the cage like a feather duster caught in a blender. Then "ZIP!" I quickly whisked it into the bunny house while simultaneously chewing, snarling, and making what I thought were maniacal "yummy" sounds into the microphone.

I don't know if Ricki Lake expected me to grab the carrot quite so violently or if she was simply acting "in the moment," but she let out a loud squeal and slammed the cage door shut. I could hear Hal Cooper and several other members of the cast and crew laughing out loud. When we finished the scene, Hal said to us, "That was great! Do it just like that at the producers run through this afternoon!"

So we did. At the end of the day when we ran through the show for the producers, Ricki and I simply repeated what we had done earlier. I did my bit with the carrot, and Ricki squealed and slammed the cage door. And the reaction was the same as before. The producers and writers all laughed out loud, confident that this bit was going to play very well in front of a studio audience on show day.

Fast-forward with me to Wednesday, two days before we would videotape the pilot in front of a live studio audience. On Thursday the "tech" crew would be coming in, and we would rehearse and refine all of the camera shots and audio cues for the show. And on Friday we would tape the show twice in front of two separate audiences; once at 5:00 p.m. and again at 7:30 p.m.*

We were on a break between scenes sometime after lunch on Wednesday when Henry Winkler, Hal Cooper, and George Sunga approached me on the set. George said, "Doug, let me ask you something. Do you have your actor's card?"

He was asking if I was a member of SAG, the Screen Actors Guild. Paramount, like all of the major studios in Hollywood, is a "union" lot. In order to work there on a film or television show, you must be a member of one of the industry's professional unions. As the associate director on *Starting Now*, I was working on the lot under a contractual agreement between Paramount and the DGA, the Directors Guild of America.

"I don't have a SAG card, George," I replied. "But I'm a member of AFTRA."† The three of them huddled quietly for a moment, speaking softly, and nodding their heads. Eventually somebody mumbled

---

* *I discuss the multi-camera sitcom production schedule in greater detail in the chapter devoted to the Golden Girls.*
† *AFTRA is the American Federation of Television and Radio Artists. Historically AFTRA represented "non- actors" in the industry such as announcers, radio personalities, TV game show hosts, singers, and journalists. In 2012 AFTRA merged with the Screen Actors Guild to create SAG-AFTRA.*

something to the effect of "that will work." George turned back to me and asked, "Are you current with your dues?"

"Yes, I'm paid in full," I said. "Why? What's this all about?"

Henry put his hand on my shoulder and smiled. "Well Doug, here's the thing. We've just spent the last few days auditioning at least a dozen actors to play the rabbit. And not one of them made us laugh the way you have in rehearsals."

"You're kidding," I said. "Not one?"

"Not one," Henry repeated. "It wasn't that they were bad. But they all just had a different take on it. The bottom line is, after watching all of them play the rabbit, we realized that we preferred the way you've been doing it. So after some discussion, everyone agreed that the best solution would simply be for you to play the rabbit in the show."

"Which is why I needed to make sure that we could hire you under a union contract," George added.

"So what do you say, Doug?" Henry asked. "Do you want to be our rabbit?"

This was an unexpected turn of events. As I said earlier, I had stood in for "day players" dozens of times in the past, so when Henry had asked me to stand in for the rabbit, it had never even crossed my mind that I might end up actually playing the part in front of the television cameras and the studio audience!

I turned to Hal Cooper, who anticipated my question before I could even ask it. "Doug, don't worry about the camera shots," he said. "I assured Henry that we can find a spot when you can slip out of the control room to go backstage to the microphone. Just make sure you get back to the booth as quickly as you can when the bit is over."

I'd really had fun doing the bit with Ricki in rehearsals. And between the three of them, they had worked out how I could do it in the show, so I thought, "Why not?" And just like that, I was suddenly the newest cast member of *Starting Now*, playing the part of the psycho-bunny!

During camera rehearsal on Thursday, Hal Cooper and I identified the spot in the scene when I could slip out of the director's booth, quickly make my way backstage to the "bunny microphone," do my bit with Ricki Lake, and quickly slip back into the control room to coordinate the camera coverage and call the stage cues for the rest of the show. We rehearsed it during camera blocking and again later that day during the camera dress rehearsal. Everything went off without a hitch.

We taped two shows on Friday, each with a fresh audience. The 5:00 p.m. taping, or "dress" show as it is usually known, went fairly well especially for a pilot episode, with only a few minor glitches (which is to be expected, especially on a TV pilot). The studio audience seemed to like both the concept of the show and the cast of characters. And most of the jokes seemed to score, including the "bunny" joke. There were just a few notes to be addressed during the dinner break while the new audience was being seated in the bleachers for the "air" show at 7:30 p.m.

Just before we were about to start taping the "air" show, I noticed Ceci Hart peeking out around the corner of the set. She was looking past the cameras and boom microphones towards the audience, who were settling into their seats for the taping. The cast members usually don't make an appearance in front of the audience until they are officially introduced at the beginning of the show, so I thought I'd better see if she needed any assistance.

"Is everything okay, Ceci?" I asked. "Do you need anything?"

"Oh, no," she replied, still scanning the audience. "Everything's fine. Jimmy's coming to the taping, so I had them reserve a seat for him. I just wanted to make sure that he found it." Then she pointed her finger towards the center of the audience. "Yep. There he is. See?"

I followed the direction of her finger across the soundstage floor and above the television cameras to the center of the audience. And there, on the aisle about four rows back, up just high enough to be able to see over the cameras and down into the set, sat Darth Vader himself, James Earl Jones.

"Okay, he's in his seat. I can stop worrying now," Ceci said.

"You were worried?" I asked.

She laughed and shot me a sideways glance. "Doug, you have no idea. Jimmy has the uncanny ability to get lost anywhere, at any time." Then she headed backstage to get a final touch up on her hair and makeup. I just stood there, looking across the studio at James Earl Jones out in the audience. I was having my own little private "Mel Brooks" moment, imagining Darth Vader getting lost on the Death

Star while trying to find the men's room (there *had* to be bathrooms on the Death Star, right?).

The "air" show went very well, and the 7:30 audience seemed to enjoy the show even more than the 5:00 audience had. After the show, we all gathered backstage for a "wrap" party. Everyone was feeling good about what we'd accomplished and were optimistic about the sitcom pilot's chances of getting picked up as a series by CBS when it would be shown to potential sponsors at the network's "up fronts" in May.[*]

I was at the refreshment table, eyeing the assortment of finger food when Ceci Hart came up, took my hand and said, "Come on, Doug. I want to introduce you to Jimmy." Ceci knew that I had been hoping to meet James Earl Jones ever since we worked together on *Mr. Sunshine*. But as luck would have it, the entire time we had been shooting that series in Los Angles, "Jimmy" had been in New York preparing for what would turn out to be his Tony-winning Broadway run in August Wilson's play *Fences*.[†] But that was all about to change, because now the adorable blonde pixie was leading me by the hand across the soundstage to meet her husband, Darth Vader himself!

Before I knew it, I was shaking hands with "one of the greatest actors in American history," trying not to embarrass myself as I stammered something vaguely resembling, "It's an honor to meet you, sir." I had barely managed to put a coherent sentence together when Ceci said, "By the way, Jimmy, Doug here is the one you've been asking about." It was like a scene out of a sitcom. I was in the middle of trying to figure out what to say next when my mind suddenly screeched to a halt. "Wait… What?" I thought. "Did she just say that James Earl Jones has been asking about *me*?"

---

[*] "Up fronts" are where the networks invite potential sponsors and advertising agencies to screen their new season of TV pilots, hoping to generate lucrative sponsorship deals. Traditionally the "up fronts" take place in May in New York City, where most of the advertising agencies are located.

[†] *Fences* also received a Tony award for Best Play and a Pulitzer Prize for Drama. The play enjoyed a revival on Broadway in 2010 starring Denzel Washington and Viola Davis. In 2016 it was adapted into a film, with Denzel Washington and Viola Davis reprising the roles they had played on Broadway.

Before I could even process that, Ceci turned to her husband and said, "In addition to being our associate director, Doug also played the part of the rabbit."

On hearing that, James Earl Jones broke into a smile that was just slightly less wide than the front grille of a '62 Buick. He pointed at me. "That was you?" he asked, his hands now gripping my shoulders.

I somehow managed to string together the words, "Uh, yes, sir, it was."

He grabbed my right hand with both of his. "Marvelous!" he grinned, as we shook hands for a second time. It was kind of surreal. I was looking directly into the beaming face of James Earl Jones, and I knew that he was speaking to me, because I could see his lips moving. But in my ears, all I could hear was Darth Vader saying, "Young man, that rabbit was inspired! I haven't laughed so hard at anything in a long, long time! Well done!" I really don't remember much after that. The rest of the evening is pretty much a blur.

Despite the enthusiastic reaction from the studio audience, the pilot episode of *Starting Now* was not picked up for production as a series when it was shown at the network "up fronts" that May. As a result, the show was relegated to that cavernous, mysterious vault of "unsold television pilots" that is rumored to exist somewhere in the bowels of Hollywood.

Ricki Lake went on to become a cast member on *China Beach*, a popular ABC drama set during the Vietnam War. She later hosted her own successful daytime talk show. Ceci Hart returned to New York, where she and James Earl Jones continued their careers in theater, on film, and on television. And I went back to *Empty Nest*, where I worked for the next six years until the show left the air after a long, successful run of 175 episodes.

Other than those few of us who were directly involved, I doubt that anyone even remembers *Starting Now*. By network standards, the project was a failure. But for me *Starting Now* will always hold a special place in my heart. Because on that night on a soundstage on the Paramount lot, Darth Vader met the psychotic rabbit. And the rabbit made him laugh.

15

DANNY THOMAS

"You should be ashamed of yourself, young man!"

A bronze statue of Danny Thomas stands in the "Hall of Fame Garden" at the Academy of Television Arts and Sciences in North Hollywood, California. The sculpture simply identifies Danny as a "performer." But I suspect that the Academy might just have easily placed the statue there to recognize his place in history as a producer of some of TV's most popular and beloved programs. Danny is in good company in that garden, nestled among statues of other television notables such as Walt Disney; Lucille Ball and Desi Arnaz; Rod Serling; Barbara Walters; and Ed Sullivan, just to name a few.

But there is also another statue of Danny Thomas you should know about. And this one's a long way from Hollywood. It's in Memphis, Tennessee. But here Danny is not surrounded by famous TV celebrities. He's surrounded by children, three to be exact. Flanking him on the right and left are a young boy and girl, looking up at him, reaching up to him, as if asking him for help. A third child, a toddler, is cradled in his arms. This sculpture is on the grounds of the St. Jude Children's

Research Hospital, facing the mausoleum in which Danny is buried. It was erected there to recognize Danny's place in history not just as the founder of the research hospital, but as a man who kept his promises, a man who believed in "paying it forward."

Danny Thomas will always have a special place in my heart. I felt as though I'd grown up with him, since he'd been an invited guest in our home every week on the TV in our living room. I admired him. I respected him. And when I worked with him, I called him "Pappy." But Danny Thomas was also the person responsible for my father taking away my TV privileges for two whole weeks when I was eleven years old, saying that Danny was "a bad influence" on me. But more on that later...

Danny, whose real name was Amos Muzyad Yaqoob Kairouz was born in Deerfield Michigan, one of ten children in a family of Maronite Christians who had immigrated there from Lebanon. By the time he was eight years old, the U.S. Census listed him under a more anglicized version of his name, "Amos Jacobs." He was confirmed in the Catholic Church by Samuel Stritch, the bishop of Toledo, Ohio. The bishop would remain his lifelong spiritual advisor. But more on that later as well...

After struggling early in his career, Amos eventually began to find work on the radio. But he quickly discovered that he could make much better money with a nightclub act. The problem was that his Catholic family would be less than thrilled if they discovered that their son Amos Jacobs was working in nightclubs. So Amos took the names of two of his brothers and came up with the stage name of Danny Thomas.

Danny began to make a name for himself on the radio, landing a supporting role on the popular radio comedy *The Bickersons* starring Don Ameche and Frances Langford. He later played the part of postman Jerry Dingle on *The Baby Snooks Show* starring the renowned comedienne Fanny Brice.[*] Before long, Danny had his own weekly 30-minute variety show, *The Danny Thomas Show*.

But it was through television that Danny Thomas became a household name. In 1953, his sitcom *Make Room for Daddy*, later re-

---

[*] *The life of comedienne Fanny Brice was the subject of the 1964 Broadway musical "Funny Girl" starring Barbra Streisand. In 1968 "Funny Girl" was made into a film, with Streisand winning the Oscar for Best Actress for her portrayal of Fanny Brice.*

named *The Danny Thomas Show,* began an astonishing 11-year run on TV. The show's success not only made Danny Thomas a bankable star in the fast-growing medium, but also afforded him a "ground floor opportunity" to become one of television's more successful producers.

With partners that included Sheldon Leonard and Aaron Spelling, Danny Thomas produced such iconic television programs as *The Andy Griffith Show*, *The Real McCoys*, *That Girl*, *The Mod Squad*, and *The Dick Van Dyke Show*. In fact, it can be argued that Mary Tyler Moore owed her career to Danny Thomas, as it was Danny who personally recommended that Carl Reiner take a look at her for the part of Laura Petrie on *The Dick Van Dyke Show*. Danny remembered her from among the twenty or so actresses who had been submitted for the part as "that girl with the three names."

I've taken the time to share this with you because it helps to provide the context for what follows in the chapter. But if I'm being perfectly honest, everything I've told you about Danny Thomas up to this point are things you could easily find out for yourself just by searching the Internet. Except, of course, the part about him getting me in trouble with my father when I was eleven. But more on that later...

I've mentioned elsewhere in this book that in 1986 I had been hired by Witt/Thomas Productions to work as both the associate director and director on *One Big Family*, a sitcom they were producing for first-run syndication.* By this time I had become a seasoned veteran as an associate director, having accrued more than a decade's worth of experience. But this would be my first real assignment as a director on a sitcom. And the star of *One Big Family* was none other than Danny Thomas. Not to mention that the show's executive producer (and my boss) was Tony Thomas, Danny's son.

In the show Danny plays Jake Hatton (perhaps "Jake" was a nod to "Amos Jacobs"), a semi-retired comedian who moves in with his nephew Don and his wife to help them raise Don's younger siblings after the death of their parents. *One Big Family* only ran one season, but for that one season I got to spend every day working with Danny Thomas. For that one season the eleven-year-old kid inside of me was living the dream.

---

* *I discuss this sitcom and the process of first-run syndication in greater detail in the chapter devoted to Suzanne Somers.*

As a matter of fact, "kid" was Danny's nickname for me, which I took to be a term of endearment. Looking back on it now, maybe it wasn't. Perhaps it was just Danny's way of not having to worry about keeping everyone's name straight. But during our time together on the set, I don't ever remember hearing him call anyone else "kid." And there was just a hint of something affectionate in the way he said it. So for that season at least, I claimed "kid" as his nickname for me. In return I called him "Pappy." He is the only one I've ever called "Pappy," that season or any other. For me it was definitely a term of endearment.

All season long we had a standing lunch date. And it was always at the same place, which was the prop room on the soundstage. From my perspective, Danny was a study in contrasts. When it came to other people, his generosity often seemed boundless. But when it came to spending money on himself, he preferred things "on the cheap." And our lunch dates were definitely "on the cheap." The prop room on the set of a TV series is equipped with a complete kitchen, which is always stocked with food paid for out of the show's budget. So every day, while the other members of the cast and crew would go "off the lot" and have lunch at any one of the numerous restaurants in the proximity of the studio, Danny and I would make our own lunch in the prop room. As Danny liked to put it: "Cheap is good, kid. But free is better."

His preferred lunch of choice was a hot dog. Yep, just a plain simple hot dog, heated in a saucepan of water and served in a bun with mustard and relish. And at least three times a week our lunchtime routine would usually begin with a series of verbal volleys. It was as if we had our own little comedy routine that we would act out together in the prop room kitchen, and would usually go something like this:

ME: "Hey, Pappy, what are you doing for lunch? You want me to make you a hot dog?"

DANNY: "Ooh, a hot dog sounds good, kid. But that's too much trouble. Don't bother. I'll just make myself a sandwich."

ME: "Okay, suit yourself. But I'll be happy to make you a hot dog if you want."

DANNY: "No, that's too much trouble. Besides, we had hot dogs yesterday. I'll just make a peanut butter and jelly. It'll be fine."

ME: "You sure?"

DANNY: "Would I say 'sure' if I wasn't sure? I'm sure! *(he pretends to look around)* Now, where do you suppose the prop guys keep the peanut butter?"

ME: "In the fridge, same as always."

DANNY: "Oh, right, right. You want me to leave the jar out for you when I'm done?"

ME: "No, thanks."

DANNY: "What, you got something against peanut butter?"

ME: "No, I love peanut butter. But I'm having a hot dog."

DANNY: "Wait. *You're* having a hot dog?"

ME: "Yeah. And I was going to make one for you while I was at it. But that's okay. I'll just make the one for myself. Enjoy your peanut butter."

DANNY: "What's this thing with you and peanut butter all of a sudden?"

ME: "There's no 'thing.' You said you *wanted* peanut butter."

DANNY: "Why would I want peanut butter when I can have a hot dog?"

ME: "You said a hot dog was too much trouble."

DANNY: "What trouble? You're already making *one*. Is it so hard to make *two*?"

ME: "See? I knew you wanted a hot dog all along! So why didn't you just say so when I asked you?"

DANNY: *(shrugging)* "I thought it would be too much trouble."

ME: "It's no trouble, Pappy."

As I pull the hot dogs from the package, there is a perfectly timed pause for comedic effect, and then a tap on my shoulder:

DANNY: "Mustard only. No ketchup. Remember?"

I just shoot Danny a look.

ME: "I remember like it was yesterday. Because it *was* just yesterday!"

I start heating the hot dogs.

DANNY: "Maybe a little relish."

I shoot him a sideways glance and grin.

DANNY: "I mean, if it's not too much trouble."

ME: *(still grinning)* "You're starting to get on my nerves, Pappy."

I go back to tending the hot dogs.

DANNY: "And don't forget to toast the bun."

I turn and give him an exasperated look.

DANNY: *(in well-rehearsed mock ignorance)* "What? Who doesn't like a toasted bun?"

ME: "Fine, I'll toast the buns. Now, do you want any potato chips with that?"

DANNY: "Chips would be nice. You know, just so long as…"

DANNY/ME *(in unison)*: "…it's not too much trouble!"

And then we'd both break out in laughter. Sometimes when you get the chance to meet a celebrity whom you've admired (especially as a child), it can be a disappointing experience. That real person just doesn't live up to the image you created (or the image they've projected through the media) over the years. But on rare occasions, that person just might turn out to be exactly as you had imagined him to be. And on even rarer occasions, you just might get to improvise some comedy "shtick" with him over a saucepan of boiling hot dogs.

It was during one of our lunches that Danny told me the story behind the founding of St. Jude's. "We were living in Detroit," he said. "And we were starving. I couldn't find any steady work in show business, and my wife was pregnant with Marlo.* I was desperate, wondering if I should give up on my dream of being an actor. One night I went to church and prayed to St. Jude Thaddeus, the patron saint of lost causes."

He put his hand on my shoulder and smiled. "I made a vow to St. Jude that night, kid. I told him, "Show me my way in life, and I will build you a shrine." And before long, I was starting to get steady work in radio, and then I hit it big in television, which opened doors I could never even have imagined." He was still smiling, but his tone became a bit more serious. "That night back in Detroit, St. Jude kept his part of the bargain and showed me my way in life. I knew I needed to keep my part of the bargain, so I built him a hospital dedicated to treating children who might otherwise be considered lost causes."

"Why did you decide to build it in Memphis?" I asked.

"Don't forget kid, we're talking about the early 1960's. Our mission from the start was to build a hospital where no sick child would ever be turned away, regardless of race. So I knew I wanted to build it somewhere in the south," he said. "And it just so happened that the priest who confirmed me in the church was originally from Tennessee. He was my mentor, and he was the one who suggested we build it in Memphis."

As we went back to our hot dogs, he smiled at me and said, "Just remember, kid. Success isn't about what you get in life. It's about what you do for others that really matters."

And I remember thinking to myself: *Just being able to sit here with you like this, Pappy, has mattered a great deal in **my** life…*

I should also mention that among his many considerable talents, Danny was an absolute master of the comedic "spit-take." Now for those of you who may not know what I'm referring to, a "spit-take" is

---

* *Margaret Julia "Marlo" Thomas is an actress, author, and activist. She has won four Emmy awards, a Golden Globe, and a Peabody Award for her work in television and recording. In 2014, President Obama presented her with the Presidential Medal of Freedom. She is married to former talk show host Phil Donohue and currently serves as the National Outreach Director for St. Jude Children's Research Hospital in Memphis, TN.*

a classic "sight gag" in movies and television shows. It occurs at the precise moment in which someone casually takes a drink of something (coffee, milk, water, beer–it doesn't matter), only to have someone else say something unexpected, catching that first person completely off guard, causing them to spit their drink out, spraying liquid everywhere. An expertly timed "spit-take" was comedy gold, guaranteed to produce a laugh. And no one did it better than Danny Thomas. Which is how I got in trouble with my father when I was eleven.

Over lunch one day I thought I'd give Danny a playful little poke and tell him the story, so I said, "You know Pappy, when I was eleven years old you got me in big trouble with my father."

He just blinked at me over his hot dog. "What?"

"Oh, yeah," I continued. "He banned me from watching TV for two whole weeks, and it was all your fault." He was expecting me to say more by way of an explanation, but I didn't. I just winked at him and took another bite of my hot dog, chewing and grinning.

He grinned back and peered at me over the top of his glasses. "So, are you going to tell me what I'm guilty of, or are you just going to sit there like a schmuck eating a hot dog?"

"Okay, okay," I said, laughing. "Here's the story. Back when you were doing *Make Room For Daddy*, every few episodes you would do a spit-take, which I thought was hysterical. As a matter of fact, I thought it was so hysterical that I decided to try and learn how to do a spit-take just like you. I mean, let's face it. No one does it better than you!"

"Flattery will get my attention, kid. Go on."

"Well, I'd noticed that in the show you were usually drinking a cup of coffee when it happened. So one day I got a coffee cup from our kitchen, and went into the bathroom I shared with my sister. I filled the coffee cup full of water from the bathroom sink, stood facing the mirror, and started practicing. I'd sip and spit, sip and spit, s—"

"—Sip and spit. I get it." He looked at his watch and grinned. "We only get an hour for lunch, kid. Cut to the chase."

"Right. Like I said, I was practicing using the mirror over the sink, trying to imitate what I'd seen you do on TV. You know, the way you sprayed your drink, your facial expressions, and everything. And as you can imagine, after about eight or nine attempts I had managed to spray the entire bathroom with spit water."

"Ahh," was all he said. He could see where this was going.

"Anyhow, my dad must have heard me spewing all that water in there, because all of a sudden, the bathroom door flew open, and there he was, standing in the doorway. He took one look at the mess I'd made and said, "What the hell is going on in here? What do you think you're doing?" I very sheepishly told him, "I'm practicing spitting." And he just stood there, looking at me, and said, "Show me." At that point I knew I was in big trouble, and the last thing I wanted to do was spit more water into the bathroom mirror right in front of him. But I'd seen that look on my dad's face before and knew that non-compliance was not an option. So I took another gulp of water, spit it out into the mirror, and then waited for the axe to fall."

Danny just smiled. "You know, kid, if you'd written this as a scene in a TV show it would be pretty funny."

"Well, it wasn't very funny at the time. My dad just stood there and said, "Who the hell put this idea in your head?" And I told him, "I saw it on *Make Room For Daddy*." And that's when he banned me from watching TV for two weeks. He said it was a bad influence on me. All because I was trying to learn how to do a spit-take just like you."

Danny stood up. "Show me, kid."

I just looked up at him and said, "What?"

He just laughed and said, "Hey, you made me the fall guy in all this! Don't I at least deserve to see what I'm getting blamed for? Come on, kid. Show me your spit-take."

So I got a glass of water, took a casual mouthful. Then I suddenly pretended to hear something shocking and spit the water out, spewing it all over the soundstage floor. Water sprayed everywhere. It was beautiful. I looked at Danny as if to say, "Not bad, huh?"

Danny just looked at me, shaking his head in disgust. "You call that a spit-take? You should be ashamed of yourself, young man!"

He had to be kidding, right? "What? That was no good?"

"No good?" he said. "To call that 'no good' would be too good! It was terrible! If I had been your father, I'd have banned you from TV for a month!"

I was crushed. But then he burst out laughing, put his arm around my shoulder and said, "But listen, kid. If you want to learn how to do it the right way, I'll teach you."

Naturally, I wasn't about to let a chance like this pass by. I was going to learn the art of the "spit-take" from the master himself!

He told me that a successful spit-take always requires a story leading up to the moment of surprise. And if there was one thing Danny Thomas knew a thing or two about, it was how to tell a story. His nightclub act did not consist of a series of rapid-fire "one liners." Instead, he would meticulously weave stories designed to engage the audience, eventually building up to a climactic punchline that would produce an explosion of laughter from the room. Simply put, Danny Thomas was a natural-born storyteller. And as he quite correctly pointed out, my spit-take attempt had no story behind it, which is why it fell flat. So he gave me one.

"Okay, kid," he said. "Here's your story. You're Prince John, a sniveling coward who can't wait for your father to die so you can be the king and loot the kingdom."

"Wait. I understand the need for a story. But why do I have to be a sniveling coward?" I asked.

He smiled and pointed his index finger at me. "Because I'm the one telling the story, kid. You got a better one?"

I just shook my head "no."

"Okay. And because you're sniveling Prince John, you order one of your lackies to arrange a 'hunting accident' for good King Richard and kill him while he's out in the forest. The lacky returns and tells you 'the deed is done,' and that good King Richard is dead. You're finally the new king. Are you with me so far?"

"I'm with you. But it seems like an awful lot of trouble just for a spit-take," I said.

Once again Danny just peered over his glasses at me, blinking, as if I were a child who didn't want to eat his vegetables. "Look, do you want to learn this the right way or not, kid?"

"Yes, I want to learn."

"Okay, then stop interrupting. Now, where was I?"

"Good King Richard is dead, and I'm now the new king."

"Right, right. So you arrange a coronation ceremony to have yourself officially crowned as the new king. Only what you *don't* know is that good King Richard isn't dead. Your idiot lacky only wounded him."

"Serves me right for being such a sniveling coward."

"And that's not all. A woodsman found him in the forest and has nursed him back to health. And good King Richard has secretly sent word to his trusted palace guard back at the castle. You see where I'm going with this, right?"

"Right."

"Good. Okay, so the story is in place. Now to set the scene. You and your knights are sitting at the round table. One of them lifts his goblet of mead and offers a toast to you saying, "King Richard is dead. Long live King John!" at which point everyone, including you, takes a drink. At that precise moment the palace guard bursts into the room and shouts, 'King Richard lives!' causing you to choke on your drink, spitting it out into the room."

I had to admit, Danny's whole "back-story" really added the right amount of drama to the moment leading up to the toast. "Okay, kid, now let's try it," he said. "You're Prince John—

"—The sniveling coward," I interrupted. Danny shot me a look.

"—And I'll be both the knight who makes the toast, *and* the palace guard who bursts in. Are you ready?"

"Ready," I answered.

Danny picked up a glass and lifted it into the air, saying, "I propose a toast to the new king." At that point I lifted my glass as well. Then he said in a loud voice, "King Richard is dead. Long live King John!"

As he started to take a drink from his glass, I took a healthy mouthful from mine. But at that moment Danny mimed throwing a door open, yelling, "King Richard lives!" I quickly spit my water out, once again spraying it liberally all over the studio floor.

"How was that?" I asked eagerly.

"Eh. A little better," he replied. I think he could read the disappointment on my face, because he smiled and said, "Don't worry, kid. We've got all season to work on it."

And we did. From time to time during the remainder of our production schedule on *One Big Family*, Danny would pull me aside and we would run his "The king is dead, long live the king!" spit-take drill. And eventually I got the hang of it, because one day after we'd gone through the routine, he just looked at me and smiled. He put his arm around me and said, "Now *that's* how you do a spit-take, kid!"

At that moment, I remember feeling a real sense of accomplishment and pure joy. But let's face it, in the grand scheme of things, knowing how to do a spit-take is pretty insignificant. No, it wasn't so much the moment as it was the journey which had led up to it. At eleven years old, I already had dreams of one day working in Hollywood on a TV sitcom. But even the eleven-year-old me could never have imagined that one day I would be working on a sitcom, doing "The king is dead! Long live the king! The king lives!" spit-take routine with Danny Thomas himself!

As it turned out, I'd be doing that same routine one more time…

....

In January of 1991, I was working on *Empty Nest*, the spinoff of *The Golden Girls*. As I've mentioned elsewhere in this book, the executive producers of *Empty Nest* were Paul Witt, Susan Harris, and Danny's son Tony Thomas. The star of the show was Richard Mulligan, who played Dr. Harry Weston, a pediatrician living in Miami "around the corner" from the home occupied by Dorothy, Blanche, Rose, and Sophia. We were working on an episode titled "The Mentor," in which Danny had been cast to play Dr. Weston's beloved teacher and mentor, Dr. Leo Brewster. I hadn't worked with him since *One Big Family* had wrapped production back in 1987. And it was great to see him again.

Danny walked onto the soundstage Monday morning for the cast read-through wearing a Miami Dolphins jacket. When he saw me, he smiled and said, "Hiya, kid. How's your spit-take these days?" We greeted each other warmly and I assured him that I'd been keeping my spitting skills "up to snuff." As we separated, I said to him, "Gee, Pappy. I would've figured you for a (Los Angeles) Rams fan. What's with the Dolphins jacket?"

He just looked at me for a second or two. "Didn't I ever tell you, kid? I used to own the team!"

I was stunned. Twice. First, I was stunned to learn that he used to own the Miami Dolphins. And second, I was stunned to learn that he *used* to own the Miami Dolphins. All I could manage in response was, "You what?"

"Oh, yeah," he said. "Joe Robbie and I founded the team back in 1965. We were the original owners. It cost us a little over seven million dollars. It was great at first, but after a while, it just got to be a drag flying from LA to Miami every other week or so for the games, so I sold my share to Joe."

My head was spinning. In 1991 the value of the Miami Dolphins was somewhere in the neighborhood of $150 million dollars.[*] And Danny had sold his share to Joe Robbie decades earlier because, in his words "it got to be a drag" trying to make it to the games.

"Pappy," I said to him, "Couldn't you have kept your ownership share and just, you know, watched the games on TV? I mean, there's no rule in the NFL that says that a team owner has to actually attend the games in person."

"Oh, sure," he replied. "But I didn't want to be an absentee owner. Besides, it was really more Joe's thing than mine. I had fun with it at first. But when it stopped being fun, I got out."

I was still having trouble processing all of this. "But do you know how much the team is worth today?" I asked.

"Of course I do," he said with a laugh. "What am I, a schmuck?" Then he smiled, put his left hand over my shoulder and patted the back of my neck. With his right hand he pointed his cigar at me. "But you know, kid, there's more to life than money." And then, with perfect comic timing he said, "Now, show me where they're hiding the maple donuts!"

And, of course, he was right. I imagine there are few, if any, who will remember Danny as the co-founder of the Miami Dolphins. But there are hundreds of thousands of children that to this day continue to receive free cancer treatment through St. Jude's who, along with their grateful families, will never forget Danny Thomas or his legacy.

It was a fun week on the set. Writer Arnie Kogen's script was strong, and he had written a wonderfully sweet scene at the end of the show in

---

[*] *The current estimated value of the Miami Dolphins would be in the neighborhood of just under $3 billion dollars. That's quite a neighborhood!*

which Danny's character of Dr. Brewster is confronted with the reality that his best years are behind him, and that his career as a practicing physician is coming to an end.*

As the week progressed, I couldn't help noticing that the story we were telling was in some ways a case of "art imitating life." In the episode, Dr. Brewster is confronted with the reality that his time as a practicing physician has passed and was now relinquishing those responsibilities to his former student, Dr. Weston. And in real life, Danny's time as a successful television producer had also passed, with the torch having been passed to his son Tony. And it made for some interesting moments during his week with us.

When writers are creating scenes on paper for a TV show, they usually have a mental image of what those scenes will look like when they're performed. But here's the thing: comedy is much, much harder than it looks. And something that seems funny at the keyboard may not come across as all that funny on the stage. Sometimes the words are the problem. Other times, it's how the words are *interpreted* that is the problem. And the only way to determine the source of the problem is to see the script being performed.

Therefore, at the end of each day, director Steve Zuckerman would have the cast stage an informal run-through of the show for the writers and the producers, in order to give them an idea of what their script will look like when it is "on its feet."†

The run-through is the writers' first opportunity to see if the director and actors have envisioned the scenes the same way they originally visualized them when they committed them to paper. Sometimes what we will come up with in rehearsal matches what the writers had originally envisioned. Other times it does not.

---

* *Arnie Kogen was also someone I had admired since childhood, as he had been a writer for Mad Magazine. In TV he wrote for The Carol Burnett Show and The Mary Tyler Moore Show, among many, many more.*
† *Executive Producer/Director Hal Cooper left the show after season one. Starting in season two, talented director Steve Zuckerman was hired by Witt/Thomas/Harris to direct the majority of episodes for the remainder of the series. Putting a show "on its feet" refers to the process of actually staging with actors what had previously only been on words on paper in the script.*

But either way, the run-through is always followed by a "note session" in which the writers and producers make suggestions to us regarding how we can adjust the staging and the performances to be more in keeping with what they intended (in other words, "Okay, you tried it your way. Now try it *our* way!").

And it was fun to see Tony Thomas attempting to give performance notes to his father after a run-through. By that time, I'd worked with Tony for the better part of ten years, and he was without question "The Boss." He was the executive producer. His desk was the place where the buck stopped. And he was the "giver of notes." And now here he was, about to give Danny Thomas notes on how to play a scene in a sitcom, something Danny had been doing ever since Tony was five years old.

In his capacity as the show's executive producer, Tony made a concerted effort to maintain a professional relationship with his father, rather than a familial one. For example, when they were on the set together (such as in this note session) he usually didn't refer to Danny as "Dad," but instead would address him as "Amos," his anglicized birth name. But there was never any doubt that the father-son dynamic was always the "elephant in the room."

At one point during the note session, Tony offered up a long-winded preamble, trying to explain *why* he felt a particular note for Danny was necessary. Tony's deferential explanation was practically apologetic in its tone and had become rather long and drawn out. So Danny, ever the comedian, seized the moment. He made a show of looking at his watch and said, "Just give me the note, son. Your mom called and says my dinner's getting cold!" His timing was perfect, resulting in a huge laugh from the writers.

But later in the session Tony expressed concern that he might be loading his father up with too many notes. Again, Tony was doing his best to keep things strictly professional. But Danny wasn't having any of it. He just took a big puff on his cigar and with a huge grin said, "It's your world now, son. I'm just living in it." As the whole room once again broke into laughter, Tony just looked back down at his notes, shook his head, and laughing along with the rest of us softly said, "You're killing me here, Dad."

On a half-hour sitcom, the cast only has five days to learn a forty-page script. And if that weren't difficult enough, each night the writing staff would re-write all of the dialogue and situations they felt hadn't quite worked during that afternoon's run-through. So there was always a stack of "fresh pages" of new dialogue waiting for the cast each morning. Sometimes it would just be a line or two here and there. Other times it might be an entirely new scene. But on a sitcom, the scripts are constantly being revised and "punched up" right up to (and sometimes during) the show taping in front of the studio audience. So it's not uncommon to see the actors still holding onto their scripts, even during the final rehearsals on show day.

I'm telling you all of this as my way of explaining why I never noticed during the week that Danny was having some trouble remembering his dialogue. As we were taping the show in front of the audience, he had some minor "fluffs" in the first few scenes, but not enough to raise any eyebrows. The challenge of doing a brand new show each week often results in actors "going up," forgetting their lines from time to time. Especially when their lines are constantly being "tweaked" by the writing staff each day.

But the last scene in the show was proving to be a challenge. As I mentioned earlier, Arnie Kogen had written a sweet, heartwarming scene between Danny and Richard Mulligan in which Danny's character of Dr. Brewster admits to Dr. Weston (and more importantly to himself) that the time has come for him to give up his practice and go into teaching medicine full time. The dialogue in the scene went to the very heart of the story, as Dr. Brewster "officially" recognizes the wisdom and compassion of his former student, addressing him as "*Dr.* Weston" for the very first time. The moment is sealed when the teacher and his student share a tender hug. It was the perfect way to end the show. But getting that scene onto videotape was turning out to be a struggle for Danny.

Both Danny and Richard were "emotionally invested" in the relationship between their characters as they played out the scene. But as it progressed Danny was starting to have difficulty remembering his next line. Or he would remember the essence of what he was supposed to say but would get the wording wrong. Each time it happened, we would "hold," pausing the taping process so that Doug Tobin, our stage manager could quietly let Danny have a look at his script while the studio audience looked on, waiting for the taping to resume. I've attempted to re-create exactly what took place in the transcript below. And as you can see, we soon found ourselves unexpectedly shooting the scene almost one line at a time:

> DR. BREWSTER
> There was a time in my life when I could do everything. In one day, I could see patients, perform a tonsillectomy, talk to the interns, and have…uh...

Realizing he has no idea what comes next, Danny immediately breaks into a loud prayer in Yiddish, hoping that his tongue-in-cheek plea to the Almighty might help him remember his lines. This produces a huge laugh from both the audience and Richard Mulligan. Doug Tobin shows him the script and we reset the cameras. On the re-take he gets the line out correctly, but then has trouble with his very next one:

> DR. BREWSTER
> Anyway kid, I'm taking your advice. I'm giving up my practice, and I'm also stepping down as Chairman of Pediatrics…um, no…

Sensing that something he just said was wrong, Danny stops. He looks out towards the cameras and says, "That's not right. It's not Chairman. It's <u>Head</u> of Pediatrics, right?" Richard Mulligan softly and respectfully cues him with the correct word: "Chief," which Danny acknowledges. "<u>Chief</u> of Pediatrics," Danny repeats. "Is that right?"

As we reset for another take, Danny again breaks into prayer, only this time in English: "Bless us, oh Lord in these thy gifts which we're about to receive…" which produces another huge laugh from the audience. Danny just says to them very matter-of-factly, "Hey, the Jewish thing didn't work. Maybe the Christian thing will." And that gets another enthusiastic laugh from Richard.

They make it through the line about the Chief of Pediatrics, but Danny stumbles again a couple of lines later, capturing the essence of the speech but again using the wrong words. Once again, we pause, and reset the shots while Doug lets Danny have a look at his script. Eventually we reach that sweet, heartwarming moment in which Dr. Brewster calls Harry "Dr. Weston" for the very first time:

>DR. BREWSTER
>I must tell you, it took guts to do what you did today. You came in, and taught the teacher a lesson. And for that I thank you… "Dr. Weston."
>
>HARRY (moved by this)
>"Dr. Weston." You don't know how long I've been waiting to hear you say that.
>
>DR. BREWSTER
>You don't know how long I've been waiting for you to earn it!

And Danny really came through, delivering his lines with such emotional honesty that it was easy to forget that they were acting. The honesty of Danny's performance also rang true in the hearts of the audience. Because as Danny and Richard hugged, the emotional reactions from the members of the studio audience could be heard in the microphones which were hanging above them to record their laughter.

All week long there had been some discussion between father and son regarding the actual ending of the show. Tony Thomas felt convinced that the episode should end on the sweet, emotionally-rich moment of hug. Danny wasn't so sure, wondering whether the scene might need one last joke *after* the hug to serve as a "treacle cutter" so that the show would end with a laugh.*

As I mentioned earlier, even though Tony was the executive producer, he respected his father and was trying to maintain a professional relationship with him throughout the process.

---

* *A "treacle cutter" is a joke or humorous situation in a sitcom which is specifically placed to provoke a laugh in moments that might be considered too sweet, tender, or emotional. The term refers to treacle, a sugary syrup. Therefore a "treacle cutter" would be anything that diminishes the sweetness.*

So he proposed a compromise deal. The writers would give Danny one more joke after the hug, and we would shoot the scene that way in front of the audience. But on show night Danny and Tony would agree to let the *audience* decide, trusting that their reactions would tell them how the show should end. Danny agreed to Tony's proposal.

So on show night, we shot the scene. Danny and Richard hugged. The audience reacted to the emotional moment. Then Danny and Richard did the "treacle cutter" joke. The audience reacted to the joke. And before we could even stop recording, Danny turned to face the audience and the camera crew and said, "Tony was right. It ends with the hug!" Both the crew and the audience burst into laughter. At that moment Tony was upstairs, watching the scene on a monitor in a room with the writers. I was in the director's control room, so I didn't witness Tony's reaction to his father's remark, but it wouldn't surprise me at all if he'd just laughed and said, "You're killing me here, Dad!"

"The Mentor" episode of *Empty Nest* aired on Saturday, February 2nd, 1991. Four days later, on Wednesday, February 6th, Danny Thomas died of a heart attack. Just two days earlier he had celebrated the 29th anniversary of his beloved St. Jude Children's Research Hospital.

We were working on another episode when word of Danny's sudden passing came down to us on the soundstage. It didn't seem possible. Hadn't he just been here with us, laughing and joking, "holding court" with the cast and crew, spinning stories as only he could? We all just kind of stood there for a while in stunned silence.

Finally, Steve Zuckerman said, "You know, we really ought to do something in honor of Danny. Something he would appreciate that might cheer us up." And that's when I said, "How about a 21 spit-take salute?" The show's writers immediately jumped on the idea. I had related my own spit-take history with Danny to Arnie Kogen, so we decided to use the "King is dead. Long live the king!" routine for the spit-take salute. Since Arnie had written the script for "The Mentor," we all felt that he should be the one to play the role of the palace guard.

We didn't actually have twenty-one people, but between the writing staff, the props department, the director, associate director, stage managers, and script supervisor, we came pretty close. Bob Church, the show's property master, arranged for bottles of sparkling cider and plastic champagne glasses, and poured each of us a glass.

Since Danny always had the utmost respect for the audience, we decided that we would stand on stage facing the bleachers where the audience is seated during the show tapings. Once everyone had their sparkling cider, Steve Zuckerman raised his glass and said in a loud clear voice, "The king is dead. Long live the king!" and we all took a mouthful of cider.

Then Arnie Kogen yelled, "The king lives!" and all of us in unison did the spit-take, spraying cider out across the stage towards the audience seats.

Afterwards there were some laughs, some smiles, and a hug or two among the group on stage. Steve Zuckerman and I just looked at each other and laughed.

But I had tears in my eyes.

> *"All of us in life are born for a reason, but all of us don't discover why. Success in life has nothing to do with what you gain in life or accomplish for yourself. It's what you do for others."*
>
> *—Danny Thomas*

16

EMPTY NEST

"Life goes on, and so do we..."
(First line from the "Empty Nest" theme song)

Richard Mulligan was waiting impatiently for the pie. And he was not happy.

We were in the middle of rehearsing a scene on the set of *Empty Nest* in the area designed to represent the medical clinic "break room." The Emmy and Golden Globe-winning actor was exactly where he was supposed to be: standing on his "T" mark in front of a row of lockers. The mark consisted of two strips of gaffer's tape that had been stuck together in the shape of a large capital "T," and placed on the stage floor by our property master, Bobby Church. Bobby had taken great care in placing Richard's "T" mark directly in front of the specific locker which I had designated for this scene. Richard's toes were resting on the piece of tape that formed the top crossbar of the "T," which was critical to both the scene and to his safety.

There were two reasons why Richard was not happy. One reason was because he knew that when he opened that locker a large pie would come springing out, hitting him in the face, covering him with shaving cream.

Despite the fact that he could play broad, physical comedy with the best of them, (as evidenced by his Emmy-winning portrayal of the outrageous Burt Campbell on the ABC sitcom Soap), Richard Mulligan was personally not a big fan of broad, physical "slapstick" humor.* As an actor, Richard delighted in scripts that contained sharp, crisp, dialogue and "smart" jokes and situations that acknowledged the intelligence of the audience. And let's face it, the hackneyed old "pie-in-the-face" gag is none of those things.

So Richard was not happy. Two days earlier, just after the table reading for that week's script, he had pulled me aside to a secluded corner of the soundstage. "They've got me taking a #*%@-ing pie in the face, Dougie," he snarled between angry puffs on his cigarette. "And on a giant #*%@-ing spring, no less. What am I, Wile E. Coyote? You know what this is, right?"

"Yes, Richard. I do," I replied. And I did. But it didn't matter. I also knew he was going to tell me what it was anyway. But that didn't matter either. At that moment, what he needed most was to be able to vent, and I completely understood. It was part of his process.

"It's the writers sending up the #*%@-ing white flag saying, 'We give up. We're completely out of ideas.'" His face was flush with anger, and he was waving that cigarette around for emphasis as he spoke. "And because *they're* out of ideas, *I'm* the schmuck who has to go out there and take a #*%@#-ing pie in the face!"

We just looked at each other in tacit agreement. He was fuming, but we both knew that on show night in front of the studio audience, Richard would take the pie. And he would take it like the pro that he was. And we both knew that as old and tired as the gag was, the audience would laugh at it.

He took a long draw from his cigarette and slowly exhaled. Then he pointed at me with both his index finger and his middle finger together, the cigarette still wedged tightly between them. I knew from experience

---

* *The character of Burt Campbell spent an entire TV season believing he had become invisible and spent another whole season inhabited by an alien look-alike, requiring Richard Mulligan to play both "Burt" and "Alien Burt."*

that when Richard used both fingers like that, he meant business. "But just once, okay?" he growled. "No second takes. You gotta promise me, Dougie. Promise me that you'll get it right on the first take."

"You have my word, Richard," I said. "I will be there with the cameras. We'll get it right on the first take. You'll only have to take the pie once." I'd given him my word, and he trusted me to keep it. I absolutely loved working with the man, and I was both grateful and humbled to have earned his trust during our time together on the show. He would do his part and take the pie. And he was counting on me to do mine.

So after that first cast read-through (and his subsequent venting), Richard had resigned himself to the fact that he was going to get hit with a pie. After all, it was right there in the script. When he opened that locker, the pie would come out. So we all knew exactly what was coming and when. But what we hadn't yet figured out was "how?"

As written, the physical description of the gag would be something along the lines of: "Dr. Weston crosses to his locker to hang up his coat. As he opens the locker, a cream pie comes flying out on a giant spring, hitting him squarely in the face." Now typing those words into a script is easy. But actually making them come to life on screen is something else altogether.

So during the first couple of days of rehearsal, our brilliant property master Bobby Church came up with an ingenious method of making the pie appear to spring out of the locker and into Richard's face exactly as described in the script.

In order to hit Richard "squarely in the face," the pie needed to come straight out of the locker. And in order to keep my promise to Richard, it had to work perfectly (and above all, safely) the first time. And despite what was in the script, we all knew that trying to attach a pie plate to an actual spring large enough to launch it would never work. A spring that large and powerful would be impossible to compress and pre-set inside the closed locker. And when the locker door opened, the decompression of the spring would not only be unpredictable but also extremely dangerous to anyone standing in front of it. Therefore, using a real spring to deliver the pie was never a consideration.

Instead, Bobby came up with a much more fool-proof (and far less dangerous) solution. We had Richard open the locker, and Bobby marked the exact spot where Richard was standing by placing that large

"T" he'd made from gaffer's tape at his feet, so that Richard's toes were on the crossbar of the "T."

Then while Richard stood there, Bobby used a tape measure to find the distance from the studio floor to the bridge of Richard's nose. Bobby then went around backstage behind the "break room" set and using that same height measurement, cut a circular hole one inch in diameter into the back of the locker.

Bobby then screwed the center of a sturdy aluminum pie plate to one end of a six-foot wooden dowel, which was an inch in diameter and painted flat black. Standing in front of the locker, he inserted the opposite end of the dowel through the hole he'd cut in the back and slid the dowel through the hole until the pie plate was all the way inside the open locker.

While Richard stood on his "T" mark, Bobby went around behind the locker again and began to slowly and carefully slide the pie plate back out on the dowel until Richard said "stop," which was about one inch from his face. That would be close enough. There would be a layer of shaving cream in the pie plate three to four inches thick, which would be more than enough to cover Richard's face from that safe distance.

It took about half of that six-foot dowel to reach Richard, leaving about three feet of dowel still extended behind the locker, which was plenty to allow for its operation. Since Bobby couldn't actually see Richard from his position behind the locker, when Richard said "stop," Bobby marked the stopping point by wrapping a strip of gaffer's tape around the operator's part of the dowel where it was now sitting, which was at the point where it met the back of the locker.

And to accommodate the writers' description, Bobby attached a large plastic "Slinky Spring" to the bottom of the pie plate and around the outside of the dowel to make it appear as though the spring was propelling the pie out of the locker. The gag was now assembled and ready.

We set up for a dry run. Bobby was behind the locker, gripping the dowel with both hands. His right hand was clenched around the "stop" mark of gaffer's tape we'd established. When I gave the cue, Bobby shoved the dowel through the hole as fast as he could until his right hand slammed against the back of the locker, forcing the pie plate attached to the other end to come to a sudden and complete stop.

We tested it several times. Richard took his position on his "T" mark in front of the locker. At the cue, Richard would open the locker and Bobby would shove that dowel through the hole as fast as he could. The pie plate would shoot out of that locker as if it had been launched. And each time as Bobby's right hand hit the back of that locker, the pie plate would abruptly stop exactly one inch from Richard's face, close enough to cover him with shaving cream, while the Slinky Spring quivered convincingly. It was the perfect solution.

Almost.

Which brings me to the second reason that Richard was not happy.

Once Bobby had rigged and tested his "cream pie on a stick," the responsibility of actually operating it fell to our assistant prop man Victor Vitartas. Now, Victor was a big, strong fellow. He had played football in both high school and college. He was definitely strong enough to shove that dowel through the hole with enough force to make that that pie come flying out of the locker as if it had been propelled by a powerful spring.

No, Victor's physical strength wasn't the problem. It was his heart. For all his size and strength, Victor was very soft-hearted, especially when it came to Richard Mulligan, whom he regarded with the utmost respect and admiration. And Victor knew that if he were just an inch off when he shoved that dowel through the hole the locker, he could potentially break Richard's nose. And that mental image turned tough guy Victor Vitartas into a quivering mass of mush.

And that is why during the rehearsal when Richard opened the locker, no pie had come springing out. Richard just stood there, exasperated. After a beat, the pie did finally appear, slithering out oh-so-slowly on the dowel. Richard just turned to us and gestured towards the pie, which was slowly creeping towards him. He impatiently looked at his watch and shot me a sideways glance as if to say, "Do you believe this?"

And it was at this point that we all fell out of our chairs laughing hysterically. "I think we missed the boat here, Richard," I said, barely able to contain myself. "We should have been filming *this*. It's much funnier than what's in the script. And better yet, this way you don't even have to get hit with the pie to get a laugh!"

Now I should note here that Victor's regard for Richard was equally matched by Richard's fondness for the big prop man, which made the following exchange between the two even sweeter and more amusing.

> RICHARD: "Victor, what the hell, man? You're killing me out here!"
>
> VICTOR *(FROM BEHIND THE SET)*: "Oh! Did the pie hit you?"
>
> RICHARD: "I'll let you know, if it ever gets here."
>
> VICTOR *(FROM BEHIND THE SET)*: "You're saying it's too slow?"
>
> RICHARD: "I'm saying my grandmother could go faster than that. When I open the locker, you've really gotta let me have it!"
>
> VICTOR *(FROM BEHIND THE SET)*: "I don't wanna hurt you."
>
> RICHARD *(SWEETLY, AS IF ADDRESSING A CHILD)*: "Vic, do you have a good tight grip on that 'stop' mark?"
>
> VICTOR *(FROM BEHIND THE SET)*: "Yes."
>
> RICHARD: "Then you're not gonna hurt me! Now this time put your weight into it and really shove that stick fast, dammit!"

We set up for another run at it. Richard opened the locker, and again the pie slid out. To be fair, it *did* come out quite a bit faster this time, but not nearly fast enough to catch the audience by surprise.

> RICHARD: "Vic, you're killing me! We don't have time for this. It's just a half-hour show, for Pete's sake!"

The voice coming from behind the lockers sounded shaky. Very shaky.

> VICTOR *(FROM BEHIND THE SET)*: "I'm scared I'm gonna hurt you, Richard."
>
> RICHARD *(AGAIN AS IF ADDRESSING A CHILD)*: "Victor, if you don't get this right the first time, then I'm gonna

have to stand out here like a schmuck until you do. Is *that* what you want?"

VICTOR *(FROM BEHIND THE SET)*: "No."

RICHARD: "Then man up and hit me with the #*%@#-ing pie, you big pansy!"

We did it again several more times, and each time Richard would harangue Victor as if he were a drill sergeant chewing out a green recruit. But by the third or fourth try, Victor had that pie plate flying out of the locker, slamming to a quivering stop just an inch from Richard's face each time. We'd nailed it, and it looked good (well, as good as a pie-in-the-face *can* look). Richard immediately went around behind the set and gave Victor, who was still visibly shaking, a reassuring hug, patting him gently on the cheek. The big prop man didn't know whether to laugh or cry.

Bobby's pie-on-a-stick mechanism performed flawlessly again that afternoon when we showed the gag to the writers at the run-through. They all laughed like loons (with the one who actually wrote the gag laughing the loudest, naturally).

On show night when the audience was in place and the cameras were rolling, the gag came off just as the writers had envisioned it. Richard opened the locker, and right on cue, a large cream pie came springing out, hitting him squarely in the face, completely covering him with shaving cream. The pie plate quivered convincingly on the spring. As the cream dripped down his face, Richard reacted with shock and surprise. Behind the locker, Victor Vitartas breathed a huge sigh of relief. And of course, the audience howled with laughter.

And we'd gotten it on the first take.

....

I have a picture of myself with Garth Brooks that had been taken on the set of *Empty Nest* back in late September of 1991. When I was teaching, that picture used to hang in my office on the wall behind my desk. Actually, I had a number of pictures from my TV career hanging in my office. But that picture of me with Garth Brooks was the one that always seemed to catch everyone's attention and drew the most comments. And it's had an interesting trajectory.

When I first began teaching in 1997, the photo would usually elicit comments along the lines of, "Holy cow! Is that you with Garth Brooks? I mean, for real? Garth Brooks? Did you really work with Garth Brooks? That's awesome, dude! Er, sorry. I mean *professor* dude!" These comments were usually followed by a request for me to tell them all about the time Garth Brooks made a guest appearance on *Empty Nest*.

But then in 2000 things changed. Garth Brooks retired from the music business to devote himself to raising his children while they were still young and living at home. And since college students are the way they are, after six or seven years had passed, if they commented on the picture at all, it was more along the lines of, "Hey, Professor Smart, who's that guy in the picture with you wearing the cowboy hat?"

I would respond, "That's Garth Brooks."

They would usually reply, "Cool. Never heard of him. What was he, like a cowboy or something?"

But then a few years later Garth Brooks "un-retired," quickly establishing himself once again as one of country music's most celebrated and iconic performers and songwriters. I could try to describe his return to music by saying, "it was as if he picked up right where he left off," but that would be an understatement. Garth Brooks was *back*, and in a big way!

But during that almost decade and a half that he was away, digital technology had made great leaps forward. I only bring this up because by this point in time, when my students would comment on that picture of us, they no longer said, "Hey, that's Garth Brooks! Did you really work with Garth Brooks?" What they were now saying was more along the lines of, "Hey, Professor Smart, nice Photoshop job of you and Garth Brooks! It actually looks like the two of you are really standing there next to each other!"

Kids nowadays…what are you going to do?

For the record, Garth Brooks and I *were* really standing there together on the set of *Empty Nest* back in 1991. And at that time, he had already become a bona-fide super-star (the first time around!). His album *No Fences*, which included the hit singles "Friends in Low

Places" and "The Thunder Rolls" had been released the previous year and had spent an astonishing 23 weeks atop the "Billboard Top Country Albums" chart. His next album, *Ropin' the Wind* had just been released and had entered the "Billboard 200" at the Number One spot, something no other country artist had ever accomplished.

Did I say he was a "super-star?" Make that "super-duper-star!"

Now, exactly *how* we managed to land super-duper-star Garth Brooks for a guest appearance on *Empty Nest* was never divulged to me. Those kinds of programming and promotional decisions are made at a level far above mine by the "suits" who run the networks.* However, I can offer a couple of educated guesses.

Educated guess #1: *Empty Nest* aired on the NBC network, and Garth had just finished shooting his first prime-time concert special titled *This is Garth Brooks* for NBC. The episode we were shooting with Garth was going to air on November 2nd, and his special was scheduled to air the following January. This would allow the network to use Garth's appearance on *Empty Nest* in November to begin cross-promoting his January special.

Educated guess #2: The Nielsen TV ratings were traditionally calculated during what were referred to as "sweeps" periods three times per year: February, May, and November. How much money the network could charge for advertising time within a show was directly related to the show's ranking in the Nielsens. Therefore, each network would try to create episodes that might be especially appealing to viewers, in order to boost the show's ratings during the Nielsen "sweeps."

Sometimes the networks would create and promote "a very special episode" of a series to air during sweeps. "A very special episode" is often network code-speak for "someone in the cast is going to be killed off." For whatever reason, a cast member was being written out of a show. Occasionally it would be one of the leads, but more often than not it was a peripheral character. But it was not uncommon to broadcast these "very special episodes" in which a cast member is killed off during a sweeps period.

---

* *"Suits" is a less-than-flattering term for network programming executives, most of whom have college degrees in areas such as marketing, advertising, and management, but have never actually produced at television program themselves, and have little-to-no knowledge of how it's done.*

Another tried-and-true method employed by the networks was what we called "stunt casting." "Stunt casting" is the practice of securing a major celebrity to be a guest star on a show. I say "tried-and-true" because stunt-casting can be traced all the way back to the early TV sitcoms of the 1950's such as *I Love Lucy*.* And let's face it, Garth Brooks was definitely a major celebrity who would "goose" our ratings during the November "sweeps!"

The episode was titled "Country Weston," and the plot was simple enough. Garth plays himself, offering Dr. Weston's daughter Barbara (played by Kristy McNichol) a job as the head of his security detail on his current tour. Garth has a couple of jokes in the show, and sings "The River," his hit single from his newly-released album *Ropin' the Wind*.

And Garth, who was with us all week long, was a total professional. Sometimes huge celebrities come in with egos and attitudes to match. Not Garth Brooks. As accomplished as he was as a musician and songwriter, he recognized that he was a total "newbie" when it came to acting on a sitcom, a guppy who was swimming around in the deep end of the pool with seasoned pros such as Kristy, Dinah Manoff, and Richard Mulligan.

So he threw himself into it, going through his blocking, memorizing his lines, allowing the cast to mentor him, taking notes from our director Steve Zuckerman, and then taking more notes from the producers at the run-throughs. Garth was like a sponge, soaking it all up.

And he did a great job. There were a couple of brief instances in which we could "see him acting," but the viewers at home would most likely never notice. However, there was one moment in the show that the viewers at home never got the chance to see, because it was edited out before the episode was broadcast on NBC.

It was about the fourth scene in the show, in which Barbara brings Garth to the Weston home and introduces him to her sister Carol (Dinah Manoff) and her father Harry (Richard Mulligan). Carol immediately throws herself at Garth, gazing longingly into his eyes and cooing seductively, "Well, rope my feet and call me dogie!" which draws a huge laugh from the audience.

---

* *I Love Lucy* featured guest appearances by some of Hollywood's biggest and most popular stars, including John Wayne, Rock Hudson, Harpo Marx, and William Holden.

Garth acquits himself nicely. He waits for the laugh to crest and then comes back with, "Hi. I'm married," which draws another big laugh.

He proceeds to give a pretty solid performance as he goes through the rest of his dialogue, telling Harry that he's offered his daughter Barbara the job as his chief of security for his tour. But poor Garth had no idea what was about to hit him.

At one point in the scene, Richard crosses over to Garth and says, "Well, it must be very exciting being in show business, huh? Having all those people cheering for you, selling all those albums…Do you know Vic Damone?"* It's a simple enough line, and the punchline reference to singer Vic Damone was intended to generate a small but respectable chuckle from that portion of the studio audience who were familiar with the 1950's crooner.

But Richard Mulligan was a brilliant and gifted comedic actor. And he had a gift for delivering dialogue in ways that could produce huge laughs. And we usually wouldn't see that delivery in the rehearsals during the week. It was a little something extra he would save up for show night in front of the audience. Richard referred to it as "loading up" the line.

So on show night when Richard crossed over to him, Garth was expecting Richard to play it the way they'd rehearsed it all week. But he was in for a surprise, because Richard decided to "load up" just the punchline - "Do you know Vic Damone?"

And load it up he did. Richard crossed to Garth just like they'd rehearsed it all week and said his line, "Well, it must be very exciting being in show business, huh? Having all those people cheering for you, selling all those albums…" But then he paused for a beat, which may have caught Garth off-guard.

You could actually see Richard physically winding up to deliver the punchline, and then in a *very* serious tone he hit Garth with, "Do you know Vic Damone?" The entire audience roared with laughter. It didn't matter whether they'd ever heard of Vic Damone or not. They weren't laughing at the joke. They were laughing at the *way* in which

---

* *Vic Damone was a popular singer in the late 1940's and throughout the 1950's. Damone appeared on numerous musical-variety shows during the 1950's, including The Ed Sullivan Show, the Texaco Star Theater with Milton Berle, and the Dinah Shore Chevy Show.*

Richard had delivered it. Afterwards, Richard just stood there locking eyes with Garth. And Garth, now caught completely off guard, did the only thing he *could* do. He burst into laughter right along with the audience.

Once Garth started laughing, the rest of the cast, including Richard, joined in. The audience also laughed enthusiastically, enjoying this "out-take" as well. We set up for another take. And just like before, Richard crossed to Garth and said his line, "Well, it must be very exciting being in show business, huh? Having all those people cheering for you, selling all those albums…"

This time Garth knew what to expect and tried to steel himself, determined not to break character. But his resolve was short-lived, because as Richard paused right before the line, "Do you know Vic Damone?" Garth was already laughing…hard. The studio audience roared with laughter again. Garth turned to the audience and said, "I did it again! I'm sorry. He's just so dang funny!" The audience laughed along with him, as did Richard.

Richard had really enjoyed working with Garth all week and had grown quite fond of him. And at that moment, he knew he had Garth "on the ropes" so to speak and decided to take some playful jabs at him.

"Come on, superstar!" he teased, loud enough for the studio audience to hear. "You ain't on 'Hee Haw' anymore!* Now suck it up!" And this just made Garth laugh even harder. Richard put his right arm around Garth's neck and patted him gently on the cheek with his left hand, like a father might do with a son. They shared a quiet laugh together in front of the audience as we set up for another take.

This time Garth got past the "Vic Damone" line without laughing… barely. We cut to a close up of him for his reaction, but we could see on camera that he was literally biting his lip to keep from cracking up again. His close up shot was unusable. After the scene was over, we played back our camera coverage from the various takes, scanning through it for a usable reaction shot of Garth. We found one that we

---

* *"Hee Haw" was a very popular country music variety show hosted by Buck Owens and Roy Clark, and featured country music's most popular artists each week for musical performances and comedy sketches. Hee Haw ran for over 20 years, on CBS from 1969-1971, in syndication from 1971-1993, and in re-runs on The Nashville Network from 1993-1997. The RFD cable network is currently airing re-runs of the show*

could "steal" from elsewhere in the scene, so we decided it was safe to move on with that night's filming.

And, of course, when the episode "Country Weston" aired on November 2, 1991, all of those "out-takes" had been removed during the edit, and in the fourth scene the close up shot of Garth's reaction to Harry's line "Do you know Vic Damone?" was the one that we'd "stolen" from elsewhere in the scene. The laugh from the studio audience was real, but the camera shot that the viewers at home saw had been faked.[*]

Once the show taping was over, we expected Garth to be the first one out the door. After all, he was a huge star with a grueling schedule of recording, touring, and public appearances. But rather than take off with an entourage, Garth opted to simply "hang" with Richard Mulligan and the crew onstage as the carpenters, electricians, camera operators, and stage hands performed their post-show "wrap." And judging by the free-wheeling banter, everyone on the crew seemed to truly appreciate Garth's acknowledgment of their individual contributions to the show.

I don't recall who exactly, but somebody there on the set had a camera with them, and before we knew it, we were all commemorating the week by having our picture taken with Garth. The beauty of a photograph is that it can capture a moment in time. And years later, when you look at that particular moment in the photo, all the events leading up to it have a way of cascading back into your memory.

And all of the events leading up to the moment in that photo with Garth Brooks make for some really fond memories.

....

"Doug," actress Dinah Manoff asked, "would you please ask Gary if he could give me some new words here?" The Gary to whom Dinah was referring was Gary Jacobs, the show's executive producer and head writer. Gary and his writing partner Arnie Kogen had previously worked on *Newhart,* and they had both joined the writing staff of *Empty Nest* in

---

[*] "Stealing a reaction" is a very common practice in TV sitcoms. The episode "Country Weston" is currently on YouTube. If you take a close look at that moment, you can see that the editors were forced to "steal" a reaction from Garth from somewhere else. It works, but it's not the reaction he gave us at the time.

season one. After the departure of Rod Parker, the show's original head writer/executive producer, Gary had become the show's head writer.

We were in the middle of an episode of titled "The Cruise," which had been written by Arnie Kogen.* It was a really strong episode, and I felt quite fortunate to have landed the assignment to direct it. In the episode the Weston's next door neighbor Charlie Dietz (David Leisure) who works aboard a cruise ship, arranges a four-day cruise for Harry (Richard Mulligan) and his daughters Carol, a neurotic, self-loathing divorcee (Dinah Manoff) and Barbara, a free-spirited, "devil-may-care" police detective (Kristy McNichol).

During the cruise, widower Harry encounters a pair of lonely widows each hoping to find "husband number two" while at sea. When they discover that Harry is both single *and* a doctor, they spend the rest of the cruise relentlessly pursuing him. Poor Harry can't get a moment's peace, as his new "entourage" follows him everywhere he goes. So much for four relaxing days at sea…

Meanwhile, Barbara wins the top prize in the ship's talent show by performing a very sultry, sensuous rendition of the song "Fever" while cavorting on top of the grand piano, much to the delight, cheers, and whistles of the passengers, but equally as much to her father's chagrin.

Carol, on the other hand, finds romance, meeting a handsome young man (Richard Burgi) who appears to be her soulmate. He is literally "Mr. Wright," possessing all of the qualities that Carol is looking for in a relationship. That is, until Mr. Wright mysteriously disappears.

The trouble begins when lowly crew member Charlie poses as the ship's captain in an attempt to seduce a passenger named Simba Katzman, a very attractive-but-gullible dental technician (Teresa Ganzel). And while doing so, Charley accidentally steers the ship off-course and into the middle of the infamous Bermuda Triangle. As a result, Mr. Wright suddenly and mysteriously vanishes. Carol frantically searches for him all over the ship, but to no avail. He is simply nowhere to be found.

The scene that Dinah Manoff, Richard Burgi, and I were working on was the one in which the insecure, neurotic Carol begins to believe that

---

* *I discuss Arnie Kogen's career in a bit more detail in the chapter devoted to Danny Thomas.*

this handsome man she just met may in fact be her "Mr. Right." It was a cute scene in which Carol discovers that Mr. Wright not only seems to understand and accept her many quirks, foibles, and insecurities, but also actually seems share most of them! For Carol, it's a match made in heaven.

As we worked through the scene in rehearsal, Dinah was having no problem with her dialogue at both the beginning and the end of the scene, feeling that it was right on the mark for her character of Carol. But she was struggling a bit with the dialogue in the middle.

She explained, "Doug, this is *the* scene for me. It's where Carol makes 'the turn.' She starts out not really believing that this guy could be for real, but by the end of the scene, she's convinced herself that he is. I'm trying to get from point A to point C, but it feels like there's a beat or two missing at point B. The turn just comes too fast." And that's when she asked me if I would talk to head writer Gary Jacobs about a small re-write in that area to help her smooth out the transition. Or as she put it, "Doug, would you please ask Gary if he could give me some new words here?"

However, Dinah was very quick to add, "But please, *please* let Gary and the writers know how much I *love* the script. It's really wonderful. I'm just having a bit of trouble with this one *teeny-tiny* area." She held up her hand, with her thumb and forefinger so close together that they were practically touching, as if to emphasize to me just how "teeny-tiny" the problem was.

There was a reason that Dinah wanted me to know how much she loved the script, and to make sure I understood how "teeny-tiny" her problem was. It was the same reason she had asked me to intercede on her behalf in the first place. And it was because Gary Jacobs just simply didn't like Dinah.

Actually, to say he didn't like her is an understatement. Gary's dislike for Dinah was intense, and he'd made no secret of it. But don't get me wrong. Dinah wasn't particularly afraid of Gary, nor was she intimidated by him. She simply knew that if she were to make the request in person, Gary would reject it outright. No, for it to have any chance to succeed, it would have to come from me.

Now, I feel that a bit of explanation may be necessary here. I've never worked on an episodic drama, so I can't speak from experience about the relationship between the writers and the cast on a dramatic TV series. But on sitcoms it's not uncommon for an "us versus them" mentality to sometimes develop between members of the writing staff and the show's cast. And as the seasons go by, this atmosphere of mutual distrust (and sometimes disrespect) will continue to percolate and bubble over.

To be honest, some actors have been known to regard writers as insensitive, uncaring people who force them to go out in front of an audience and deliver what they feel are "stupid" jokes, "expository" dialogue,* or to act out silly, demeaning situations (such as getting hit in the face with a pie!). And even actors who show great respect for writers often will chafe at the prospect of risking their fragile careers on what they consider to be "lazy" writing (which quite often requires them to appear in silly costumes in order to try and generate a laugh).

Conversely, many sitcom writers feel that actors often have no appreciation for how difficult it is to come up with "quality" comedy scripts week after week and come to regard actors as "those spoiled children who are never satisfied with anything we do," or "those egomaniacs who don't like the dialogue we just stayed up all night working on."

And from my vantage point, this appeared to be the way Gary Jacobs regarded Dinah Manoff. I could be wrong here, but I don't think so.

And I could understand how Dinah might at times be perceived as "nit-picky." She was indeed a perfectionist, but I mean that in the most complimentary of terms. And she certainly came by it naturally. Her mother Lee Grant is an Oscar-winning actress and director, and her father Arnold Manoff was himself a screenwriter. By the time *Empty Nest* debuted in 1988, Dinah had already won a Tony award on Broadway for her performance in Neil Simon's comedy *I Ought to Be in Pictures*.

She reprised her role for the film version of the play alongside Walter Matthau and Ann-Margret. Before playing Carol Weston on *Empty Nest* Dinah had been featured in the Oscar-winning drama *Ordinary People* with Judd Hirsch, Mary Tyler Moore, and Donald Sutherland, the movie musical *Grease* with John Travolta and Olivia Newton-John, and on television in her recurring role as Elaine Dallas

---

* "Expository" dialogue is dialogue that someone in the cast must deliver in order to explain the situation to the audience. As such, expository dialogue is rarely funny, which is why the actors often complain about it.

in the Witt-Thomas-Harris sitcom *Soap*. When it came to acting for the stage and screen, Dinah Manoff was a consummate professional.

I loved watching her at work on stage. And I loved working with her. And I completely trusted her instincts as an actress. And in this particular moment, her instincts were telling her that her dialogue in the middle of the scene didn't quite "track" smoothly through to the end. So if Dinah wanted me to intercede on her behalf with Gary Jacobs, then that's exactly what I would do. I just had to plan my approach carefully…

When we broke for lunch, I grabbed my script and walked across the studio lot to the *Empty Nest* offices and up the stairs to the writers' room, where Gary and the writing staff were hard at work on the following week's script. As usual, the room was organized chaos. A dozen writers were all sitting around the large table. Some were pitching jokes, while others were criticizing those same jokes. Some were "spit-balling" story ideas for future episodes, and still others were barking out lunch orders to the production assistant who was frantically trying to keep track of exactly who was ordering what amid the commotion.

Gary, in his position as head writer, was sitting at the head of the table. When I entered the room, his "antenna" immediately went up, and the chaos began to subside. As a rule, directors don't just drop into the writers' room to "shoot the breeze" or talk sports. There's too much work to be done, and there are always deadlines looming. So when a director comes into the room, it's usually because there's an issue with the script. Gary just sat there, arms folded, reading me with his eyes, trying to figure out what *my* issue was and how aggravating it might be.

"So, Doug, how's the mood onstage?" he asked. Gary didn't really care what kind of mood the actors were in. He was just giving me a lead-in so I would tell him why I was there.

"It's great," I replied, which was the truth. "Rehearsal is going very smoothly. This is going to be a terrific episode. Everybody loves the script." Again the truth.

"Really, everybody?" he said, still eyeing me suspiciously. "Even Dinah?"

He'd phrased it as a question. But it wasn't really. Gary sensed that whatever I was about to say next, it would involve Dinah.

"Yep," I replied. "As a matter of fact, Dinah asked me to be sure and convey that to you. She *loves* the script." I was sticking with the truth.

Gary just sat there for a beat, still trying to read me. He unfolded his arms and gestured, voicing a drawn-out, sing-songy, "Buuuttt--"

And there it was. The moment had come for the intercessor to intercede.

""But," I replied, "In Act One, Scene Five she's just asking for a few new words."

Gary threw his hands into the air, making a gesture as if to say "I knew it!"

"Just hear me out," I said. "She loves her dialogue at the beginning and the end of the scene, but she's just struggling a bit with her wording in the middle." I then explained to Gary, Arnie, and the rest of the writers that all Dinah was asking for was simply another sentence or two that would help her make the emotional "turn" from doubting Mr. Wright to falling for him.

Arnie Kogen nodded thoughtfully, as if he understood Dinah's problem and was open to considering her request. Gary was deep in thought as well, but from the scowl on his face, it was very clear what he was thinking.

"Look, Gary," I said. "We're having a good week. A very good week. You've a strong script and a happy cast, and we're going to have a great show. I mean, we're talking about a sentence or two here. Is that really worth digging your heels in and starting a fight over? Really?"

Gary just sat there for a beat, and then suddenly broke into a wide grin, although in hindsight it might have been more of a sneer than a grin.

"I tell you what, Doug," he said. "If I give Dinah some new words, will you promise me that she'll choke on them and die?"

"Well, Gary," I shot back, "There's only one way to find out, isn't there? Give her the new words, and we'll see." And with that, I turned and left the room. I had no interest in knowing what was going to be said around that table.

After lunch Dinah asked me if I'd spoken to Gary. I told her I had, assuring her that I had conveyed her request accurately and let it go at that. She knew better than to press the matter any further. We both knew that it was now up to Gary Jacobs and the writers. Later that afternoon, a production assistant brought us revision pages for Act One, Scene Five. Dinah read her revised dialogue, walked over to me, and gave me a big hug.

"Thank you, Doug," she said. " I don't know what you said to Gary, but this new dialogue is perfect. Perfect!"

"No prob," I replied. "I just presented it to him the way you explained to me." I was still sticking with the truth.

"And he didn't get upset?" she asked.

"Actually, he was smiling. But you know with Gary it's kind of hard to tell sometimes. But he *did* offer to write you this new dialogue." Okay, so this time the truth may have had a bit of "elastic" in it.

The rest of the week came off without a hitch, and on show night the entire cast and crew "hit it out of the park." The studio audience was completely invested in the story and roared with laughter as joke after joke "collected." And at the end of the night, we all knew we had a really good episode "in the can." Everyone went home exhausted but happy. It had been a good week, and to this day "The Cruise" remains one of my favorite episodes of *Empty Nest*.

....

In my opinion, there are two kinds of people in the world: those who iron their jeans and those who don't. I had been working for Tony Thomas over a span of fifteen years on *Benson, Condo, The Golden Girls,* and now on *Empty Nest*. And during that decade-and-a-half I had noticed that the jeans Tony wore were always meticulously (and professionally) pressed, with sharp creases down the center of each leg.

Personally, I fall into the "no ironing" camp. I just think jeans look better without the creases. But please understand that I'm not trying to infer any kind of judgement either way. I only bring it up because I find it interesting that something as simple as a crease on a pair of blue jeans can represent a physical, tangible manifestation of two people who live in the same world, but who view it through very different lenses.

We were working on an episode titled "Brotherly Shove." In the episode the Weston's annoying neighbor Charley Dietz (David Leisure) loses his job on the cruise ship. Adding insult to injury, Charley's smarmy younger brother Dieter Dietz finds out and offers him a menial job at his place of business, "Used Auto Delights." The dealership turns out to be a rather shady outfit that prides itself on taking advantage of wealthy customers who may be in the market for a unique, high-end exotic used car. And the unethical Dieter is not above taking advantage of his brother Charley along with his customers.

Dinah Manoff was directing the episode, and I was serving as her associate director. The talented actor Peter Scolari had been cast as Charley's smarmy brother Dieter. Peter's resume was impressive, including co-starring with Tom Hanks in their early 1980's sitcom *Bosom Buddies* and later on *Newhart* for six seasons. Hanks had also cast Peter in the role of Troy Chesterfield, the host of the "Hollywood Television Showcase" in his hit film *That Thing You Do!*

Several of the scenes between Charley and Dieter took place in the showroom of "Used Auto Delights." Ed Stephenson, our production designer, had created a lovely "swing" set* for the dealership that looked terrific on camera. His staging crew had "dressed" the set with several classic (and expensive) cars, including a Porsche 356 and a Mercedes 230 convertible, and a Studebaker Avanti coupe. The cars had been driven onto the soundstage through the large "elephant doors" at one end, and then strategically placed within the set so that they could be seen on camera at all times during the scenes.

We had finished the day's rehearsal, and the cast and crew were getting ready to run the show from top to bottom for the writers and producers, who would make notes. After the run-through they would discuss their notes with us, making suggestions based upon what they'd seen. This run-through and note session was the last item of business scheduled for the day.

I was standing at my script podium which happened to be in the "Used Auto Delights" set, working on some camera notes as the writers and producers began drifting down from their offices for the run-through. Our executive producer Tony Thomas† got himself a cup

---

* A "swing" set is one that is not used in every episode but is designed to "swing in and out" as needed. It may be a recurring set used multiple times, or it may only be used in a single episode, depending upon the script requirements.

† I discuss Tony Thomas in greater detail in the chapters devoted to *The Golden Girls*, John Rich, and Danny Thomas.

of strong "5:00 p.m." coffee from the large stainless-steel urn on the craft service table and walked over to me.

"Doug, how's everything going?" he asked. The question had been general in nature, but what Tony was *really* asking was, "Doug, how's Dinah doing?" As part of her contract negotiation at the end of season five, Witt-Thomas-Harris had agreed that Dinah Manoff would direct two episodes each in seasons six and seven, with me serving as her associate director.

Although she was an accomplished actor, Dinah had been eager to try her hand at directing. And while she was very comfortable working with the actors, she was still in "the learning curve" when it came to filming a show with four cameras shooting simultaneously. So it was understandable that Tony would be checking in with me to make sure that we would have all of the proper camera coverage necessary for the episode.

"It's going well, Tony," I replied. "Dinah's doing great. She has an excellent sense of what she wants, and she's picking up on the technical aspects very quickly. The cast and crew are being really supportive. It's going to be a good show."

"Good, good," he nodded, sipping his coffee. Then he threw me with a question that came from out of nowhere. He gestured towards the set and said, "Which one would you pick?"

"Beg your pardon?" I asked.

"The cars," he repeated. "If you could have any one of these three cars, which one would you pick?"

"Oh," I said. "Well, the Avanti really intrigues me, maybe because there are so few of them. But I guess if I had to pick just one to keep, I'd choose the Mercedes."

"Interesting," he said, smiling and sipping his coffee.

"Why's that?" I asked.

"Because you picked my car," he replied. "That's my Mercedes. I'm renting it to the show for this episode." I just looked at him for a beat. My boss Tony Thomas, whose company had produced such notable sitcoms as *Soap, Benson, It's a Living, Blossom, The Golden Girls,* and *Empty Nest* was renting his Mercedes convertible to us for a few measly dollars.

"Really?" I said with a big grin. "Well, Tony, I think it's great that you have a little income on the side. You know, just in case the whole 'TV' thing doesn't work out."

Tony just grinned back at me and took another sip of his coffee.

"Seriously, though," I said, pointing to the Mercedes. "I had no idea that was your car. I've never seen you drive it."

"That's because I don't really drive it much these days," he replied. "It was my car in high school." I was trying to visualize a world in which a teen-age kid drives a Mercedes to school when he said, "So Doug, what did you drive to school?" At that instant, a whole menu of possible responses popped into my head. I chose the one labeled "poke the bear."

"Oh," I said nonchalantly, "I had a driver."

"Really? You had a driver take you to high school?" he asked.

"Well, I don't know how it was for you kids in Beverly Hills," I grinned, "But over in Santa Monica, students weren't allowed to drive the school bus!"

He just looked at me as if to say "Okay, you got me" and laughed. I laughed with him, enjoying the moment. As we went back to work, I couldn't help but marvel at how the two of us could share the same physical space each day, working together towards a common goal, and then each night go home to completely different worlds.

....

In many ways Richard Mulligan was a man of simple tastes. He didn't own a house in one of the city's "star enclaves" such as Beverly Hills, Malibu, or Bel-Air, preferring instead to live in the Larchmont neighborhood of Los Angeles, where he enjoyed being able to walk to his favorite shops and restaurants. Sometimes during breaks at work Richard would share a sweet story or two about his childhood growing up in New York City, the son of a police officer. I can't help but think that those formative years influenced his choice of "neighborhood," even in a city the size of Los Angeles.

He was always quite well dressed, but his taste in clothes were simple and understated. And his preferred cologne wasn't actually cologne at all. It was after-shave. Old Spice, to be specific, available at any drugstore or supermarket. It was the brand of after-shave my own grandfather had worn, and its pleasant familiar scent seemed perfectly suited to Richard.

I'm sharing all of this with you because it lays the groundwork for the front half of my next story…

We were beginning our first day of rehearsal for a new episode, and I had been given the assignment to direct. As was the custom, we all helped ourselves to a cup of coffee from the craft service table and proceeded to sit down around the folding banquet table on the soundstage for the first read-through of this week's script. As we sat there reading the script scene by scene, I noticed that the scent of Richard's Old Spice was a bit more fragrant than usual. And that may have been because our guest star that week was Morgan Fairchild.

The beautiful blonde actress had risen to fame playing glamorous, seductive leading ladies in popular prime-time "soap operas"* such as *Dallas*, *Flamingo Road,* and *Falcon Crest*. And as a result, Morgan Fairchild had become synonymous with both physical beauty and desirability. In his recurring *Saturday Night Live* comedy sketch, "Tommy Flanagan, The Pathological Liar," cast member Jon Lovitz would compound one blatant lie on top of another, eventually leading up to the outrageous claim that he was married to Morgan Fairchild. Then he would smirk knowingly into the camera and add "whom I've seen naked." This joke worked numerous times on *SNL*, but only because of its utter implausibility.

And looking across the table at Morgan Fairchild as she read through her scenes, it was easy to see how she had come to be regarded as that symbol of beauty and desirability. She was, in a word, stunning. So I could understand why Jon Lovitz had chosen Morgan to represent the epitome of a "trophy wife" for his *SNL* comedy sketch. And I could

---

* "Soap opera" is a nickname given to the long-running serialized dramas that were a staple of daytime television for years. These included such popular programs as Search For Tomorrow, Days of Our Lives, and General Hospital. Many of these dramas originated on the radio and migrated to the new medium of television. Many were sponsored by companies that manufactured and sold soap and household cleaning products, hence the nickname "soap opera." Today only a few, such as The Young and the Restless, remain on the air.

also understand why Richard Mulligan may have decided to treat himself to that extra splash of Old Spice.

In the episode Morgan plays the part of Zoe, Carol Weston's best friend from childhood. Zoe has returned to town having completed a lengthy overseas assignment as a reporter for CNN. In a private moment before dinner at the Weston home, the now grown-up and divorced Zoe confesses to Harry that back when she was a teenager, she'd had a crush on him. She tells Harry that he reminded her of Mick Jagger of the Rolling Stones. Zoe also lets on that she still has a crush on Harry.

Harry is doubly surprised. First, he is surprised and flattered that this beautiful young woman finds him attractive. But he's equally surprised to find himself attracted to Zoe as well. But they both worry about how Carol will react when she finds out that her father and her best friend are "dating." Therefore, the two decide to keep their budding relationship a secret from Carol. It was a good, solid story premise on which on which to create comedic conflict among the characters.

There were two scenes in the script which called for Richard and Morgan to share a romantic kiss. By this point in time, *Empty Nest* had been on the air for five seasons. And over the course of those five seasons, there had been a number of episodes which featured Richard's character of Harry Weston involved in a "romantic" situation. So doing a scene in which Richard would called upon to kiss a lovely guest actress was nothing new. After all, it was simply two professional actors playing out their parts. But in all of those previous shows with all of those lovely actresses, I don't ever remember noticing that extra splash of Old Spice.

But then again, none of those guest stars had been Morgan Fairchild…

I was impressed with Morgan's work ethic throughout the rehearsals and at the show taping at the end of the week. She was a total "pro." She always came prepared, hit her marks, processed the notes she was given, and turned in a performance that was right on the money. As the director for the episode, it was obvious to me that over her years in the industry she had acquired a seasoned professional's grasp of the entire production process, which was refreshing.

But as pleasant as she was to work with (and she definitely was!), it seemed to me that she maintained a kind of "invisible wall" around her, probably as a result of situations that had occurred throughout her career. I could be mistaken about this, but I don't think so. I just chalked it up to the price of "being Morgan Fairchild."

Let's face it: Hollywood has been known to be cruel to those who make their living in front of the cameras. And it can be especially cruel to actresses whose public image is that of the "glamorous, sexy ingenue." It can often make for a very short "shelf life" on-screen, and it can play havoc in your personal life off-screen. I have no idea what kind of emotional toll "being Morgan Fairchild" had taken from Morgan, but I could certainly understand why she might want to put up some pretty thick walls to protect herself.

Which brings me to the back half of my story...

After *Empty Nest* finished its seven-year run in 1995, I left Hollywood to begin my second career as a college professor, teaching classes in television production. In 1999 I was on the faculty at Southern Illinois University, and in addition to my teaching responsibilities, I was also the internship coordinator for the school's "Hollywood Studies" internship program.

As such, I had spent the first part of my summer back in Los Angeles as the on-site supervisor for a group of students whom I had placed in various internships around Hollywood. My friend and faculty colleague Joey Goodsell had just arrived in LA to relieve me as the on-site supervisor for the remainder of the summer internship program.

Before heading back to Illinois, I thought it would be fun to take Joey to dinner at what had been my favorite neighborhood "hang out" back when I lived in North Hollywood, the Aroma Café. A small group of students had the night off, so we invited them to join us.

The Aroma has always had a reputation not only for their delicious food and coffee, but also as a neighborhood place where "industry people" can gather for food, coffee, and good conversation. Day or night, you can find actors, agents, writers, producers, directors, musicians, and other industry folk at the Aroma Café. Some get together there to discuss business, but most are there simply to enjoy a pleasant conversation over a coffee, latte, or cappuccino.

It was just after twilight on a warm summer evening, and we were sitting outside in the Aroma's garden patio, enjoying an after-dinner coffee. Joey, the students, and I were engaged in some light-hearted conversation when Morgan Fairchild stepped out from inside the café, a cup of coffee in her hand. Her eyes were scanning the patio, searching for an empty table. All the tables were occupied except one, which the busboy was in the process of clearing and re-setting. Morgan stood near the table, waiting for him to finish.

Joey tapped me on the arm. "Hey, that's Morgan Fairchild!"

"Yes, I know."

He tapped my arm again. A bit harder this time. "Didn't you used to work together?"

"No," I replied. "I worked with her once. For a week. It's not the same thing."

"Still, I'll bet she remembers you." he said.

"I doubt it."

"One way to find out, huh?" He was grinning. A big grin. The students were all looking at me, wondering what I would do next. I could see where this was going.

"Fine," I said, putting my coffee down. "I'll just go over and say 'hello.' That way you can all see for yourselves."

I got up and walked over to the table where Morgan was waiting. As she sensed me approaching, her demeanor changed. Her eyelids closed halfway, as if she were pulling a window shade down for privacy. And the expression on her face said, "Oh, please! Can't I just enjoy my coffee in peace without some fan coming up and bothering me?" It was as clear as if she'd written it across her forehead in bright red lipstick.

Nevertheless, I put my hand out and said, "Hi, Morgan. It's Doug Smart. You probably don't remember, but I directed you in an episode of Empty Nest."

As soon as I mentioned that I'd been her director on *Empty Nest*, her expression did a complete "180." Just like that, the "window shades" flew open. And with a dazzling smile she took my hand, shaking it firmly. "Oh, yes, of course!" she said, her eyes now sparkling. "I thought you looked familiar. So nice to see you again, Doug. How are you?"

"I'm fine, thank you."

"What are you up to these days?" she asked. "Are you currently on a show?"[*]

"Actually Morgan, I'm no longer working in Hollywood. I'm a college professor now." I gestured to Joey and the students. "I'm out here with a group of students who are working as interns around town."

And just as quickly as they'd gone up, the "window shades" snapped back down. The "please just let me enjoy my coffee in peace" expression had returned to her face. It was an amazing transformation to witness, one that would have made Lon Chaney proud.[†]

"Well, listen, I don't mean to bother you," I said. "I just wanted to say 'hello.' Enjoy your evening. It was lovely to see you again."

"You, too." Her response had been very polite, but there was a hollowness in her voice. Those "invisible walls" I remembered from our time working together were now once again protecting her.

Without really meaning to, I had trespassed on Morgan's privacy. After all, we weren't really friends, and since I was no longer working in Hollywood, I had nothing to offer her professionally. She had been working in television for decades, and I was just "that guy from that show who'd directed her." But in that moment, I had become the guy who was keeping her from enjoying her coffee in peace. Like I said before, it was the price of "being Morgan Fairchild."

I went back over to my table and sat down. Joey just looked at me with an astonished grin. "Wow!" he said. "That was amazing! It was like—"

"—A window shade opening and closing?" I asked.

"I was going to say a door slamming shut, but window works, too," he replied. "Man!" he added. "That was brutal to watch!"

I turned to the group of students. "You all just got to witness the entire arc of my Hollywood career, going from nobody to somebody and then back to nobody. All in about thirty seconds! I hope you were

---

[*] Quite often when an actor asks a producer or director, "Are you working on a show?" there can be another question tacitly implied: "If you are, is there a part in it for me?" It's a polite way of asking about a potential job without putting the producer or director on the spot.

[†] Lon Chaney was a silent-movie actor, known as the "Man of a Thousand Faces." Chaney was famous for his facial transformations in classic films such as "The Phantom of the Opera," "London After Midnight," and "The Hunchback of Notre Dame." His son, Lon Chaney Jr, rose to similar fame with his portrayal of "The Wolfman."

taking notes." And with that we all shared a good laugh and went back to our conversation.

I've been back to Hollywood a number of times in the years since, and I always make it a point to stop by Aroma Café for breakfast, dinner, or just coffee. But that night back in 1999 was the last time I saw Morgan Fairchild. To this day I'm still just "that guy from that show who directed her."

But I love this story, both for the wonderful way it all began in the front half, and for the equally wonderful (and humbling) payoff in the back half. It's a good story. It's a real "Hollywood" story. And to this day, the scent of Old Spice evokes nothing but fond memories of the time that I was "that guy who directed Morgan Fairchild in that show." But unlike Jon Lovitz's *SNL* sketch, my Morgan Fairchild story is true!

....

I was walking across the studio lot with Dave Leisure, who played the Weston's annoying neighbor Charlie Dietz on *Empty Nest*. It was late afternoon, and we were heading back to our soundstage to get ready for the writer's run-through. During the break between rehearsal and the run-through, I had gone up to the office of executive producer Tony Thomas to "pitch" an idea I had regarding the staging of a particular scene. I was walking back to the stage when I ran into Dave, who had gone across the lot to retrieve something from his car.

Dave and I had met six years earlier on the pilot episode of *Empty Nest*, and we hit it off right from the start. We had been amazed to discover that we had both attended San Diego State University at the exact same time, graduating in the same class! Dave had been a Theater major, while I had majored in Television and Film Production. Even though our two majors had been closely aligned, somehow our paths had never crossed at SDSU.

A number of moments from my years between graduation and the *Empty Nest* pilot are relayed in the chapters of this book. During much of that same period Dave was, in his own words, a "struggling actor." He had made appearances in some television shows and had landed small but memorable roles in popular films such as *Airplane*,* but steady work had been scarce until 1986. That's when he suddenly shot to fame in what became an iconic series of television commercials for Isuzu cars, trucks, and SUVs. In those ads, Dave played "Joe Isuzu," a pathological liar who would make the most outrageous (and hilarious) claims about Isuzu automobiles.

The commercials were designed as a combination of unfounded hyperbolic exaggeration and truth in advertising. As "Joe Isuzu," Dave would smile directly into the camera with mock sincerity and say completely ridiculous things like, "The Isuzu Trooper II. It has more seats than the Astrodome!" or "So inexpensive you can buy one with your spare change!" while graphics appeared on the screen (purportedly from Isuzu's "legal" department) informing the viewers that the loveable Joe was in reality lying through his teeth.

Dave's embodiment of the smarmy, dishonest TV pitchman was spot on, much to the delight of the viewers. An Isuzu commercial was even broadcast during the Super Bowl, and the character of "Joe Isuzu" quickly became a part of the cultural landscape. *Daily Finance* ranked David Leisure at number 15 on their list of "Top 25 Celebrity Spokespeople of All Time." He had become so ubiquitous that in 1988 (the same year Empty Nest went on the air), during a presidential debate between candidates Michael Dukakis and George H. W. Bush, Dukakis said, "If Bush keeps it up, he's going to be the 'Joe Isuzu' of American politics."

With his portrayal of "Joe Isuzu," David Leisure had gone from anonymous actor to instantly-recognizable celebrity almost overnight. But as we walked together across the studio lot, Dave was reminded once again how that recognition can be a two-edged sword…

On the soundstage next to ours, the Fox sitcom *Married With Children* was about to tape an episode of their show. Like the majority of sitcoms that use a live audience, *Married With Children* would videotape a show at 5:00 p.m. with one audience, then tape a repeat performance at 7:30 p.m. with a fresh audience. Later during the editing process, they would combine the best performances from each taping for broadcast on the Fox network.

---

* *In the film, Dave turns in a very funny performance as a Hari Krishna. He likes to say that he got the part because he was willing to shave his head!*

As Dave and I walked past their soundstage, the "five o'clock" audience was standing in line outside the stage door, waiting to be seated for the show. From behind us we could hear a man's voice yell, "Hey, yo! Joe Isuzu!" Dave turned to see a man in the line waving at him. A few others around the man now recognized Dave and started waving as well.

Dave forced a smile and waved back politely. At this point in time, he had appeared in a number of television series, movies, and had played Charlie Dietz in more than a hundred episodes of *Empty Nest*. But the public wouldn't allow Dave to put "Joe Isuzu" behind him.

The guy in line yelled, "Hey, Joe, tell us a lie!"

Without missing a beat, Dave smiled and as "Joe Isuzu" said, "You're a very handsome guy! You have my word on it!" The guy laughed enthusiastically at this, as did those in line around him. Dave turned back towards me, the forced smile disappearing instantly.

"I swear, Doug," he said softly through clenched teeth, "They're never gonna let go of it. They'll be carving #*%@#-ing 'Joe Isuzu' on my tombstone!"

"Would that be so terrible?" I asked. He just stopped and looked at me quizzically. Actually, he looked at me like I'd lost my mind. "I mean, at least they'll remember you for *something*," I said. "Most of us never even get *that*. Plus, people like Joe Isuzu, so you've got that going for you." He sort of nodded in the affirmative, so I went on. "The way I see it, Dave, is without 'Joe Isuzu' you may never have gotten *Empty Nest*. And your tombstone might just say, 'Here lies that Hari Krishna dude from *Airplane* who shaved his head'!"

Dave just laughed and said, "Okay, okay. I see your point." He put his arm around my shoulder as we started to walk. "But just between us, sometimes you can be a real pain in the ass, you know?" He laughed again.

"I know," I replied. "That's what you can put on *my* tombstone!" And we laughed together.

....

There she was, staring up at me from the card table. The dreaded "Queen of Spades." I was suddenly about to pick up a whole lot of unwanted (and completely unanticipated) points, courtesy of Richard

Mulligan. And there wasn't a darn thing I could do about it. Richard just sat there to my left, grinning at me. A wisp of smoke was curling up from the cigarette tucked between the first two fingers of his left hand.

Ironically, just moments earlier I'd passed the queen to *him*. We'd all chosen three cards that we wanted to rid ourselves of and "passed left."* One of the cards I'd passed to Richard had been the queen of spades. But after just one hand, Richard had tossed her right back to me. Only now there were points attached. Thirteen to be precise.

It was my own fault, really. In the game of Hearts, the first hand always starts with whoever is holding the two of clubs, and you're not allowed to play a heart or the queen of spades on the first hand. So in theory that first trick is "safe," and I had taken it with the ace of clubs, a card which had the potential to hurt me later on.

But as a result I now had the lead, which I didn't really want. Director Steve Zuckerman was sitting to my right, and thanks to the three "loser" cards he'd passed to *me*, I was holding a pretty weak hand. I needed to play a low card to get rid of the lead. Then I could just sit back with my weak hand and comfortably play on everyone else's lead.

We'd only played the first trick of that hand, which had been clubs. So I threw my little four of diamonds down on the card table. After all, there were only *two* diamonds in the deck lower than my four, and there were *three* other people at the table. I thought, "Hey, everyone has to have at least *one* diamond in their hand, right?"

That's what I get for thinking. I looked down at the queen that was now sitting on top of my four. Then I looked at Richard. "Are you kidding me? You're void in diamonds?"

"It would appear so," he said, still grinning.

Richard just took a drag from his cigarette. I looked across the table at Dave Leisure and then to Stevie Z. They were both grinning like Cheshire cats. Between them, they held the remaining twelve diamonds. And from the grins on their faces, I knew they were both holding cards lower than my four. As if to emphasize that point (not to

---

* *In Hearts it is customary to pass and hold cards on a rotating basis. On the first hand in the rotation, each player will pass three cards to the player on their left. On the next hand they will pass three cards to their right. And on the third hand, each player will "hold them," playing the cards they are dealt. This rotation will repeat throughout the game.*

mention gleefully rubbing it in), when Dave played his three and Steve played the deuce, they didn't just lay their cards down on the table. They made a point of slowly and deliberately sliding them *under* my four.

"Wow," Richard said in a mocking tone as I picked up the queen. He grinned and took another drag from his cigarette. "That had to hurt." His eyes twinkled. "It's still your lead, Dougie."

I can't tell you who won the game that day (although I'm fairly certain it wasn't me!). But it didn't matter. None of us ever really cared who won or lost. We were too busy being friends.

We had a running game of Hearts that lasted almost as long as the show itself, and we played every chance we got. We played during lunch. We played during the breaks between rehearsal and the writers' run-through. We played on taping days before the first show, while most of the cast was in makeup and wardrobe and while the tech crew was setting up. If we weren't working, you would find us around that card table behind the *Empty Nest* set.

The game was open to anyone, but there was a tight-knit group of "regulars" who played every day. These included Richard Mulligan, Dave Leisure, Steve Zuckerman, prop men Bob Church and Victor Vitartas, and me. Call it what you want: "bonding," "blowing off steam," "friendly competition," or even "ritual." Our running game of Hearts probably contained elements of all of those things. But to me it also contained another essential element: "family."

Over the course of seven years and 170 episodes, we had become like a second family. We had experienced births and deaths, marriages and divorces, good times and bad. And like a family, during those times we had always been there for each other. And just like a family, when the time eventually came for us to say "good-bye," it hurt.

A lot.

In March of 1995 *Empty Nest* filmed its final episode. Those on the show who were closest to me were aware that this marked the end of my time in Hollywood. They knew that I was making the transition into teaching and would be looking for a faculty position at a college or university.[*]

---

[*] *That faculty position turned out to be in the Department of Radio and Television at Southern Illinois University in Carbondale, IL. Go Salukis!*

Even on our last day, while the cast was in make-up and the tech crew was getting ready for the taping, the "regulars" gathered backstage and played Hearts. As you might imagine, that day it was a mixture of both joy and sadness. We all knew this would be our last game together. Whatever the future held for each of us, we would never again share this same experience. As always, we laughed and made jokes, and we said rude things to each other as we played.

And we all knew that we would miss it terribly.

At the "wrap party" after the show that night, as the cast and crew were shaking hands, hugging each other and promising to stay in touch, Richard Mulligan came up to me. He had a gift-wrapped package in his hand. "This is for you, Dougie," he said, handing it to me. "Just a little something to remember me by."

I pulled off the wrapping paper, revealing a display of the "perfect" hand of hearts, mounted in a picture frame. Thirteen cards, beginning with the five of hearts and running all the way up the suit to the ace, along with the aces of clubs, diamonds, and spades, all beautifully fanned out in an arc. Beneath the cards Richard had written "Dear Doug – Your "hold 'em hand" for life. With love and thanks. Richie."

As I held Richard's gift in my hands, I was overwhelmed by that same mixture of pure joy and tremendous sadness that I had experienced earlier that day. Richard said, "I'm really gonna miss you, Dougie," to which I replied softly, "I'm gonna miss you, too."

I was close to tears as he put his left hand around the back of my neck and kissed me on the forehead, the way a father might kiss his son. He clasped my right hand in his, perhaps for the last time. But even though my eyes were wet, as we shook hands, I suddenly burst out laughing. I could feel him pressing something into the palm of my hand, and I immediately recognized what it was. "You son-of-a…I don't believe this! You did it to me **_again_**!" I said as I broke our handshake.

There, in the palm of my hand was the queen of spades. Richard had stuck me with her one last time!

I saw Richard several more times after that night. Each summer when I was back in Los Angeles with my student interns, we would meet at a restaurant or coffee house in his beloved Larchmont neighborhood. And as soon as we sat down together, it was as if no time had passed.

Our conversation would simply pick up where we had left off. Richard would fill me in on his latest project, and I would talk to him about the joys and challenges of teaching college.

During one of these conversations Richard paused and said, "Look at you. 'Professor' Smart. You made it, and now you're paying it forward. I'm so proud of you, Dougie." At that moment all I could manage was a very sincere "thank you." But I hope that I was always the kind of teacher that Richard would be proud of.

On the evening of September 26, 2000, I was at home practicing the guitar in my basement. The phone rang. It was former *Empty Nest* director and Hearts "regular" Steve Zuckerman. I was really happy to hear from my old friend. "Stevie Z! This is a nice surprise! What's going on, buddy?"

I was expecting the usual light-hearted banter, interspersed with rude remarks. But Steve's voice was quiet and somber.

"Doug, I'm afraid I have bad news," he said. "We lost Richie today. It was cancer."

It was as if someone had just punched me in the stomach. Hard. My head was spinning, and I could feel the tears welling up in my eyes.

In the handset I could hear Steve saying, "I thought you should hear it from me. I didn't want you to have to find out about it on the news." I thanked him for that.

He said that he'd been in contact with a couple of the other "regulars" Dave Leisure and Bob Church, and that they had all decided to chip in to take out a full page ad in Daily Variety[*] to commemorate Richard. Steve knew how I felt about Richard and asked if I would like to contribute as well. I told him, "Absolutely. Yes."

Since time was a factor, Steve graciously offered to go ahead and pay for my portion of the ad, saying I could just repay him in installments. I think he probably suspected that since I was now living on a college professor's income, money would be tight. He just didn't know *how* tight.

But as the old saying goes, "Where there's a will, there's a way," and I managed to find a way raise the money. Each month I would go down to the local blood bank and sell my blood, one pint at a time, and then send my "blood money" to Stevie Z. It took me well over a

---

[*] Daily Variety is an entertainment industry trade paper.

year pay back my share of the ad. I never told Steve exactly *how* I was coming up with the money, and he never asked or gave me a deadline, for which I will always be grateful.

And looking back on it now, it seems kind of weirdly and ironically appropriate.

I have a bit of a confession to make. When I was teaching, I hung my "perfect" hearts hand on the wall of my office at the university, along with the rest of my "Hollywood" pictures. When I retired in 2017 and cleaned out my office, I packed all of my pictures into boxes and brought them home.

It had always been my intention to mount it on the wall of the home office I have above the garage. But in that life-changing transition from career to retirement, I just never seemed to get around to it. So my gift from Richard was sitting in a cardboard box in the basement.

Until now.

Writing this chapter reminded me of just how much I treasured my time on *Empty Nest*. And Richard's gift had been a tangible reminder of the bond of friendship we all shared. So I went down to the basement and dug through the boxes labeled "office" until I found it. As I write this, my "perfect" hand of hearts is now right where it belongs, in my home office where I can see it every day. And every time I look at it, it brings back warm, happy memories of my "second family" on *Empty Nest*, and of my friend, Richard Mulligan.

And by the way, in my wallet you will still find that last queen of spades he snuck into my hand.

Made in the USA
Monee, IL
25 April 2025